D0325739

For Verner -

GROWING UP WITH MY GRANDFATHER

GROWING UP WITH MY GRANDFATHER

MEMORIES OF HARRY S. TRUMAN

Clifton Truman Daniel

With a Foreword by Margaret Truman and Clifton Daniel

A BIRCH LANE PRESS BOOK
Published by Carol Publishing Group

For Polly and Aimee and Wesley

Copyright © 1995 by Clifton Truman Daniel
All rights reserved. No part of this book may be reproduced in any form except by a newspaper or magazine reviewer who wishes to quote brief passages in connection with a review.

A Birch Lane Press Book
Published by Carol Publishing Group
Birch Lane Press is a registered trademark of Carol Communications, Inc.
Editorial Offices: 600 Madison Avenue, New York, N.Y. 10022
Sales and Distribution Offices: 120 Enterprise Avenue, Secaucus, N.J. 07094
In Canada: Canadian Manda Group, One Atlantic Avenue, Suite 105, Toronto, Ontario M6K 3E7
Queries regarding rights and permissions should be addressed to Carol Publishing Group, 600 Madison Avenue, New York, N.Y. 10022

Carol Publishing Group books are available at special discounts for bulk purchases, sales promotion, fund-raising, or educational purposes.
Special editions can be created to specifications. For details, contact:
Special Sales Department, Carol Publishing Group, 120 Enterprise Avenue, Secaucus, N.J. 07094

Manufactured in the United States of America
10 9 8 7 6 5 4 3 2 1

Library of Congress Cataloging-in-Publication Data
Daniel, Clifton Truman, 1957–
Growing up with my grandfather : memories of Harry S. Truman / Clifton Truman Daniel.
p. cm.
"A Birth Lane Press book."
Includes index.
ISBN 1-55972-286-X :
1. Truman, Harry S., 1884–1972—Family. 2. Truman family.
3. Daniel, Clifton Truman, 1957– . 4. Presidents—United States—Biography. I. Title.
E814.D28 1995 95-8084
973.918'092—dc20 CIP

Contents

Foreword

Margaret Truman and Clifton Daniel

Having children is like shooting craps: When you roll the dice, you know what you want to come up, but often you don't get it; sometimes it's better, sometimes worse.

We, the authors of this introduction, Clifton Daniel and Margaret Truman, husband and wife, and parents of four, have been lucky: We are pleased and satisfied and now resting on our laurels, so to speak.

When we started this business of procreation, we agreed on one thing: Our first daughter would be named after Margaret's mother, Elizabeth, better known later in life as Bess Wallace Truman.

The result in our case was that every child was named Elizabeth in the womb, but every one emerged as a boy.

We hadn't even discussed boys' names and had to think them up after the boys were born. Another thing we agreed on: All of them would have family names, chosen from one branch of the family or the other or both.

Father rather assumed that the first boy would automatically be called Harry Truman Daniel. He hadn't counted on the fact that Mother, although she adored her father, did not particularly care for the name Harry. So number one became Clifton (for his father and paternal grandfather) Truman (for his mother's family) Daniel. He was born June 5, 1957. His birth certificate was initially issued without any name except his last one while the parents came to an understanding.

Number-one kid, as he now announces himself to his parents on the telephone, was followed by three others in this order:

William Wallace, born May 19, 1959, and named for his paternal great-grandfather and his maternal grandmother's family. (When he visited Edinburgh Castle in Scotland, he found at the front gate a monument to William Wallace. Sir William was known as "the Hammer and Scourge" of the English in the struggle for Scottish independence in the thirteenth and fourteenth centuries. Eventually betrayed to the enemy, he was hanged, drawn, and quartered.)

Harrison Gates, born March 3, 1963, and named for his grandfather Truman's favorite uncle and the family of his grandmother Truman's grandmother. ("Mama" Gates, as she came to be called, was born in 1839 in the district of Rounds in England. She was christened Elizabeth Emery. As a child of eight, for reasons unknown, she was sent alone to join her older sister in Vermont. There she met her husband, George Porterfield Gates, and traveled with him to Missouri, where they settled in Independence. There, in 1867, he built a fine Victorian "mansion." The house, which became known as the "Truman Home," is now administered by the National Park Service, and is open to the public on a limited basis—limited because the wooden structure has now become quite fragile.)

And finally, Thomas Washington, born May 28, 1966. (When he arrived, somwhat unexpectedly, we had run out of family names, but Father wanted Washington to be in there somewhere. As a child he had played happily on the farm of his great-grandmother Washington, a relic of the Civil War, in Granville County, North Carolina. His maternal grandmother, who had taught him to walk and had been a second mother to him, was born a Washington. Her favorite cousin was Tom Washington, and his name was given to our fourth son.)

This genealogical survey, as the reader can see, is so far more of an introduction to the family into which the author was born than an introduction to the book he has written.

Now to the book: It is the story of a young man who remade himself. He had a rare role model—a distinguished grandfather known the world over, a man loved and respected by millions.

The young man, our eldest son, did not try to remake himself in the image of his grandfather, but to make himself worthy of him.

They were not really much alike, except possibly in their sense of humor, their capacity for enjoying life, and their close attachment to family and friends.

There was, of course, a vast generational gap between them; Clifton was fifteen when his grandfather died at the age of eighty-eight. Still, President Truman took great delight in his grandsons and showed them off to news photographers, much to the annoyance of their mother, who tried to shield them from too much publicity.

As Clifton says in his book, he was not even aware that his grandfather had been president until he went to school and other children started asking him about it.

Now Clifton is beginning to attract some public attention on his own and has made us proud of him, but we have reason to be proud of all of our boys, although they are not conspicuously alike in looks or manner, ability, or interests. They are individualists who happen to share a common ancestry.

Clifton, in another era, might have been called a good-time Charlie, or later on a playboy, in his early years. He himself started the process of remolding his character. Without any prompting from his parents, he announced one day that he wanted to move out of New York and put its temptations and pitfalls behind him. He went to Wilmington, North Carolina, his father's home state.

In this book he tells his own story of what followed. We can only say that he has amazed and delighted us by his accomplishments as a newspaperman, an actor in the Wilmington community theater, one of the country's oldest, and as a loving husband and father.

His grandfather Truman would have been proud of him, too.

Acknowledgments

I would like to thank my parents for writing the foreword to this book and my father for helping edit out bad grammar, lousy punctuation, and blatant falsehoods in the manuscript. I would also like to thank my brothers, Will, Harrison, and Thomas, for letting me include parts of their lives in the book and helping me get it right.

Thanks also to Ted Chichak and Hillel Black for their skill and guidance and for remaining steadfast in the face of monumental moaning and handwringing; Clark Clifford, George Elsey, Gen. Donald Dawson, and the late George Tames for not only helping me get started, but for their kindness as well; and Mary Shaw Branton, Hugh Hill, Irv Kupcinet, Jack Brickhouse, Edwin Darby, Bill Hannegan, and Bob Wiedrich for their wonderful stories about my grandfather.

Last, but certainly not least, I thank Jack Harrison, Jim Weeks, Bill Coughlin, Charles Anderson, *The New York Times,* and the *Star-News* for giving me the second chance that made all the difference.

GROWING UP WITH MY GRANDFATHER

1

Presidential Pajamas

I was six when I first learned that my grandfather had been president of the United States. It was a simple thing. Someone at school asked me about it—and I had no idea. That was the first I'd heard of it.

I had many other things to think about that year. That was the year I got a pair of six-guns, a cowboy hat, and boots for my birthday, taught my younger brother, Will, to read, and was sent out of class at school for picking my nose.

I went home the afternoon I was asked about my grandfather and found my mother sitting in her chair in the living room, reading. "Mom, was Grandpa president?" I asked.

Mom put her book down and looked at me. She had sworn to keep Grandpa's fame from interfering in our lives—or from letting that fame spoil us.

"Yes," she said, smiling. "But anybody's grandfather can be president. You must remember that. You mustn't let it go to your head."

It was out of my head fast, in fact the minute I wandered off to the library to watch television. The significance of what she had told me didn't sink in until the following year, when I saw Lyndon and Lady Bird Johnson in their pajamas.

The Johnsons invited my grandparents to the 1965 inauguration, but my grandparents declined. They liked the Johnsons. In 1968, they would even let President Johnson bring a horde of reporters into their Independence living room to sign the United Nations Day proclamation. But not only were my grandparents getting older and more weary of the hoopla involved with traveling; they had seen enough inauguations to last them a lifetime.

"Mr. President, I think we're going to stay in Independence," my grandfather told Mr. Johnson. "But if you don't mind, maybe Margaret and Clifton and the boys could do in our place."

Mr. Johnson said he didn't mind at all. As a matter of fact, he set things up very nicely for us.

Early in January, we boarded a train for Washington. I couldn't have been happier. I was out of school for two days, fresh on the heels of Christmas vacation. The only dark cloud on the horizon was that I had to write an essay about the trip for my second-grade teacher, Miss Foster. I had already begun to show a distaste for schoolwork that would dog me for the next fifteen years. But I figured the trip was worth the extra work. As my grandparents' representatives, we went first-class. Not only did our travel arrangements come with a limousine and deluxe accommodations at Blair House, but there was one perk you won't get, even at the finest hotels—a uniformed military aide. About the only thing we didn't get was a sign with our names on it for the side of the limousine.

Such signs were for dignitatries in the inaugural parade. They had worked very hard to get to where they were, and they didn't want to ride in the inaugural parade without the thousands of spectators knowing they'd been invited.

Also, the spectators often liked to know whom they were applauding so they could stop in case it was someone they didn't like. Alas, my parents rode without a sign. The sign painters, expecting the Trumans, hadn't had time to make a new one. It served Mom and Dad right, because they didn't take us along. Actually we had not been invited. Our only consolation was that no other kids had been invited, either.

The day we arrived, the limousine picked us up at Union Station and ferried us to Blair House, which sits catty-corner from the White House across Pennsylvania Avenue. I got out in a state of high anticipation. I loved being away from home, not having to make my bed. And I was fascinated by hoteliers' habit of wrapping everyday things in paper—butter pats, sugar, soap. I couldn't get enough of drinking glasses with paper hats. So I looked at Blair House like a smorgasbord. More than that, though, I liked being in hotels because my parents were different away from home.

At home, everything was very prescribed, very strict. Up in the morning, off to school, home in the afternoon—the same thing every day. Dad came home at six thirty, had a scotch and soda, and watched the news. Dinner was at seven. Then homework, TV, and bed. There were few breaks from the routine. More than that, Mom and Dad themselves were more rigid at home. They both had high-powered careers and stuck to their schedules like glue. There was no family time; in the evenings we didn't all take a break and spend time together reading or playing. When Will and I were done with homework, we played in our room or watched TV.

To be fair, I don't remember craving play time with my parents. I could sit in front of the TV until my eyes glazed over. I still can. My wife calls it the "Daniel Stare." But away from home, all that changed. Without the pressures of their careers, Mom and Dad were more playful, more spontaneous. They seemed to like hotels for the same reason I did: Everything was wrapped up neatly by someone else.

But if I expected Blair House to be the same kind of place as a Howard Johnson, I was disappointed. Howard Johnson was the kind of hotel I liked—exotic, but not too fragile. Blair House was too damned elegant. The soap wasn't wrapped, and I don't remember finding any hats on drinking glasses. The sugar wasn't those great little wrapped cubes or in packets I could swallow in a gulp; it came in a bowl. The butter pats weren't wrapped, but made up for it somewhat by being stamped into seashells. Overall, Blair House just didn't have that wrapped-and-packaged atmosphere I preferred.

It was more like a palace or a museum, the kind of place I was used to looking at from behind a velvet rope. All we needed was a tour guide.

"And now, ladies and gentleman, you're entering the bathroom. Note the Louis the Sixteenth commode and the gold-leaf toilet paper."

The rooms were decorated with antiques, and I remember seeing a lot of four-poster beds, which reminded me for some reason of sleeping in tents. Where the floor wasn't covered with a richly patterned Oriental rug, it was polished to such a high gloss you could see your face in it. Run too fast and your legs went out from under you. There was crystal everywhere. To a seven-year-old, the house screamed "Don't touch!"

Blair House is actually two town houses, Blair House and Lee House. They're welded together so seamlessly that you can't tell from the inside unless someone shows you where one leaves off and the other begins. Someone showed me and Will, because I remember jumping back and forth over the threshold between the two. "Look, I'm in Blair House. Look, I'm in Lee House. Look I'm in Blair House again."

In the late 1940s, my grandfather's chief of protocol, Stanley Woodward, persuaded the Blair family to lease the house to the government as a guest house for visiting dignitaries. The government later bought the house outright. Lee House, which belonged to members of Robert E. Lee's family, was annexed not long after.

When my grandfather scooped up Blair House, he had no idea he was going to have to live there himself. But early in 1949, a piano leg went through the rotting floor of Mom's sitting room in the White House. At about the same time, Grandpa noticed that the chandeliers in the huge East Room on the first floor swayed ominously whenever people were moving around upstairs. So he and my grandmother and mother packed their bags and moved across the street to Blair House while the White House underwent a full-scale renovation. They lived there for about two years while the White House was completely gutted and its interior rebuilt around a new steel frame. Only the outside walls, which had been in place since about 1799, remained standing.

In 1965, it was my mother who led me and Will up to her old room in Blair House. "This is where I used to live," she said, taking in familiar sights in the sitting room. By the window, she ran her hand over the top of a polished writing table. "This is where I used to do my homework. You could write your paper here," she said to me.

"Great," I said.

Will was in the bedroom, checking the firmness of the mattress on one of the twin beds.

"Stop dat!" said a sharp voice from the doorway. "Beds are for sleepink, not jumpink around like a monkey."

The command came from Miss Deutler, the German nanny my parents had brought along to keep an eye on us. When I mentioned earlier that the essay I had to write was the only dark cloud on the inauguration trip, I'd forgotten about Miss Deutler. Before I savage her character completely, let me say that she was a good nanny, despite the fact she scared me half to death. She was actually a substitute nanny, brought up from the farm team after our starting nanny, Miss Nutzmann, went home to Nebraska.

It was actually Miss Nutzmann's going home to Nebraska for what she meant to be a visit that caused my parents to send her home to Nebraska for good. During an earlier trip to Independence, Miss Nutzmann had flown as far as Kansas City with us, then unexpectedly hopped the next plane home to stop in on her family. This infuriated my mother, who had planned on having Miss Nutzmann—not herself—chase us all over my grandparents' Victorian mansion for two weeks.

"If she wants to go home," Mom said after that, "let her just keep on going."

That was the last straw as far as Miss Nutzmann was concerned. She and my parents hadn't gotten along for years. Though she doted on me and Will—we called her "Sooker" after the German word *Zucker*, meaning "sugar"—my parents found her "quite impossible," as Mom says. My parents didn't tolerate much dissension in the ranks, from us or the nannies, and Sooker had her own way of doing things. Mom and Dad were also concerned that Sooker, a highly trained professional, seemed to have trouble relating to and caring for my second brother, Harrison, who was born with developmental problems.

"She was only used to dealing with perfect little Park Avenue babies," Mom said. "She didn't know what to do with Harrison."

Mom also blamed Sooker for letting Will fall headfirst off the Hans Christian Andersen statue in Central Park. He wound up with a concussion. In Sooker's defense, it is my own experience that stopping children from falling is like trying to defy gravity. One second they're standing firmly on two feet; the next, they're flat on their tushies. You can be standing right next to them and not be able to stop it.

For us, Sooker was a pushover, a marshmallow. We could do no wrong. We loved her. Miss Deutler, on the other hand, was made of steel, covered in a vast expanse of blindingly white uniform with razor-sharp creases—like an operating table with a fresh sheet. To heighten the effect, she was a German-born immigrant with a strong accent. What she said was law; there was no getting around her. She was strict for the sake of being strict. At Blair House, when Will and I discovered a bowl of fruit in our bedroom and partly devoured a bunch of grapes and several apples, Miss Deutler was beside herself. "Don't touch ze fruit!" she snapped. "You vill schpoil your dinner."

Whatever we had for dinner, I don't remember it. Aside from my fascination with wrapped butter and sugar packets, food was not a priority. Since my parents would be taking part in inauguration festivities, they arranged a full slate of amusements for us, including a tour of the Smithsonian's Air and Space Museum on the day we arrived.

By age seven, I had already developed a rich fantasy life, I guess in response to my parents' busy lives. The Smithsonian visit stoked my love of anything to do with space. I was fascinated by hoses and helmets and gauges and dials and small, cramped spaces. For years to come, my parents would pay the price for sending me on such a trip by having to buy me hordes of Major Matt Mason Lunar Crawlers, model rockets, and plastic replicas of the *Gemini* space capsule for my G I Joes. (Warning: Do not stage a splashdown in the bathtub using an old-style, foot-tall G I Joe. Their joints rust, and they make a sloshing sound for weeks afterward.)

Oddly enough, I remember very little specifically about the Air and Space Museum, though I recall vividly having to sit at my mother's writing desk in Blair House and compose a detailed account of the visit on a sheet of lined paper. The strongest image I have of the museum itself is of a set of giant rocket boosters. Each was about as big as a house, and they must have blotted everything else out of my mind, including a tour of the White House the Johnsons arranged for us the next day.

We went with Miss Deutler and our military aide, like a little band of house hunters with a real estate agent. ("You'll love the space for entertaining. It's solid, too. The whole place was redone in the late forties by a previous owner.") We sneaked in while everybody else in Washington was at the Capitol, listening to Mr. Johnson's speech. We saw the White House swimming pool and got a lick from the Johnsons' beagles, Him and Her. But as nice as that tour was, it is a dim memory compared to that of the tour we took the next morning, when the Johnsons went above and beyond the call of duty by inviting us to the White House living quarters. And this at a time when both of them were recovering from being out half the night. They had been to five inaugural balls.

"We made an appearance at just as many as we could," Mrs. Johnson said. "We even got to dance at one."

That was the ball at the Mayflower Hotel, where my mother was the official hostess. As hostess, she got the first dance with the president when he and his party arrived. Her entrance onto the dance floor was more spectacular than his.

The hotel's ballroom floor was ringed with boxes where ballgoers could sit and watch the dancers. But it was a bit problematic if they wanted to dance themselves. There were none of the customary waist-high doors in the fronts of the boxes to the dance floor. This was not, as I thought, a Secret Service idea to keep people from crowding around the president when he arrived, but to keep people from swinging the doors open and bashing dancers—possibly including the president—on the shins. So would-be dancers had to duck out the back door of their boxes and walk along a corridor to a main dance floor entrance.

The president had no time for such shenanigans. He had other balls to attend, other light fantastics to trip. So when he arrived at the Mayflower and it came time to dance with my mother, he did not say, "Go on around, Margaret. I'll wait." With the help of another man, he simply hauled Mom out of the box, set her down gently on the parquet, and waltzed off with her. And he waltzed off very well, too. Despite his size and strength, Mr. Johnson was a heck of a dancer.

When he had finished waltzing with Mom, he passed her off to Vice President Hubert Humphrey and segued into a fox trot with Mrs. Johnson. Mom was delighted, since Mr. Humphrey was one of her all-time favorite people. But delightful though he was, the vice president didn't have the heave-ho his commander in chief possessed. When it came time for the presidential party to leave, he couldn't lift Mom back into her box. Rather than send her around back, he gallantly ordered a chair so she could use it as a stepladder.

The president was evidently wearier from his evening's celebration than the first lady. He was nowhere in sight when we arrived upstairs at the White House at about nine o'clock the next morning. We had left Miss Deutler behind at Blair House. She had finished her duties and was on her own. The last we saw of her, she was sitting at the desk in her room, furiously writing letters to all her relatives in Germany on White House stationery.

Though the president lingered in bed that morning, Mrs. Johnson was more chipper than people have a right to be after a night of dancing. She greeted us wearing a canary-yellow dressing gown over her nightgown.

"Good morning," she said cheerfully. "Pardon the way I'm dressed, but we had quite a night last night. Weren't the parties just wonderful, Margaret?"

"Oh, yes," my mother said. "Lovely."

My mother was smiling, but she had been a crab earlier on while we were dressing and packing. Not only does she hate traveling, but she hates getting up in the morning, something Grandpa always found both amusing and annoying. That morning, her misery was compounded by a slight hangover. I didn't know then what a hangover was, though I would someday become an expert, but I was so struck by the difference between Mom's crabby attitude and the first lady's sunny disposition that I was driven to comment on it later, when we were settled in at home again in New York. "You know, Mom," I said. "Mrs. Johnson may be a lot older than you are, but she has more pep."

Fairly bursting with pep that morning, Mrs. Johnson had showed us up and down the living quarters. It was the first time Will and I had seen where our grandfather lived while he was president. We saw the Lincoln Bedroom, which Grandpa Truman thought might have been haunted by the ghost of Mr. Lincoln himself. He appreciated its historical significance, but his mother, my great-grandmother Truman, wouldn't have anything to do with that room on her first visit to Washington. She came from a family of Confederate sympathizers. Mom knew that, and in the car on the way from the airport, she teased Mama Truman about it. "We've got you all set up in the Lincoln Bedroom," she said with a grin.

Mama Truman gave her an icy stare. "I'm not going to sleep in there," she said with finality. "If there's no place else, I'd prefer the floor."

Grandpa Truman slept in the Lincoln Bedroom for a short time in 1948, when it was found that the White House was falling apart. His own bedroom and bathroom were shaky to the point of being unsafe. During a press tour at the start of the renovation, *New York Times* photographer George Tames remembered Grandpa showing reporters the steel rod that had been driven from the ceiling through his bathroom floor next to the toilet. The rod was intended to hold up the floor at their feet, but Grandpa wasn't sure it was strong enough for the job.

"One day I'm going to flush this thing during a diplomatic reception and wind up in the Red Room while the band plays 'Hail to the Chief,' " he said.

My grandfather's changes to the White House have been the most sweeping of the twentieth century. Mrs. Johnson also showed us onto the second-floor balcony, the Truman Balcony, which my grandfather had built prior to the renovation so he and "Gammy" could sit outside with a degree of privacy.

"It's one of my favorite places," Mrs. Johnson said. "I love to come out here on a nice day."

The Johnsons had made some minor changes of their own, as had the Kennedys before them. Mrs. Kennedy had turned my mother's sitting room and bedroom into a dining room and small kitchen, which the Johnsons used to entertain family and close friends.

"You are not cozy down on that first floor," Mrs. Johnson said. "Up here, you can put on your bedroom slippers and your old robe and you're home."

My mother had never been at home in the White House, but she kept the thought to herself as Mrs. Johnson showed us to the East Sitting Hall, where we all plunked ourselves down in front of the large, crescent-shaped window. No sooner had we sat down than Mr. Johnson came out of the bedroom. I was astounded at the sight of him. Not only was he huge compared to my short parents, but, like Mrs. Johnson, he was dressed for bed. He had on a royal-blue robe over a pair of scarlet pajamas. And, to my amazement, he was wearing a pair of bedroom slippers just like mine.

"Good morning'. How are ya'll this mornin', Clif?" he said, shaking hands with my father. "Margaret," he added, giving my mother a hug. Then he turned and looked down—way down—at us. "And who've we got here?"

"This is Clifton and William," my mother said, pulling us both forward.

The president smiled and bent down to shake hands. It was like having one of those California redwoods bend down to offer you a branch.

"Hi there, boys," he said. "How're you?"

"Fine . . . okay . . . how do you do, sir," we muttered.

"Good, good. Nice to have you here. Well, sit down, sit down," he said. "Did you have a look around?"

We nodded.

He took a seat on the end of the couch next to me and Will.

We were in a couple of chairs with our backs to the crescent window. Mrs. Johnson was at the other end of the couch, talking to my parents. "You know, Margaret," Mrs. Johnson was saying. "I love to gather tales of what it was like in the White House when another family lived here."

"Oh, I can tell you plenty," my mother said.

Mr. Johnson leaned toward me and Will. "You boys get a chance to see the dogs yesterday?" he asked.

We nodded energetically. The biggest pet my parents would allow in our New York apartment was a hamster.

"Margaret, didn't you have a dog while you were here?" Mrs. Johnson asked.

"Oh, that awful Mike," Mom said with mock disgust. "We could never train him. The staff liked him so much they fed him candy until he got rickets."

Mom knew a lot about presidents' pets, beyond her terrier, Mike, and she would one day write a book called *White House Pets.* To my horror and dismay, the book became required reading in one of my grade-school history classes.

"The Coolidges had a beautiful white collie," she was telling Mrs. Johnson. "And one morning, President Coolidge was up here having breakfast with Senator Pat Harrison of Mississippi, and the collie walked over and sat down by the senator's chair and stared at him for the longest time. 'He wants your bacon,' President Coolidge said. So Senator Harrison gave the dog his bacon, expecting that the butler would bring him some more. But the butler never did. The senator spent the rest of the meal looking over his shoulder for the butler, but he never showed up."

At about that time, Mr. Johnson suddenly leaped up from his seat and disappeared into the bedroom. When he reappeared, he had a couple of handfuls of pens, medallions, and matchbooks all bearing either his signature, the presidential seal, or the logo THE PRESIDENT'S HOUSE.

"Here you go, boys," he said, handing them over to us. "A little something to remember your visit by. You can use those pens for your schoolwork." He never got around to telling us what we might use the matches for, because my mother and Mrs. Johnson practically yanked them out of our hands.

At about this time, my father started looking at his watch. It was about twenty minutes to ten, and our train left at ten. And if there's one thing Dad is, it's punctual. If you're late meeting him for lunch, he'll spend the appetizer course telling you five faster ways you could have come than the one you chose. "Mr. President, I don't mean to be rude, but I think we must be on our way," he said. "Our train leaves at ten o'clock."

Mr. Johnson smiled. "Aw, Clif. Relax. Have another cup of coffee," he said. "The train'll wait."

"Mr. President, the train will wait for you, but it won't wait for me," Dad said.

Nevertheless, nobody made a move toward the door. Being around the president and first lady must have done something to my mother, because she is normally even more time conscious than my father, especially when traveling. We sat and talked and talked and sat, and time wore on. Finally my father couldn't stand it anymore. It was nigh on ten o'clock. "Mr. President, if you'll forgive us, we really must be going," he said.

"Well, all right, Clif. I hate to see you rush off like this."

"Well, sir. You've been very kind to have us," my father said, shaking the president's hand. "I hope we haven't taken up too much of your time."

"Not at all, not at all," the president said. "We enjoyed seeing you."

"Have a safe trip back to New York," Mrs. Johnson said, giving my mother a hug.

"Boys," the president said, turning to us, "it was nice to meet you. Come see me again sometime."

Will and I nodded and shook his hand, trying at the same time to keep a grip on our pens and medallions.

We left the Johnsons at the end of the East Sitting Hall, trying to walk nonchalantly down the hall to the elevator. Once out of the elevator on the first floor, however, we damn near broke into a run. There were only a scant few minutes before the clock struck ten.

"Come on, boys, don't dawdle," Mom said, practically dragging us through the Diplomatic Reception Room on the basement level. We piled into the limousine, and my father told the driver to break all land speed records. I thought he might also try giving the guy directions to the station, which is a service he provides for taxi drivers in New York. Dad carries around a map of Manhattan in his head.

"We're not going to make it," Dad said, exasperated.

My mother patted him on the knee, nodded, and sighed. As the limousine shot through the gate, I turned to her. "Mom, why does the president talk like a cowboy?"

Concentrating on the train, she was caught off guard. She stared blankly at me for a long second, trying to come up with an answer. "Well, uh . . . he, ah . . ."

"He talks like a cowboy because he comes from cowboy country," my father said calmly. "He even owns a big ranch down in Texas."

"Oh, boy!" I said. "Maybe we can visit him there next time!"

The car screamed around corners and hurtled over potholes in our dash for Union Station. At every red light, my parents looked like they might explode.

"What time is the next train?" my father said, anticipating defeat.

"I don't know," Mom said, suddenly rummaging in her purse. "I think I've got a schedule in here somewhere. There's probably one later this morning."

Neither of them noticed the driver's radio crackling or his answer.

Then Union Station was there, its massive, columned façade looming in front of us. To my father's astonishment, the driver shot past the front entrance and wheeled around the side. "Aren't we going in the front?" he asked the driver.

"No, sir. This'll be a little faster."

With that, he swung the car to the left, through an enormous arched door, drove right into the station itself, and pulled up at the gate to the platform. To my parents' astonishment, the train was still there. Dad flung himself from the car and, with the driver's help, started hauling bags from the trunk and handing them to a redcap with a baggage cart. The redcap had not appeared out of nowhere, nor had my father flagged him down. He had been standing there, waiting for us when the car pulled up.

Sprinting after the redcap, we made a dash for the train, sure it would pull out of the station just as we reached the doors. We must have looked frantic to the conductor who met us. He was a big man, tall and wide, and as calm as we were agitated. He shook his head and smiled as we panted up in front of him.

"No hurry, folks," he said, eyeing an enormous pocket watch he had pulled from his vest. "The White House called."

I learned a lesson that day, though it wasn't a very good one. I decided that, despite what my father said, I might be the kind of person a train should wait for.

2

So What?

My mother started having contractions at about two thirty in the afternoon of June 4, 1957. Having never had a child before me, she wasn't sure at first what was happening, maybe a little gas from bad cold cuts at lunch. Her cook and housekeeper, however, were more expert in such matters and quickly convinced her that she was in labor and should call my father at his office at *The New York Times.* After talking to her, he hesitated only long enough to put in two quick calls of his own: one to his parents in Zebulon, North Carolina, and one to his in-laws in Independence, Missouri.

"I just want to let you know Margaret's in labor and we're on our way to the hospital," he told my grandmother Truman. "We'll call you when the baby's born."

"Is everything all right?"

"Yes, fine," he said. "Nothing to worry about. I'm just on my way to get her now."

"Well, go on," she said. "We'll wait to hear from you."

My father took a cab home, picked up my mother and her suitcase, and drove to Doctors Hospital on Manhattan's Upper East Side, just a stone's throw from the mayor's house, Gracie Mansion. It was a small hospital by New York standards, founded by a group of well-known doctors so they could administer to their more affluent patients in pleasant surroundings. My parents liked Doctors Hospital enough to have three out of four sons delivered there. Visiting hours were relaxed, and the food, while not great, was a cut above the usual hospital fare. The best thing about the place for Dad was that he could order up a cocktail and some dinner while visiting Mom after work.

But that was after I was born. The night I was born, he had no such luxury. Mom started hard labor at around 6 P.M. and all Dad could do was cool his heels and smoke cigarettes in the waiting room. At about midnight, Mom's obstetrician, Louise Dantuono, came to see him.

"I'm concerned about Mrs. Daniel," she said. "She's been in hard labor for six hours, and yet her cervix hasn't dilated one bit. She is in a lot of pain and I'm worried the stress is going to be too much for her and the baby."

"What do you suggest doing?" Dad asked.

"Well, I'd like to perform a cesarean section. That would save her any more painful labor and relieve the stress on the baby."

Dad thought for only a moment. "You do what your professional training tells you to do," he said.

Dr. Dantuono started to leave, then hesitated, as if she were unsure of something. Slowly, she turned back to my father and leaned in close, as though she were about to pass on some gossip. "Do you think we should call President Truman?" she asked in a low voice.

My father was astounded. Not only was the doctor suggesting that she go over the head of the actual father in favor of the grandfather, but she was about to make a monumental blunder as far as the grandfather was concerned. It was midnight in New York, 11 P.M. in Independence, and my grandfather was fast asleep. He could always sleep, even under tremendous stress. And I did not fall under the category of "tremendous stress." As my mother said years later: "Did you think any man who slept through his own election to the presidency was going to stay awake for a mere grandson?"

Dad smiled at Dr. Dantuono. "No, I don't think we should call President Truman," he said. "President Truman is asleep. He's probably been asleep for several hours. He will be amazed if you call him in the middle of the night to ask his opinion on a medical matter he knows nothing about. He will probably tell you, 'You're the doctor. You handle it.' "

Dr. Dantuono considered this for a second or two. It certainly seemed liked sound advice. And she was loath to wake up an ex-president. So she did as Grandpa would surely have suggested. I was born by cesarean section at 12:11 A.M. the morning of June 5. My mother thinks it was 12:10, but (a) she was out cold at the time and (b) it says 12:11 A.M. on my birth certificate.

I work for a newspaper, but I am not a journalist the way my father is a journalist. He is a Journalist with a capital J. He's been at it since he was a teenager, and I have never heard him talk about considering any other career. He is a natural imparter of information. In this regard, my father has no equal. If he knows something, everyone around him will know it, too. As an adult, I've learned to appreciate Dad's skill at telling a story.

As a teenager, however, I considered his storytelling a negative trait. Four out of five times when I asked a question, I had to be prepared for a long answer, always prefaced by "Let me tell you something . . ." To this day, he communicates with his far-flung sons not with long letters but with short notes glued to news clippings. News is in his blood.

So it wasn't surprising that the first person my father called on the night I was born was not his parents or his in-laws but Lou Jordan, the assistant news editor at *The New York Times.* At the time, my father was the assistant to the managing editor.

"Lou, I just wanted to let you know Margaret had a boy."

"Oh, that's great, Clifton. Congratulations. Everything go all right?"

"Just fine. Margaret had a cesarean."

"She okay?"

"Yes, thank you."

"Okay, let me get a pencil, and give me the details."

Mr. Jordan was smiling as he hung up the phone and dialed the press room. He had been in the newspaper business twenty years and had never had the chance to utter the one phrase that sends chills up and down a journalist's spine.

"Press room" came the reply from downstairs.

"Stop the presses," Mr. Jordan said.

Not that I was any big deal, as my parents have always been quick to remind me, but I made the front page of *The New York Times* the next day.

Before my father went home from the hospital that night, he had one more call to make. It wasn't to my grandmother and grandfather Truman. He wouldn't call them until he was sure they were up the next morning.

"I didn't think it was necessary to wake them up that night," he said. "They were getting older, and they weren't as excited about this whole thing as we were."

He had no qualms, however, about calling his own parents, E. C. and Elvah Daniel in Zebulon, North Carolina. They were getting older, too, but apparently they kept later hours than the Trumans, as my father found when he dialed the number. And dialed the number. And dialed the number. He glanced at his watch and saw that it was half past midnight. For the next half hour he called and called but still got no answer. Finally, just as he was beginning to be truly concerned, my grandmother answered the phone. "Mother? Good Lord, it's nearly one o'clock in the morning," he said. "Where have you been at this hour?"

"Visiting my aunt in Louisburg," she said. "What's going on? Is everybody all right."

"Everything's fine. I just thought you'd like to know you have a grandson."

"Oh, my! That's wonderful! How's Margaret?"

"She's fine. She had some trouble with the labor, so they performed a cesarean. But everything turned out fine."

"Oh, dear. How's the baby?"

"He's fine."

"How much does he weigh?"

"Six pounds, eight ounces."

Normally my grandmother would have been relaying all this information to my grandfather, who would have been sitting nearby. But he wasn't there. Grandpa Truman occasionally liked to hold a fishing pole and kill some time in the company of friends, but Grandpa Daniel was a true fisherman. He even had a bait pond out back of his house, under a wooden trapdoor next to the garage. Will and I loved to open the trapdoor and chase the silvery little fish around with our hands. We also loved to dig worms from the dirt nearby. One of the earliest memories I have is of fishing on a North Carolina lake, in a scuffed aluminum rowboat, with Grandpa Daniel. I think I caught a catfish that day.

Grandpa Daniel was out for bigger game the night I was born. Apparently completely unconcerned about my impending birth, he had taken off for an overnight fishing trip off the North Carolina coast. He didn't hear about me until the next day, when the fishing boat skipper's wife, who had been listening to the news of my birth on the radio, started shouting to him from the dock as they sailed back in.

After my grandmother hung up when my father told her the news the night before, she found herself sitting all alone, at nearly one o'clock in the morning, with the knowledge that she was a grandmother for the first time—and no one to tell it to. She couldn't call her friends or wake up her neighbors. Yet she wanted to celebrate in some way.

So she took the bottle of cooking sherry out of the kitchen pantry and poured herself a small glass. Up until that moment, she had been a teetotaler, but she thought that if there was ever a time to take a drink, this was it. So she sat in the kitchen for a few minutes, sipping the sherry by the light of the fluorescent lamp overhead. Then she went to bed. She and my grandfather were not to lay eyes on me for a couple of months.

My other grandparents were less patient. My grandfather Truman, particularly, had been waiting for this moment for years. Although he supported my mother's desire to have a career of her own—partly, I think, because she had had to live so long in his shadow—he was nonetheless an old-fashioned father. Sometime after he left the White House, a reporter asked him how he felt about my mother's singing.

"Frankly, I'd rather have a grandchild," he said, to my mother's chagrin.

Both he and my grandmother had known Mom was in the hospital since the previous afternoon, so they had half-packed their bags and made travel arrangements. When the call came from my father, they left like the wind, undaunted and unhampered even by reporters, some of whom called the house while the sun was still below the horizon.

"What's it feel like to be a grandmother?" one asked when my grandmother picked up the phone in the pantry between the kitchen and dining room.

"We're very happy," she answered.

"What did President Truman say when you gave him the news?"

My grandmother started laughing. "Don't ask me that," she said. "I can't remember what he said."

"Are you going to see the baby anytime soon?"

"Yes, we're leaving by train this morning for New York."

An hour or so later, she and my grandfather were at the Independence station, saying farewell to friends and well-wishers, among them members of my grandmother's bridge club who had come to see them off. Much to my grandmother's dismay, they also found themselves answering more questions from a hastily mustered group of reporters. My grandfather, however, was delighted when the newsmen started calling him "Grandpa," and he spent the time before departure shaking hands and accepting congratulations. "Mrs. Truman and I are both very happy," he told the reporters.

"Any ideas on a name for your grandson?" a reporter for the *Kansas City Star* asked.

"No, I'm going to stay out of that department," my grandfather said with a sly smile. "There are too many grandmothers."

"What's that you're reading?" another asked.

My grandfather held up the thick book he'd brought to read on the train. He'd already finished several hundred pages. "*Soviet Russia and China* by Chiang Kai-shek," he said. "It's very good."

With that, they were on their way. They had left so fast, they missed getting my first birthday present, a baseball glove from Robert P. Weatherford Jr., the mayor of Independence. Mr. Weatherford had sprinted for the Independence station when he got the news, but he was no match for my grandparents. So he sent the glove ahead to St. Louis.

"Mr. President," Mr. Weatherford wrote in a note accompanying the glove. "Of course, Mrs. Truman hurried you so much you forgot the boy's ball glove. Here it is with my best wishes and prayers for all."

"Dear Bob," my grandfather wrote back nineteen days later, "That young man is going to be in a bad way—the Boston Braves gave him a cap, you gave him an Athletics glove, and the mayor of St. Louis gave him a National League baseball."

In St. Louis, Mayor Raymond R. Tucker handed over Mr. Weatherford's glove and kindly threw in a couple of presents of his own, including a copy of Stan Musial's *How the Majors Play Baseball.* I did not read the book, but I wound up meeting Stan Musial years later in Florida, after he had retired. Unfortunately my grasp of baseball was no better than it is today, and I had no idea who in the world I was shaking hands with.

Despite the baseball theme running through my first batch of presents, my grandfather had no wish for me to take up the game. "I'd like to see him become a United States senator, but not president," he told reporters during the stopover at the St. Louis Union Station. "The presidency is the most demanding job in the world, so I have no desire to see him hold that office."

"How does becoming a grandfather compare with becoming president?" a reporter asked.

My grandfather smiled broadly. "They're different types of experiences," he said. "But since the mother and baby are doing fine, this is a delightful experience. And there's no controversy over this one."

"How'd you like the baby to be named after you?"

My grandfather said he wouldn't like it at all. "That's up to the parents," he said. "But if he's named Harry, he'll never live it down. The boy would be under a handicap the rest of his life."

My grandparents arrived in New York the next morning and were met at Penn Station by my father, who found himself in the middle of a press melee. Answering questions on the run, my grandparents were whisked to the street by Dad and a redcap and piled into a cab. Dad rode with them uptown to the Carlyle Hotel on 76th Street and Madison Avenue and saw them to their suite on the top floor. After my grandparents had a chance to put down their bags and freshen up, Dad took them over to Doctors Hospital.

First they checked in with Mom and were amazed to find her living in a what looked like a hothouse. The room was stuffed with flowers of every kind, a sea of roses, lilies, daisies, mums, and orchids. The flowers eventually became so abundant that Dad drove most of them down to Bellevue Hospital in a cab and gave them to the nurses on duty to distribute to their patients.

Having called on my mother, my grandparents went down to the nursery, where they were keeping us newborns under glass. As they stood by the window, a masked nurse lifted me out of my basket and held me up. My grandfather got a good look at me through all that glass, yet minutes later he went outside to an impromptu press conference and told a huge lie.

The reporters were waiting for him on the steps of the hospital. Since he had practically run from them at the railroad station, he decided to settle in and let them take their time with this one. Dad couldn't have been more put out. When he walked out behind my grandfather, he was muscled aside by his own colleagues and had to stand in the background. On top of that, he was overdue at the office and Grandpa wouldn't stop talking. And not only was he talking; he was telling fibs.

"What's the baby look like?" a reporter asked.

"He has red hair, just like my side of the family," Grandpa said proudly.

This, to put it kindly, was sheer wishful thinking. Grandpa Truman wanted very badly to see some of the red hair that ran in his family, but unfortunately it did not run down my personal branch. Though my mother has pale red hair, what she's always called strawberry blond, I was born with a thick mop that was nearly jet black.

When my father finally pried Grandpa loose from the press, it didn't occur to him to bring the ex-president up short for telling so obvious a falsehood. He thought that in addition to the wishful thinking, the light in the hospital might have played tricks on Grandpa's eyes, which had never been good.

Grandpa obviously reconsidered the remark on his own, because the red-hair statement never came up again. Though Dad would never have mentioned it, I'm sure my grandmother and mother were not so shy.

And Grandpa had plenty of other chances to boast about his family. While he and my grandmother were in New York, reporters made a habit of greeting him at the hotel every day so they could follow him on his habitual morning walk. Since his schedule for the rest of the day was usually full, it was the best time to catch him. And more often than not he was in a good mood.

The only problem with walking with my grandfather was his speed. He walked a military mile—120 paces a minute, two steps every second. That's not bad when you're on your own. You would be blown off the sidewalk by those people you see power-walking around malls. But when you're trying to walk and write on a notepad or lug around a few extra pounds of cameras, canisters of film, and extra lenses, two steps a second is quite a pace.

And my grandfather, while glad to have the press along for the ride, wasn't about to stop for them every few feet. He walked for exercise, not photo opportunities. So when he came down for his walk in the morning, the press would be waiting for him, like a pack of hunters unwilling to give the fox a head start. "Morning, Mr. President," they would say, poised on tiptoe, ready to break from the gate.

"Morning, boys," he would say with a smile. "Ready to go?" And they were off, Grandpa in the lead at first. Then it was Grandpa back in the pack as the reporters swarmed around him, jockeying for a position next to his elbow.

"How're you feeling, Mr. President?"

"Fine, fine. Beautiful day," he would say, and plow ahead.

The photographers had the worst of it. If they wanted anything better than a shot of his backside, they would have to sprint out in front of him, shoot, then reload as he strode past. Then they would have to sprint past him again for another shot.

Though he wouldn't stop, Grandpa was usually otherwise accommodating. He despised most publishers but had a soft spot for working reporters. And he especially liked the photographers, whom he rescued from the elements when he was president. President Roosevelt had given the reporters a press room, but he had made the photographers stand outside the side door.

To honor him for bringing them in from the cold and making them what *New York Times* photographer George Tames called "first-class citizens," the photographers made Grandpa president of the Just One More Club, which they formed just for him. The title also acknowledged his willingness to honor their frequent request: "Mr. President, just one more?"

But his largesse didn't extend to photographers who took risks to get a shot. Two days after I was born, when the pack took off from the Carlyle at the crack of dawn, my grandfather noticed that one of the photographers seemed a little speedier and more adept than the rest. Tired of running a series of wind sprints every morning, the man had strapped on a pair of skates and was gliding backward in front of the group, snapping away. To my grandfather's horror, the shooter rarely glanced over his shoulder. Grandpa cringed as the man barely stopped in time for a curb or squeaked past a pedestrian by the slimmest of margins. After several minutes of near heart failure on the man's behalf, my grandfather could stand it no longer. "All right, that's it," he said, stopping dead in his tracks and wagging a finger at the daredevil. "You're going to kill yourself. I'm not taking another step until you take those things off."

"But Mr. President . . ." the man pleaded.

"No buts. Take 'em off or I don't budge."

I was born on a Wednesday. My grandfather left that Sunday morning to make a commencement address at Brandeis University in Waltham, Massachusetts. My grandmother stayed in New York, visiting my mother daily. She and my grandfather both especially liked to be around at feeding time, when they could look at me up close. They could do that because Mom had taken to feeding me formula out of a bottle. She had tried breast-feeding the first time but quickly soured on the idea because it hurt. Besides, she noticed I wasn't getting very much milk. This whole business of having children was still very foreign to her. It had not been her idea, but my father's. And he had wanted a girl.

I didn't realize that I and my brothers had come up with the wrong chromosome combination until years later, when I was school age. I happened to be poking around in my dresser drawers one day, probably looking for something my parents had thrown away. The bottom drawer wasn't one I used, so it had become a repository for stuff that wouldn't fit anywhere else. My whole room is like that today. Since I left home, it's become one big walk-in closet for Mom and Dad. Anyway, I came upon something in that bottom drawer that I never expected to see in a house full of boys: a little lacy white dress.

"Hey, Will! Look at this!" I yelled, holding it up for him to see.

"Whose is that?"

"I don't know. Hey, Mom!" I yelled, taking the dress into my parents' room. "What was this thing doing in my bottom drawer?"

"Why shouldn't it be in your bottom drawer?" she said. "It's your dress."

My mouth dropped open. Will had come up behind me and was snorting with laughter.

"It is not!" I said.

"Well, it would have been if you'd been a girl. And what are you laughing at?" she asked Will, who was still snorting. "It would have been yours, too. We thought both of you were going to be girls. You were going to be named Elizabeth, after your grandmother."

"Oh, gross."

"What?"

"Nothing."

Though she had no namesake to care for, my grandmother pitched in to help my parents anyway, staying in New York for a couple of weeks after I was born. When she wasn't with Mom at the hospital, she lent a hand at home, where my father was busily preparing my bedroom.

One of the first orders of business was buying a crib, which had been put off until after I was born. My parents had acted not out of laziness, but because of my mother's superstition. My grandmother Truman had suffered two miscarriages before my mother was born, and both times afterward, she and my grandfather had drawerfuls of clothes that would never be worn and an empty crib to remind them of their loss. So, during her third pregnancy, my grandmother refused to have any baby trappings in the house, fearing they might jinx her chances of having a healthy baby. As a result, my mother spent the first night of her life in the bottom drawer of my grandparents' dresser.

I was luckier. I was born in the 1950s, when women were kept in the hospital for a week or so after giving birth, giving my father plenty of time to buy a crib. It was a sturdy crib, made of wood, and it lasted through all four of us. The only problem was that it came disassembled. So, one evening, my father and grandmother fell to the task of putting it together. The weather was scorching hot, and my parents' new apartment had no air conditioning. Plus the crib, like all of its ilk, wasn't going to give in easily.

I've put more than my fair share of these things together, since I married a woman who owns a baby-clothing-and-accessories store. Cribs either don't come with all their parts—or you finish and find you've got four or five small but vital-looking pieces left over. The instructions come with pictures—of a crib that's completely different from the one you've bought—and nothing quite fits the way it should. Construction requires keen eyesight, muscle, and a vocabulary rich in profanity.

My father wanted very much to swear several times during the evening he and my grandmother put my crib together, but here was Bess Truman looking over his shoulder, so he couldn't. He would find he was missing a part and have to say, "Gosh darn it! There are supposed to be five of those blessed things!" Or he would pinch his thumb in the pliers and mutter "Phooey!" under his breath.

And he was melting, too. Today that apartment has an air conditioner in every room, but back then the only air came from the open windows, and that night the air wasn't moving. Finally the heat got so bad that he asked his mother-in-law if he could remove his shirt, which she didn't mind in the least. Not that this was such a big deal. My father has always worn an undershirt.

When he worked in London during World War II, Dad picked up the nickname the Sheik of Fleet Street because of his habit of wearing custom-made shirts and Savile Row suits. He was probably the most elegant American reporter working in England at the time. He and my grandfather Truman shared a penchant for good clothing, though it never would have occurred to Dad to buy any of those loud Hawaiian shirts Grandpa liked so much.

Dad is, by nature, slightly more formal than Grandpa. I rarely catch him without a jacket and tie, and that's when he's just working at his desk at home all day. If I'm up early enough, I'll find him in his pajamas. But where I look rumpled from sleeping in shorts and a T-shirt, he looks almost freshly ironed. So Gammy Truman had nothing to worry about that hot day she and Dad put the crib together. Dad is so impeccable that even in his undershirt he looks almost formal.

My grandfather arrived back in New York several days later and came to visit me at home, in my new bedroom. The big thrill of the event was watching my mother change my diaper. It had been a very long time since he had had to deal with an infant, so he was content to be an observer, as my mother discovered.

"Do you want to hold him?" she asked when she had finished inserting the little duck-head safety pins in my diapers.

"Well, uh . . . I, I, uh . . . sure," he said, and stuck out his arms. He looked more like a coatrack than man accepting a baby.

Mom frowned. Being a new mother, her natural instincts were finely honed. She could smell fear on my grandfather. "Not so fast," she said, her eyes narrowing. "Are you sure you know how?"

The inference that a former U.S. president, a man who survived the Argonne battle, might not be able to handle a baby brought him back to himself.

"I think I can manage," he said sarcastically. "Nothing's changed, has it?"

"Well, . . ." my mother said. Despite his bluster, he still didn't look completely sure of himself. "Sit down over there and take off your jacket."

"Why should I take off my jacket?"

"It might be dirty."

"Oh, for . . . All right, all right."

He took off his jacket and settled into the armchair in the middle of the room. Carefully Mom handed me to him. He received me like a package with the words CAREFUL, MIGHT GO OFF stamped on the side. For a few seconds, he simply sat there, getting used to it. Then, when he saw I wasn't going to explode, he began to bounce me gently up and down and smiled from ear to ear.

Because I had such problems as a young adult, I sometimes looked back to my childhood, and even my infancy, for clues to why I felt driven to make certain choices. It's all hindsight, and some of what I remember may not be accurate, but I have gained some insight. None of this, by the way, is accusation. People did things differently in the 1950s.

To begin with, I was a bottle baby, as were all my brothers. My mother wasn't keen on the alternative, which she found painful. Today doctors stress breast-feeding as the best source of nutrition for infants. Mother's milk is also believed to help boost an infant's immature immune system. The act of breast-feeding, the touch of human skin, is thought to create a closer bond between mother and child. But in 1957, the nuclear age, the age of whiz-bang gadgetry and medical miracles, bottle-feeding was often considered a fine alternative, if not preferable, to breast-feeding.

In 1957, it was also normal to let babies cry when they couldn't be soothed quickly. Even in 1987, when my daughter was born, Polly and I took our cue from Dr. Spock's book and let her cry herself to sleep for three nights in a row to wean her off her midnight feeding. It took an hour the first night and half an hour the second.

My father has told me of his frustration with trying to get me to sleep at night when I was a baby. I cried, and he would come upstairs, lift me out of my crib, and walk me back and forth across my bedroom until I dozed off. Then he would lay me back in the crib and try to tiptoe back downstairs. The instant his foot hit the bottom step, I would start crying again and he would have to start over. Pretty soon he gave up. Having been through that kind of thing myself, I can understand if he was aggravated.

I'm not interested in second-guessing my parents on how they raised me. I don't think they let me cry and bottle-fed me because they wanted to give me a bad start in life. I think I—and they—were more likely victims of the times. And who is to say being bottle-fed and left to cry had any effect on me? I might just have come into the world an impossible, cranky, needy baby. Who knows? These are just things I have thought about.

In July 1994, I spent about five days at the Truman Library in Independence, poking through decades of old newspaper clippings and correspondence belonging to my parents and grandparents. It is a strange thing to be in a building entirely devoted to your own family. I feel a very close connection to the Truman Library, but there's also a sense of unreality when I'm there. I walk around the building, looking at the exhibits, seeing Grandpa's face at every turn, and I find it hard to believe I'm related to him. Not that I feel unworthy, just sort of in awe. What's even more strange is going through the correspondence and finding all sorts of letters discussing my life, particularly my birth. The folders are filled with tons of yellowing cards and telegrams sent to my parents and grandparents, all dated around June 5, 1957.

Some were a little sneaky: Earl Zimmerman of the Connecticut Mutual Life Insurance Company sent a letter of congratulations to my grandfather that read, in part: "I would very much like to send you some information in regards to setting up an insurance estate for your grandson."

Some were funny: Congressman Merwin Coad telegrammed: "Congratulations on the birth of your new grandson. Hope mother and son are doing fine. Hope father and grandfather survived."

A couple made me feel that perhaps I should have tried harder in school: "You must all be very pleased with this new heir to a great American Democratic tradition," said a telegram from Congressman John F. Shelley. "With this background, I'm sure he will be a credit to his parents, his grandparents, and his country."

"The Governor's office of Kansas wishes to offer congratulations on the arrival of the future Democrat president of the United States in the year of 2000."

There's one I'm going to hold on to in case I ever need a theatrical agent. Joe Magee of the William Morris Agency wrote: "Please register new client with this office if he has no other agent."

But the one I like best was the telegram from my grandfather's old friend and close adviser Charlie Murphy. Mr. Murphy was as direct and no-nonsense as Grandpa and even more down to earth. Not one to let Grandpa get his head stuck in the clouds over me, he cabled exactly two words:

"So what?"

3

Florida Bound

Whenever they came to New York, my grandparents always stayed at the Carlyle Hotel, which was very convenient, since it was about a block from our apartment. During my grandfather's presidency, when my mother had flown the coop in Washington to try her wings as a singer, she eventually settled in the Carlyle, on the twenty-seventh floor, overlooking Central Park. When she married Dad, they found a new co-op apartment not far from her old digs.

When my grandparents visited the Carlyle, they stayed in a top-floor duplex, which is now known as the Presidential Suite. But it wasn't so named because my grandparents stayed there. It was called the Presidential Suite only after my mother recommended the hotel to President John. F. Kennedy.

My mother actually regretted doing that. Much as she liked Mr. Kennedy, she did not like the way he got around in our neighborhood. The motorcade he brought with him came with a pack of big, noisy police motorcycles that surrounded his car. Whenever President Kennedy was in the suite and announced he was coming down, the motorcycles revved their engines, rattling the windows and sending an acrid cloud of exhaust up the street and often into our living-room window. The racket always went on for at least ten or fifteen minutes because the president was invariably delayed on his way to the lobby.

Finally my mother could stand it no longer and called the Carlyle. She did not ask for the concierge or even the manager. Not my mother. She went right to the very tippy top. "Hello, this is Margaret Truman, may I speak to the president, please?"

There was a pause of less than a minute before Mr. Kennedy came on the line. "Margaret, how are you?"

"Fine, Jack," she said, "but I wonder if you could do me a favor? Those motorcycles of yours are driving me crazy. They're making a horrible racket and spewing exhaust fumes up the block. I'm right up the street, you know."

"I'm very sorry, Margaret, I had no idea," the president said.

"Well, I don't think it would be so bad if they'd wait until you get downstairs, but they're always starting up twenty minutes before you get there."

"I think that's just the way they do things, Margaret."

"Well, I wish they'd learn to do things a little differently."

"I'll talk to them."

"Thank you, Jack. I'd appreciate it." She hung up and walked into the next room to pick up the book she'd been reading. Before she sat down, the motorcycles stopped.

My grandfather caused a lot less racket than President Kennedy when he visited. Each day, he was up about five thirty, dressed, and out of the lobby door for that brisk one-mile walk, his handful of reporters in tow. Afterward he sat down for a light breakfast of half a grapefruit, some toast, and coffee. Then he usually strolled up to our apartment and let himself in with his own key. If no one was up, which was usually the case, he settled into my mother's living-room chair and read the paper. That's where Will and I found him one morning when we came down early.

"Well, good morning," he said, folding his paper. "I'm glad to see somebody's up in this house. Is your mother awake?"

We, standing in our pajamas with the feet in them, shook our heads. We didn't see Grandpa that often, so this was sort of like having a stranger in the house. Plus he had that stern demeanor, as if he were on the verge of giving an order. We were always a little uneasy around him.

"Well, if your mother's not up, what are you up to?" he asked.

I pointed to the library, which was where we kept the television set. "We're going to watch cartoons," I said.

He frowned and shook his head. "You don't want to do that," he said, getting up. "Why don't we read a story instead. Here, I've got something I think you might like." And he went into the den and pulled a book down from the shelf. He did not take it from the kiddie books section.

"Come sit by me," he said, settling again in my mother's chair. We climbed up on either side of him. "Now, let's see what we've got."

He opened the book and began to read.

Five minutes later, my mother came down, her feet in fuzzy slippers, her hair on end, her eyes half open.

"Good morning," my grandfather said, looking up from the book. His tone implied that she had wasted the better part of a day.

"Good morning," she said slowly, not sure of what to make of our trio. "What on earth are you reading to them?"

My grandfather said not a word, but held up the spine of the book so she could see. Her eyes narrowed as she read the title, then widened. "Thucydides?" she said. "Good God!"

"And why not?" my grandfather said. "They're enjoying it just fine."

It never occurred to him as strange that Will and I, a three-year-old and a one-year-old, would willingly give up our morning cartoons for a dose of Greek history.

The next time my grandparents came to stay with us wasn't long after, in the spring of 1960. My parents were taking off on a nine-week tour of Europe. Dad had been assigned by *The New York Times* to cover the Big Four conference in Paris between the United States, France, Russia, and Britain. When the conference failed to convene in the wake of the Russians' downing of Francis Gary Powers's U-2 spy plane, Mom and Dad took an extended holiday. My parents left us in the hands of Miss Nutzmann and a cook and housekeeper and a former U.S. president and first lady. My grandparents stayed for at least two weeks to help baby-sit. This time they stayed not at the Carlyle but in the apartment with us. One morning, I walked into the dining room to find my grandfather reading the paper at the table. My grandmother and the cook were in the kitchen, discussing lunch.

"Hi, Grandpa," I said.

He lowered his paper. "Hello there. What are you up to?"

"I'm gonna ride my horse."

"Well, good. That's a fine thing. You go right ahead."

The horse sat by the window. It was plastic, brown and white, mounted on a wooden base with heavy springs. It was one of my favorite toys, and I loved to ride it hard. Sturdy as it seemed, I had already come close to tipping the whole thing over several times.

"You're going to kill yourself on that thing," my mother had told me at least a dozen times. "Don't ride it so hard."

But she wasn't there that morning. And my grandfather, engrossed in his paper, took little notice of me as I whipped my stallion into a lather.

Seconds later, in the kitchen. my grandmother and the cook heard a loud thump. They came spilling through the swinging door to find me on the floor of the dining room, half under the overturned horse. My grandfather had done little more than lower his paper again.

"Oh, my goodness!" my grandmother said, rushing forward to pull the horse off me.

The second I saw the concern on her face I knew I must have suffered a dire wound, and I knew dire wounds were good for at least a hug and, possibly, a cookie, so I started to cry. I did not get a chance to produce more than one or two teardrops.

"Stop right there!" my grandfather said, putting up his hand. "Don't touch him."

At the sound of his voice, my grandmother stopped dead in her tracks. My tear ducts dried up instantly, and my mouth clapped shut of its own accord.

"You're not hurt," he said sternly. "You've just had the wind knocked out of you. Now pick up that horse, get back on it, and start riding it again."

I didn't argue, didn't let out another whimper. I did as I was told. It was, after all, an executive order.

My grandfather had been much nicer to me than his own father had been to him. At age six, he had fallen off his pony while his father was leading the animal through the fields by their house. His father, disgusted, made him walk the rest of the way home.

"Any boy who can't stay on a pony at a walk deserves to walk himself," he said.

The following year, 1961, my parents and grandparents, and my brother and I, took a month-long trip to Bermuda. It was the first of what would be a string of spring vacations together, most of them to Key West, where my grandfather had had his "Little White House" on a U.S. naval base.

The Bermuda trip was completely uneventful as far as my parents and grandparents were concerned. For them, it was just a nice month of reading, visiting, and sitting by the ocean. Well, it was a nice month for Mom. Dad had to go back to work after two weeks. Gammy and Grandpa got the better end of the deal. They came for the second two weeks, after my father had left. When they arrived from Independence, they brought the sun with them. It had rained almost the entire time Dad was there.

I was four, and there are three things I remember about Bermuda: the winding path from our house on the cliff down to the sea; the knotted tree stump Will and I used as an imaginary sailing ship; and a lizard named Mr. Dubious who lived in our room for the first few days of the trip. He was named Mr. Dubious because when I saw him, I turned to my mother and said, "I don't know, Mom. I'm kinda dubious about this."

There were other memorable things about Bermuda, namely, the day the sunken patio flooded in a storm because the drain was clogged with leaves, and the night Miss Nutzmann burned up Will's and my underwear. She had hung it to dry in front of the fire, and it got riddled with hundreds of tiny holes from sparks flying off the sputtering cedar we were burning. Bermuda was also the first place I got drunk, off a teaspoon of sugared whiskey Miss Nutzmann gave me after I threw up at a birthday party. It was a harbinger of things to come. My father said I was having such a good time dancing, yelling, singing, and acting like an idiot that he and my mother had to hold me down to get me to go to bed.

The next Daniel-Truman family vacation was in 1962, when I was five, to a tiny dot in the Florida Keys named Duck Key. The island had only one hotel, because that's all there was room for. We had gone down there at the suggestion of Senator John Spottswood, a leading citizen and politician in Key West.

Duck Key was where I think I fell in love with hotels. The hotel there had a swimming pool and a private beach where we swam and built sand castles. There was also a restaurant, and my father let us go down early each morning and order our breakfast. It was a big thrill for a five-year-old. Also, there were plenty of elevators. I loved the elevators. There was nothing better than making something work by pushing a button. What I liked even better was the approval I got from adults for pushing the button for them. I went out of my way to ride the elevator, even to the point of doing it while wearing nothing but my beach towel.

Will and I had nothing to do but play in the pool and at the beach with two kids from Milwaukee, a boy named Fritz and his older sister, whose name I can't remember. Will probably remembers it. She had a crush on him and followed him everywhere, which drove him crazy.

A few days into the trip, my mother woke us up a little earlier than usual. The sun hadn't yet hit the window of our room. Normally this was an extreme breach of vacation etiquette. Like my mother—and unlike my grandfather—I hated getting up in the morning unless it was Saturday and cartoons were on. When I got older, I used to bunch up against the wall in my top bunk so Mom or the nanny wouldn't be able to poke me awake in the morning. Sometimes Mom would even leave me alone for a while. This morning, however, she was all business.

"Come on, let's go," she said. "You're going for a walk with your grandfather today."

Will and I staggered out of bed and started feeling around for our clothes, which Mom had laid out for us. Our uniform for the day was the one we had worn—with some variations—for all public events: matching shirts, ties, jackets, shorts, and kneesocks. I have lost count of the number of pictures we have that show me and Will in some kind of cute, coordinated outfits.

At my grandparents' suite, we found Grandpa in the middle of the living room, in a chair, waiting, idly fingering the curved handle of his cane. "Good morning," he said when he saw us. "How are you boys this morning?"

"Fine," we said, looking and sounding like a fraternal-twin variation of Tweedle Dum and Tweedle Dee.

"Are you ready to go for a little walk?"

Well, actually no. We would rather be sleeping. Then we would like to play on the beach. But what are you going to say to your grandfather the ex-president?

"Yessir," we said.

"Good. You just stick with me."

We were driven to a small bridge less than a mile from the hotel. Waiting for us when we arrived was a small crowd of spectators and television and newspaper reporters. The bridge in front of us was to be the Truman Bridge, dedicated in Grandpa's honor. What we were going to do was help him cut a ceremonial ribbon at one end, then walk with him from that end to the other.

The bridge isn't the only Truman monument in the Keys. It's not even my favorite. That would be the Margaret Truman Laundromat in Key West, so named because it stands at the intersection of Margaret Street and Truman Boulevard. It is not named for my mother, otherwise she would have demanded dividends—or at least a free roll of quarters when she visited.

After a few minutes of standing at the bridge, shaking hands and having his picture taken, Grandpa turned to us. "Let's go," he said.

We followed him as he strode forward, cut the ribbon with a pair of scissors, and walked across the bridge. Even at the tender age of six, I was conscious of publicity. I loved seeing my face in the paper. And with all the cameras going off in my face, I was sure I was going to make it into the local papers the next day.

When morning came, I spilled out of bed to get the paper and forced my parents to look for a picture of the bridge-dedication ceremony. I was bitterly disappointed when they found it, though. It was a great picture of Grandpa and Will as they walked across the bridge. Will looked like Grandpa's shadow, a tiny, short-pants version of Harry Truman. I, however, was nowhere in sight. I began to wonder if Will and Grandpa had gone to some other bridge-dedication ceremony without me. Then my mother noticed a small black lump sticking out from just above my grandfather's knee.

"Oh, look," she said. "There's your shoe."

That photo, good as it was, dogs me to this day. When I submitted a bunch of photos for the jacket of this book, that's the one the publisher's art department chose.

"It's perfect with you following in his footsteps like that," they said.

"Yes, it is," I said. "There's only one problem. That's not me. See that lump by his knee? That's me."

"Oh," they said. "Well, never mind."

I didn't have much time to worry about publicity. During the rest of our vacation, we had a full slate. One of the things I enjoyed most was the deep-sea-fishing trip we took in the hotel charter boat. Just before the trip, I had gotten a hold of a book on sharks from the school library and had been mesmerized by the section on hammerheads. When I went out on that boat, I was determined to catch one.

Our family was pretty evenly divided into sportsmen and spectators. My mother and grandmother set themselves up in the shade of the wheelhouse, avoiding both the sun and any chance they might have to touch a fish. My father, being more game, was fishing alongside me and Will. Grandpa secured himself a deck chair and offered advice on baiting and casting. Dad hardly paid attention to his pole, preferring to talk current events with my grandfather. But I watched the water, straining through the dark blue for a glimpse of a hammer-shaped silhouette.

Suddenly, there was a tug on my line—a hard one. The pole jerked in my hands, startling me.

"Dad, I got one!" I yelled. "I got a shark!"

Bowed by the fish on the other end of the line, the tip of the pole arched toward the water. The handle nearly jumped out of my hand. Dad saw I was in trouble and took the rig from me, then started reeling in the fish. I stood by, jumping from foot to foot and nervously clapping my hands, waiting for the monster from the deep that I knew was going to come thrashing up at the end of my line.

The fish broke the water, long, sleek, and fat. His blue sides glistened; his tail churned the water. Then Dad pulled him clear, and he landed on the deck at my feet, twisting furiously.

He was beautiful. But he was no shark. It was a big, old bluefish.

"Throw him back," I said.

"Why?" my father said. "That's the best fish anybody's caught all day. We're going to eat this fish for dinner tonight. I'm not going to throw it back."

And he wrested the hook from the fish's mouth and dropped my catch to the deck, where it seesawed feverishly toward me, as if it were spring-loaded. I got the hell out of the way.

"Pick it up so I can get a picture," Dad said, camera in hand.

"No," I said, moving as the fish lurched in my direction again. "It'll bite me."

"It won't hurt you," my grandfather said. "It's just a fish."

I watched the blue fish thrashing on the wooden deck, rattling the gunwales with each slap of its tail, its jaws opening and closing. I could have sworn I saw hundreds of tiny teeth in there.

"I'm not touching it," I said again as the fish backed me into a corner.

"Oh, for heaven's sake, Clifton . . ." my father began.

But my grandfather stopped him. "Put it in the bucket," he said. "He can pick it up in a minute."

My father grabbed the fish and dropped it into a Styrofoam cooler at the stern. And we sat and waited, me on the gunwales with my feet pulled up, watching the fish. When it died, my father walked over to it and slipped his fingers under its gills.

"Is it dead?" I asked.

"Yes. Now you can pick it up," he said, offering it to me.

"Not by its mouth!"

"All right, then. Grab its tail if you want."

And he stood back and took the picture—a boy with a devil-may-care grin, one hand on his hip, the other holding a fish nearly two feet long. It was cooked that night by the hotel chef and served to us. I didn't eat one bite of it. Still, by the end of the fishing trip, I had decided that not catching a shark was all right. Everyone seemed much happier with the fish I had caught.

The day would have ended perfectly except for the fact that near the end of the trip, Dad had the temerity to go and catch a baby hammerhead shark. A baby hammerhead! Just the right size for a five-year-old. I still think someone switched fish on us. Dad should have gotten the bluefish. He liked eating it, anyway.

Most of the rest of our Florida spring vacations were spent in Key West, at least the ones I remember. The visit I recall most vividly occurred in 1968, when we stayed on the grounds of a 1920s, Spanish-style hotel owned by Senator Spottswood. The senator was having the hotel renovated, so my family and I moved into what would become the maid's quarters, a duplex on the grounds. We had the rest of the hotel grounds to ourselves, including a pool and a pool house, which came complete with billiard and Ping-Pong tables. Will and I were forbidden from playing in the hotel itself because we might fall through the old floorboards, just as the piano leg had in the White House. My grandparents stayed in a rented house nearby. By this time we had added the third and fourth brothers to the family roster. Harrison Gates Daniel had been born March 3, 1963, and Thomas Washington Daniel had been born May 28, 1966.

I was eleven in 1968 and growing more and more conscious of my grandfather's place in history and the effect his fame had on me. At home and at school, being Harry Truman's grandson was no big thing. But on vacations with him, there were cameras and reporters and onlookers everywhere we went. Occasionally Mom couldn't keep me and Will from basking in the extra attention.

My grandparents rented a villa-style house with a stone courtyard and a tiled roof overlooking the beach. It was at the end of a dead-end street so the police could keep tabs on who was coming and going. Only those who lived on the street or their friends and family could get around a set of police sawhorses at the mouth of the street. Walking over to see my grandparents one day, we watched as two boys on bicycles tried to ride past the policeman at the barricade.

"Whoa, whoa! You boys can't go down there," he said. "President Truman is staying down there."

Both boys came to an abrupt halt and walked their bikes back toward him. This was just as Will and I were rounding the corner. They frowned at us as we waved to the policeman and walked down the street.

"Hey! How come they get to go down there?" one of them asked.

"Those are Mr. Truman's grandsons," the policeman said.

I felt very smug and superior at that moment. Thinking about it now, I'm ashamed of myself. But at the time, the feeling was enough to keep me walking on air for a few hours. There was none of that kind of feeling at home. In fact, we lived under conditions that were the very opposite. I've often thought my parents were harder on us because of chance encounters like the one with the boys at the barricade. They didn't want us to get the idea that, just because of our grandfather, we could go through life getting something for nothing. Looking back at the way I felt that day, I can see what they were worried about. But keeping us from getting swelled heads often meant bruising our egos.

My grandfather held one press conference while we were in Key West that year, on the lawn of the hotel where we were staying. The reporters gathered near the pool, where we had been swimming and playing with the Secret Service agents. At the start of the press conference, my mother shooed us away, toward the pool. "Just stand over here and watch," she said. "Don't get in the way."

But as the conference got going, I had the idea that I could lure a reporter or two away from my grandfather if I tried showing off a little bit. It was not an unconscious act. I intended to get some attention. So I found a tree with a fat, level branch, climbed up, and sat down where everyone gathered around my grandfather could see me. It worked. Within a minute or two, a lady reporter spotted me and walked over.

"Hello there," she said. "What's your name?"

"Clifton Truman Daniel," I said, noting with glee that she wrote my name in a notebook.

"Are you the oldest?"

I nodded.

"And where do you live?"

"New York."

This went on for a couple of minutes, with her writing down everything I said. I was scared to death, but thrilled to have someone paying such close attention to me. It was the same feeling I get going onstage today. In fact, if the truth be known, it's the reason I act. I guess I've come to appreciate the craft of acting, but that's not what I do it for. During rehearsals, I'm like a bulb on the lower end of a dimmer. I don't put my heart and soul into a play until there's an audience.

That day in Key West, I lost my audience quickly. Will had climbed a tree nearby and was not just imitating my act, but going me one better by hanging upside down by his knees. This was just too much for the reporter to pass up, and she threw me over. I was mad at Will for stealing her, but my anger was nothing compared to Mom's. She had been watching the whole thing. After the press conference was over, she pulled us angrily aside. "I thought I told you to stay out of the way," she snapped. "You're not the important ones here. Your grandfather is."

At the time I didn't make that much of the comment. It was in keeping with the way Mom sometimes talked to us, so I just took it in stride. But over the years, whenever I've thought of that particular trip to Key West, that's the incident I remember first. My mother was trying to tell us not to get too big for our britches, but I took it to mean "You're not as good as he is."

Come to think of it, that was a gloomy vacation all around. Will and I and Senator Spottswood's son, Robert, did get to tour Cape Kennedy with Gemini astronaut Tom Stafford as our guide. We even wound up posing for photos in the trainer for the *Apollo* capsule. But on top of it all, the second week we were there was the week Dwight D. Eisenhower died. I didn't then know the history of the animosity between the general and my grandfather. Grandpa didn't say anything that I remember, so I can't say exactly how he took the news of Eisenhower's death, but he became withdrawn and moody after hearing it. In fact, a cloud seemed to settle over our whole family for a while.

Earlier Key West vacations had been more festive. On one of the first, my grandfather was invited to have lunch at the naval base where he had had the Little White House. Will and I got to tour a destroyer and a submarine, after which we were served lunch in the commandant's quarters. Will and I had a separate table. The adults ate in the main dining room. That lunch was the first time I ever saw an artichoke.

In Grandpa's day, he and his staff used the Little White House as a place to escape Washington and let their hair down. These were working vacations, but not so strenuous that they couldn't find time to lounge around in loud shirts and play poker.

Many people know of my grandfather's penchant for loud Hawaiian shirts. Presidential aides and advisers also wore such shirts in the warm climate, but Grandpa's were the loudest. Until recently I thought the ones I had were a couple of the wilder ones—a silk one with an Aztec sun on the back and a black one with purple and green all over it. But when they opened the storage bins at the Truman Library, I was awed by the sheer garishness of some of my grandfather's Florida shirts. Most of them were printed in colors not found in nature. There was a green one there that I could have sworn was still glowing as they shut the cabinet.

Grandpa's poker game was a strong as his shirts. He actually had two games. One he played with the big boys—senators, judges, maybe Clark Clifford, men who could afford to lose. The high-stakes games weren't played at the White House because my grandfather considered that sacrilegious. They were usually played in a rented room at the Statler Hotel.

Grandpa played a less strenuous game with his staff. At these games, the betting limit was one hundred dollars, and a backup kitty was kept in a hat in case someone lost his stake. Staff games were played often at Key West or on the presidential yacht, the *Williamsburg.*

There's been a lot made of my grandfather's drinking while playing poker, but he actually had tremendous self-control. He had been known to belt back an entire bourbon in the middle of the afternoon, but then not have another drink the rest of the day. He has also been known to have more than one drink, but was never seen to be drunk, unlike his grandson. George Elsey, one of his administrative assistants, said he usually nursed one bourbon and water through an entire four-hour poker game.

Still, he liked a man who could hold his liquor and distrusted those who didn't drink. The first time he met my father, he thought Dad fell into that category. Dad had just returned from Russia, where he had been bureau chief for *The New York Times.* This was in the mid-1950s, when communism was in full swing and the Russians were extremely suspicious of Western journalists. Everything Dad wrote had to pass through Soviet censorship. For most of his time in Moscow, he was the only American newspaper correspondent based there. The rest of the American press relied mainly on news agency correspondents. It was a tough, twenty-four-hour-a-day job, and Dad lost thirty pounds working at it. If he got a good story out of Moscow, he felt that he had really done a day's work.

All the haggling, late nights, and some vodka left Dad exhausted. The combination also gave him an ulcer. So when he got home, his doctor prescribed plenty of rest and no alcohol. When my mother took him up to meet my grandparents in their suite in the Carlyle, the first thing she did after she sat him down was ask if anyone wanted a drink.

"Bourbon," my grandfather said.

"Make it two," said my grandmother.

"Clifton?"

"I'll just have a glass of milk, please."

Both my grandfather's eyebrows went up. Here he was, faced with a prospective son-in-law who was not only a newspaperman but a teetotaler to boot. My mother was laughing so hard at the sight of his face, it took her a couple of minutes to explain.

But as I've said, it was publishers my grandfather didn't like. He got along fine with reporters, even editors. In Key West, he often encouraged the reporters to have fun, even when they turned unruly.

My grandfather liked to swim, but the naval base had no natural beach, just a small cove near the Little White House. So the Navy brought in several truckloads of sand and made a beach. They even built a small wooden cabana on it so my grandfather could change into his trunks. One night, a couple of the reporters were weaving down the street after barhopping in downtown Key West when they stumbled across an old man with a small burro. In a flash of drunken inspiration, they bought the animal on the spot.

When the guard at the naval base gate waved them through in the taxi that brought them home, he didn't notice the squirming lump under the jackets at their feet. The next morning, my grandfather walked out to his cabana and flung open the door. There, braying at him, was the burro. And that wasn't all. With nowhere else to go, it had used its small wooden prison as a toilet—repeatedly.

My grandfather stared, astonished, for a few moments, then burst out laughing. The chief of security didn't take it so lightly and ordered a full-scale search for the culprits. Grandpa had to go over and calm him down—and practically order him to call off the search.

4

219 North Delaware Street, Independence, Missouri

For a place to explore, nothing could top my grandparents' house in Independence, Missouri. I grew up in a big apartment on Manhattan's Upper East Side which had more room in it than my own house—and maybe some of my yard—in North Carolina. I'm always a little in awe of the size of the place when I go home to visit my parents. (The building has one other distinction: It and my father are the same age. Of the two, Dad's in much better shape. At least he's not cracking or peeling.) But for all its size and grandeur, that New York apartment could never compare to my grandparents' home at 219 North Delaware Street in Independence. That was a great treasure chest.

My grandmother's grandfather, George Porterfield Gates, was a lumberman who would become one of the richest men in Independence as part owner of the Waggoner-Gates Milling Company. He had the house built in 1867, and in 1885, his wealth allowed him to expand the existing house to what it is today, a fourteen-room Victorian mansion. For me, it has always been a place of gables and turrets, nooks and crannies. There are bedrooms you have to step up to walk into, stairs that lead nowhere, an attic full of draped shapes, and a secret storeroom through the back of a closet. No matter how many times I was there as a child, it was always a place to explore.

The first place Will and I headed when we hit the door was perhaps the plainest place in the house, the kitchen pantry. Still, it held a treasure all its own. On the shelf was a red-and-white cookie tin. If we were lucky, which we always were when it came to that tin, Gammy and Grandpa's longtime cook, Vietta Garr, had filled it with brownies. Vietta made some of the best brownies I've ever had in my life, thick and chocolaty and undercooked just enough so they were perfectly gooey. And she was very free with them, too. All you had to do was ask.

When she knew we were coming, Vietta baked some of those brownies and put them aside on the second shelf in the back of the pantry. After saying hello to my grandparents—and sometimes before—Will and I went to see if there were two stacks of brownies separated by a sheet of wax paper.

My parents and grandparents worked hard to keep all our visits "normal." Their house was the kind of place where you could find a tin full of brownies in the pantry, a place that was filled with the smells of good food at mealtime. Rules were relaxed, we didn't keep up any kind of public schedule, and there was plenty of time to play.

On early visits, there were photographers and reporters at the airport or train station when we arrived. That's because Grandpa always insisted on meeting us. We, in turn, greeted him by yanking at his jacket or climbing up his leg. But as we and my grandparents grew older, there was obviously less leg climbing, and consequently, less was made of our arrival.

As Grandpa got older, he often stayed at home, where it was safer. Gammy usually came out to meet us with their bodyguard and driver, Mike Westwood, or a couple of Secret Service agents. But though Grandpa chose to stay at home, he didn't expect to be ignored. When we got to the house, Mom's first order was: "Go say hello to your grandfather."

It was never hard to find my grandfather. In his later years, he was almost always in his study, leaning back in his big leather armchair, walled in by stacks of thick books. It's a small room, and it's been tidied up some by the Park Service, which now administers the house, but in Grandpa's day, it looked like the whole Library of Congress had been stuffed in there. Books were crammed into every square inch of shelf space. Table-size picture books, well-thumbed old history books, thick biographies, faded magazines, all bulged from the floor-to-ceiling shelves. If you tried to slip even a pamphlet into the pile, it would all come crashing down.

I thought of that study as kind of an inner sanctum, and I didn't just wander in there anytime I felt like it, though I was always welcome. After the pantry, it was usually the next stop. One Christmas, however, when Will and I were fourteen and twelve respectively, we forgot our manners and completely ignored Grandpa. So he had to come looking for us. And he was not at all happy about what he found.

It is no secret what my grandfather thought of long hair. There's a story I've often heard—and told—about the morning he was on one of his walks with Mike Westwood and crossed paths with a long-haired young man.

Recognizing my grandfather, the young man stopped and said politely, "Good morning, Mr. President."

My grandfather did not waste time with pleasantries, nor did he employ tact or feel that he needed to withhold judgment. "Young man," he said directly, shaking the young man's hand and smiling. "You'd look a lot better if you went to see a barber." And he was on his way without another word.

Imagine his dismay that day in late 1971 when Will and I cruised past the study door. My parents, trying to be open-minded when it came to our fashion and coiffure choices, had let both of us grow our hair down to our shoulders.

Seeing us go by, Grandpa frowned and put down his book. He made his way to the study door for a better look, but he was eighty-seven and did not move as quickly as he once had. By the time he reached the door, we had disappeared around the corner and headed upstairs. So he beckoned to my mother, who was at that moment coming through the kitchen.

"Who are those two young men with the long hair?" he asked.

Mom stared at him for a second, wondering what in the world

he was talking about. Then it struck her. "Those are your two oldest grandsons," she said carefully, waiting to see what his reaction would be.

He did not say a word.

We were upstairs, sniffing around our old bedrooms and opening up boxes. This was part of the ritual whenever we went to visit. Over the years, my grandmother had amassed for us a treasure trove of old and new toys, store-bought and hand-me-down: guns, blocks, trains, building sets, footballs. They were kept upstairs in anything that would hold them, including my mother's old toy chest and a big, sagging cardboard box. No matter how old I got, one of the first things I did when I visited that house was go through my old toys. Will and I were in the middle of such an inventory when Mom called from the foot of the stairs.

"Come say hello to your grandfather," she said.

I don't know about Will, but I walked down the stairs with mild apprehension. By that time in my life, I was a little afraid of my grandfather, afraid of not knowing how to act or what to say. I didn't share his interests in history and government. In fact, I didn't share his interest in self-enlightenment in general. (At that particular time, my chief interest was where I might hide so I could smoke a cigarette.) As a result, I usually avoided talking to my grandfather at all, which was why I neglected to say hello when I arrived that day. I don't know what I expected to happen if I did sit down and talk to him; probably that he would lecture me. What a horrible fate, I thought.

So, worried about being summoned to the inner sanctum, I followed Will downstairs, through the dining room, and to the study door where Grandpa was still standing, one hand on his cane, the other on the doorway. His dark gray suit seemed too big, his tie and collar loose around his neck. His face was gaunt, and his eyes looked huge behind his thick glasses. But there was something about him that made him seem anything but frail. As we approached, he didn't say anything, just looked us up and down, his mouth set.

"Hello, Grandpa," I said.

"What was that?" he asked, cupping his left ear and leaning forward a little.

"We just came to say hello," I said, louder.

He straightened up again and nodded once sharply.

"Well, do it, then."

As younger children, Will and I were left pretty much to our own devices in Independence. We weren't expected to spend a lot of time sitting around talking to Gammy and Grandpa. They, in turn, did not expect to spend a lot of time playing with us. Though Gammy had been a standout high school athlete, she wasn't keen on chucking a baseball around the yard or playing hide-and-seek. Grandpa, though he liked to fish, was not in a position—or of an inclination—to grab a pole and a can of worms and drive us all to the nearest stream.

Will and I also got the impression that Grandpa didn't want to have much to do with us while we were there. He spent much of his time in his study, reading. I think it had a lot to do with his age and increasing infirmity. He just couldn't keep up with us the way he had when we—and he—were younger.

It was not that I never read a book in my grandparents' house. Even among the thick, scholarly volumes in the study, I could find something to interest me. One spring, when I was about eleven, my parents decided we would drive from New York to Independence to visit Gammy and Grandpa. Along the way, hoping to cram some history into our heads, Dad stopped at the battlefield in Gettysburg, Pennsylvania. As far as I was concerned, the ploy worked. I was fascinated. I had been able to walk over the battlefield, crouch down in the snipers' nests and see where cannons had stood to hurl shells at advancing troops.

When we got to Gammy and Grandpa's house, I went to the study and found a big Civil War picture book, which included lots of photographs of the places where I had stood and things I had seen in Gettysburg. I spent an hour in the study when no one else was around, just thumbing through the pages. I preferred to look at the book alone, without an adult hovering over me, telling me what

This is me at age five in 1961. I'm smiling, so I must have done something really horrendous. This is the kind of photo my friends see and say, "Oh, you were so cute then! What happened?"

Cartoonist Jim Berryman heralded Grandpa's impending grandpahood in 1957 in the *Washington Star.*

On the afternoon of June 5, 1957, Gammy and Grandpa were photographed leaving the Independence depot for New York and their first glimpse of little old me. (*Courtesy UPI*)

In St. Louis, on my grandparents' way to New York, Edward Golterman, assistant to the mayor, presented them with a baseball and glove on behalf of the mayors of St. Louis and Independence. My grandparents left Independence so fast that neither mayor had a chance to see them off. (*Courtesy UPI*)

Dad took this photo of nurse Adele Day holding me up so I could get my first look at Gammy and Grandpa.

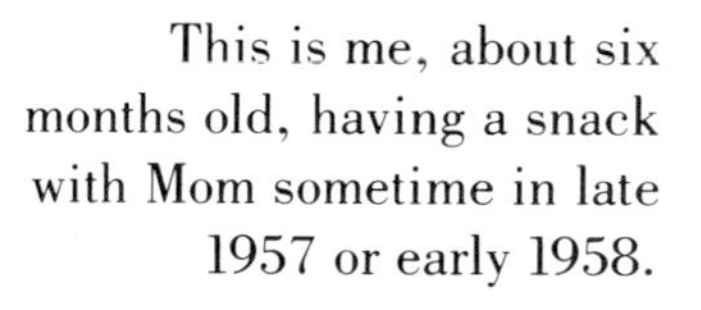

This is me, about six months old, having a snack with Mom sometime in late 1957 or early 1958.

This photo was taken during a party for my third or fourth birthday. I'm sitting in what has always been my mother's traditional seat at the dining-room table. Whenever Grandpa visited, it became his seat, and from there he had watched me tip over my rocking horse a year or so earlier. The horse is out of frame in front of us.

What a cute family—
Mom, Dad, and me.

We arrive in Independence for a Christmas visit. If I look bewildered, it's because I had just woken up and wasn't sure who the heck was carrying me.

My first visit to the Truman Library, on December 31, 1959. I was given a special tour by the custodian.

On April 14, 1960, Mom and Dad prepare to leave the country for nine weeks. Mom is holding Will, age eleven months, and Dad is holding me, age two, while Gammy and Grandpa look on. Dad was supposed to cover a summit conference attended by the United States, France, Great Britain, and the Soviet Union, but the conference was canceled, so my parents had to make do with an extended vacation. They left us with some very overqualified babysitters. (*Courtesy The New York Times*

The first thing the sitter did after my parents left was show me and Will off to the press, which had gathered outside my parents' living-room window. My mother, who was afraid we'd be kidnapped, is still mad at him for getting our faces plastered all over the newspapers. (*Courtesy Wide World Photos*)

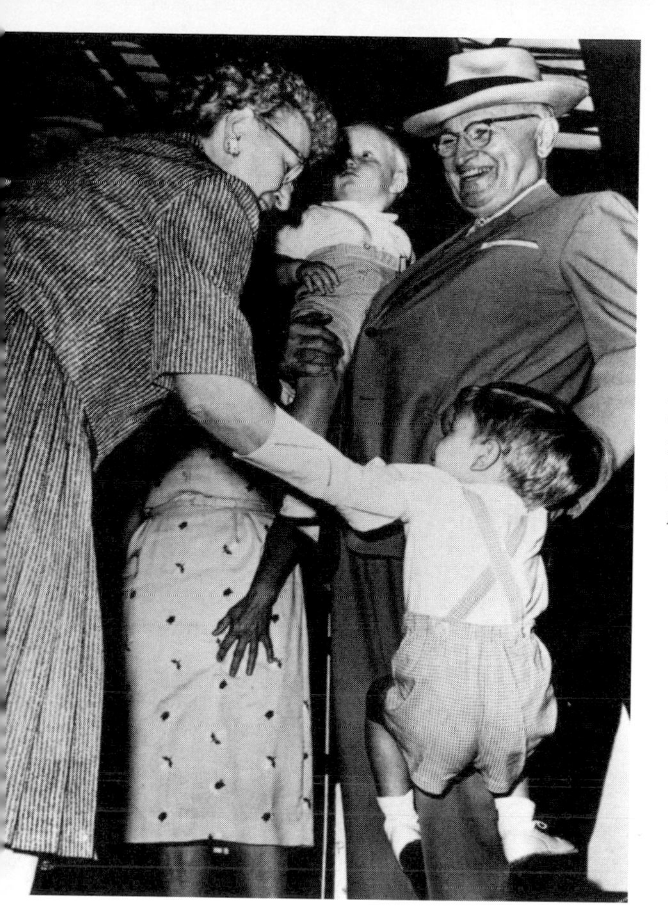

When my parents returned from their nine weeks in Europe, we all went to meet them. By that time, I had begun to see Grandpa less as a baby-sitter and more as a jungle gym. (*Courtesy Wide World Photos*)

Christmas Day 1961 in Independence, when I was four. I had asked for a band uniform like those I had seen in the Macy's Thanksgiving Day parade. This Marine dress uniform was much better. Where Gammy and Grandpa got it, I don't know. Probably from a small Marine.

My parents and grandparents posed with the Kennedys in 1961 prior to a disastrous White House dinner featuring overbaked grouse. Dad said we once had a better copy; when this one was taken, Dad had turned to whisper something to Mom, and Mrs. Kennedy was in the middle of a long blink.

was what. Now, of course, I could kick myself for not asking my grandfather to read it with me. At the same time, though, I don't know what his reaction would have been if I had. Will isn't sure he would have wanted to take the time.

As much as I avoided having anyone teach me history, it never occurred to me that Will and I were playing in a historical treasure trove every time we went to visit our grandparents. They kept so much exotic stuff in that house that every visit was like a trip to a museum—a museum where you could touch everything.

Among my favorites were the marbles my grandmother kept in an ornate thingamabob on the dining-room sideboard. The Park Service has this item listed as an *epergne,* something in which you keep flowers. But it looks more like a nineteenth-century bowling trophy. It was given to my great-grandparents, David and Madge Wallace, as a wedding gift by their groomsmen. It is about two feet high and silver-plated with a small bowl at the top, supported by two stems. Another small bowl hangs on slender chains beneath it. The bowl at the top is where my grandmother kept the marbles. She kept them there because I kept putting them down the heating vents, and she hoped the top bowl would be out of my reach.

I first found those marbles when I was about three or four years old. They were nothing spectacular, just a batch of red and blue marbles my grandmother had bought specifically for me and Will. Only I found them a few years earlier than she had hoped I would.

Before the marbles made it to the heights of the thingamabob on the dining-room sideboard, they were in one of two larger silver bowls on the sideboard, both of which were closer to the floor. When I discovered them peeking from over the scalloped lip of that bowl, I dug out a handful and walked off. Not knowing how to play marbles yet, I improvised my own game.

The heating system in my grandparents' house was an old dinosaur fueled by an oil furnace in the basement. Its fat ducts snaked throughout the house, each ending in a substantial vent in the low end of a wall. These were not vents like you have today—little louvered, rectangular things. These were square, almost a foot long on each side, and covered with an iron grille.

The granddaddy of these gratings was over the return duct in the floor of the entrance hall. It carried cool air back to the basement to be reheated, but it looked like a hatch people used to put over their dungeons. Leaning close to it, you would half expect to hear a plaintive voice saying, "Please let me out. I've been down here since 'forty-eight. I promise I'll never mention Dewey again."

This return-duct grating was also mere feet from the dining room and the bowl of marbles. So, naturally, when I wandered out of the dining room with my handful of marbles, within seconds I had discovered those little square holes were just big enough for a marble or two . . . or three or four. . . .

One by one I would put the marbles through the vent and listen to them clang against the tin wall of the heating duct and disappear into the dark. I didn't know where they were going, nor did I care. There was just the contentment of fitting them through and watching them drop. My fascination was as endless and bottomless as the duct seemed to be. I could have gone on forever—or at least until I ran out of marbles—if my grandmother hadn't rounded the corner just as I was letting go handful number five or six.

"Here, now! What are you doing?"

I didn't answer. The tone of her voice told me it wasn't a question.

"That's not what those are for," she said sternly. "Let me have those things."

I gave her the few marbles I had left in my hand, and she glared at me. Well, *glared* isn't the right word. Gammy never glared. I've only seen her glare once in my life, years later, when Will and I got up on the roof. That was the maddest she has ever been around me, and her glare was like stone glazed with ice. Most of the time, though, when we misbehaved, she fixed us with an almost comical frown, part frustration, part resignation. You knew you'd blown it, but you also knew you weren't in too much trouble. That was the look she gave me before she walked off and moved the marbles from the low bowl to the high bowl. I couldn't reach them again until I was about eight or nine.

A few years ago, I began to wonder what happened to the twenty or so I dispatched. I thought the Park Service must have found a chunk of blue-red melted glass in the old furnace, but they never did. So those marbles are still rattling around in the ducts somewhere.

The duct system was much more efficient at carrying voices than marbles, as I discovered one night about seven years later while using the upstairs bathroom. No sooner was I comfortable than I heard voices just inches from my dangling little legs. At first I thought the toilet was talking to me, but I soon discovered the voices were coming from the heating duct next to the toilet.

As soon as I could, I called Will into the bathroom, and the two of us put our ears to the vent, which was no mean feat, since it's sandwiched between the toilet and the bathtub.

We went downstairs, looking to see which room the adults were in. Through the grating, we'd been able to hear every word they were saying. Now it was just a matter of seeing which room our tin intercom was picking up. At the bottom of the stairs, I peered around the corner into the living room, then walked through the hall into the dining room. In the study I found Mom, Dad, and Gammy and Grandpa enjoying a quiet after-dinner chat. I found the vent I was looking for about two feet from Grandpa's desk, in the wall next to the arched doorway into the music room.

If I had just shut my mouth, Will and I might have learned all sorts of plans my parents had for us. We might have heard their thoughts on discipline or how they hoped to make us better students—maybe even what they thought of us. Instead, I pointed to the register and said, "Hey, we can hear you guys through that thing. Cool, hunh?"

My mother hadn't discovered the heating-system intercom as a child. Will and I were the first and last generation to use it. I tried it again when I was at the house in 1994, but the Park Service has installed central air conditioning to protect the fabrics and furniture. The constant flow of air through the ducts kills their ability to carry voices.

There were plenty of legitimate toys to play with at 219 North

Delaware, including all those construction sets, trains, and planes my grandmother bought for us over the years. But beyond them, behind the toy chests, tucked into drawers and closets, peeking out of dust-covered boxes, were even greater treasures. The house abounded with knickknacks and baubles, thingamajigs and what-nots—items made exotic by where they were kept and the fact that most of them dated to an era Will and I saw portrayed only on television. A lot of the things we played with in Independence are now museum pieces.

Because my grandparents were public figures, people were always giving them these knickknacks and mementos, like lighters embossed with the seal of the Protective Order of Elks, Rotary pins, campaign buttons, Optimist ribbons and five-inch Statues of Liberty. Apparently one of the hottest political gift items of the 1940s was the money clip. My grandparents had scads of them.

There were two repositories for this stuff. One was the attic. The other was a storeroom above the kitchen, which you could get to either by going up the back steps from the kitchen or through a door in my grandfather's dressing room upstairs. That was how Will and I found it.

We were poking around Grandpa's dressing room one day—we were about eight and six—when we discovered that what we had always identified as a closet was actually the entrance to the storeroom. It was like having a way into a secret room. Of course, everyone else in the family knew about the storeroom, but no one else seemed interested in it but Will and me. Gammy and Grandpa had chucked all the clutter in there years earlier and shut the door. Will and I also shut the door, but we stayed inside, spending an hour at a time poring over hundreds of small boxes arranged in haphazard piles on the shelves and floor.

We took home a little of that treasure, with permission. I've still got a money clip given to my grandfather from some fraternal order and one or two other knickknacks. The remainder was taken to the Truman Library after my grandmother's death in 1982. Now each one has an information sheet, its own plastic bag and little tag. The curator handles them all with white gloves.

When George Curtis, the library's acting director, showed me a handful of those baubles when I was there in July of 1994, the first words out of my mouth were: "Hey! You guys have my old toys!"

As I've gotten older, the storeroom has lost its grip on my imagination. If I had to pick one room of that house I think of more than any other, it would be the room on the other side of the upstairs storeroom door, my grandfather's dressing room.

The room is at the back of the house, across a short hall from what was my mother's room when she was a child. My grandparents' bedroom is on the other side of my mother's room, which was entirely separate from my grandparents' room until just after she was born. She was a frail child and caught every dangerous virus going around, so my grandparents enclosed part of the sleeping porch to make a passage from their room to hers.

My grandfather's dressing room is a small room with a single bed, two dressers, and a closet with an accordion door. Next to the door leading to the storeroom are a couple of wall racks absolutely clogged with ties. My grandfather also had one of those wooden "silent butlers," a three-foot-high rack for his suits. A wooden chair and wooden rocking chair sit in the alcove formed by the room's three floor-to-ceiling windows.

After Grandpa died, that was my room whenever I went to visit my grandmother. I liked being in there for some reason. The strongest image I have of that room comes back to me from a Christmas visit to Independence. I don't remember the year. But I do remember, clearly, standing in the doorway, watching snow drift past the windows. The room was silent. The rocking chair was empty, and there was a gray suit on the rack. That memory is very comforting to me, the thought of the silence and the cold outside. I loved being in that big, warm house, watching the snow blanket the small town outside and feeling alone, like I was the only one in the house, maybe the only person in the whole town.

The storeroom beyond the dressing room didn't have half the accumulation held by the attic.

You got to the attic by climbing a set of stairs off the second-floor hall. They lead past a huge attic fan that once pulled a breeze through the open windows on hot summer days. The attic itself is a high-ceilinged split-level room, big enough to be a studio apartment. When I was a child, the place was piled with furniture covered with yellowed sheets. There were stacks and stacks of dusty hatboxes and a dozen or so plain, round-handled canes, as if my grandparents planned to open a Harry S. Truman spare parts store.

When I was thirteen, old hats were the rage at my school in New York. That Christmas, I took home one of the spare hats, ripped the band off it, turned the brim down, and added a red bandana. It was well received at school as a work of art, but now I feel that I committed sacrilege. I've lost more museum pieces that way.

But the hats weren't the best part of the attic. The attic's best feature was that it was a conduit to an even more fascinating part of the house, the roof. Rising from the middle of the cavernous and dusty room was a shaky old ladder fully one story tall. At the top was a wooden trapdoor that led out onto the flat roof of the main part of the house.

Will and I discovered that ladder when I was about eleven. The two of us were poking around in the attic by ourselves when we decided to climb it. We went up once, then came back down. The second time we went up, we were following our mother.

Why she came up to the attic that day, I can't remember. We may have gone to get her to tell her of our great find. The way Will remembers it, we had actually been up on the roof once already, with permission. But I don't remember getting anyone's permission. For me, that was not standard operating procedure.

Mom may also have arrived in the attic simply as a reaction to the eerie quiet that descends on a house when children have found something to do that is potentially dangerous or horribly messy. But the even greater mystery is why, having found us in the attic, she not only didn't stop us but joined us in moving on to greater heights.

Except for when she was young, Mom has not been known for spontaneity. Having children probably helped make her cautious by bringing out in her all the latent fretting her own parents did when she was a child. So it was a shock to me and Will when she arrived in the attic and didn't immediately send us packing back downstairs.

"What on earth are you doing?" she asked me, seeing that I had one foot on the bottom rung of that big ladder.

"Look, Mom!" I said excitedly, hoping to infect her with my enthusiasm. "This ladder leads to the roof!"

"I know where it leads," she said. "Just where do you think you're going?"

"To the roof?" I said.

I just knew that the next thing out of her mouth was going to be "*Oh, no you don't . . .*" But she didn't say it. She stood there for a long second, looking up at the ladder and the trapdoor, as if she were an engineer considering a rickety bridge over a gorge. "How steady is that thing?" she asked.

I rattled it and stamped on it a couple of times with as little force as I could muster.

"Real steady. See?"

She stood for a moment longer, hands on hips, looking at the ladder and the trapdoor. Then she took a step or two forward.

"I haven't been up there since I was about twelve," she said, the ghost of a smile on her face.

"You used to climb on the roof?" I asked.

This was a major revelation, that my mother had actually done something risky—that she'd even had a childhood, or played or jumped or did any of the things Will and I liked to do.

"You want to go up with us?" I asked.

This time, Mom didn't hesitate or examine the ladder again. She just shrugged. "Sure," she said. "But let me go up first. I don't know how safe this old thing is."

So up we went, Mom in the lead. I can't express how much of a major character deviation this was for my mother. As I climbed, I might have considered the idea that my real mother had been abducted by aliens and replaced by a duplicate identical in every way except that she would climb rickety old ladders.

Pushing the trapdoor aside, the three of us crawled out

onto the roof and stood up. We were at the highest point of the house, and the view was magnificent. The whole of Independence stretched out before us. The yard below was a dizzying three stories away.

Standing there, Mom seemed a little unsteady; perhaps she thought the whole house might give way beneath us. She stayed near the trapdoor while Will and I immediately went to the edge of the roof to stare down at the gables and the yard below. We were so caught up in our adventure we didn't notice the Secret Service cameras swiveling in our direction. There were two of them, one on my grandparents' garage and one on the corner of a commercial building across the alley from the house. The minute our heads peeked over the edge of the roof, they started whirring around like a couple of tops.

Seconds later, Paul Burns, the head of my grandparents' Secret Service detail, came charging out of the Secret Service command post in a small house across North Delaware. We called and waved to him as he came through the front yard, but though he obviously saw us, he didn't smile or wave back; he just plowed forward, head down, into the house. Mom understood immediately what was happening and said something like "Uh-oh."

We walked to the other side of the roof like people watching a shark glide from one side of their boat to the other. Less than a minute later, Mr. Burns reappeared in the backyard with my grandmother. Both of them walked to a spot on the grass near our swing set, looking up over their shoulders the whole time until they got us in view. Then they started gesturing and yelling. I couldn't hear what either of them were saying, but I understood the point: *Come down now.* Mom got it even faster than I did.

"Come on, we'd better get down," she said, practically running for the trapdoor. "Your grandmother doesn't want us up here."

That was an understatement. After we came down, Gammy locked the attic door and threw away the key. I have never—before or since—seen her that mad. She didn't say anything directly to me and Will, but I can bet she chewed Mom out thoroughly. Probably even more thoroughly than when she went up there the first time.

The Park Service didn't find the attic key until after Gammy died. It was tucked in the back of a file cabinet drawer on the second floor.

Most of the time Gammy was our champion. She loved spoiling us and often gave us toys that my parents wouldn't have dreamed of buying. For example, for Christmas one year, when I was ten or eleven, she bought us a pair of toy guns, each about three feet long and made of heavy green plastic. Before we lost all the red bullets, each gun fired five rounds with a spring. You popped them into the magazine on top, cocked the gun, and—twang—one came flying out. The guns had a range of about fifteen feet and were not in the slightest bit accurate.

Will and I mostly played with the guns outside, as we were supposed to, but one rainy day, trapped in the house and bored, we pulled them out of the toy chest upstairs and headed down to the living room. The only other person in the house was Grandpa, who was, as usual, sitting in his study and reading.

In the living room, Will and I set up on the carpet facing the coffee table and the bay window looking out on Delaware Street—one of my favorite places in the house. The bay window is framed by two smaller stained-glass windows, and during a sunny day that corner of the room looks like the inside of a kaleidascope. On that rainy day, our target was a soft-drink can, which we set up on the coffee table, not bothering to move anything else around it that might be fragile. Then we sprawled out at the other end of the room like a couple of sharpshooters. In seconds, red plastic bullets were flying all over the room, bouncing off curtains, furniture, lamps, paintings, and bric-a-brac.

In the study, Grandpa heard a twanging sound and looked up from his book. He knew exactly what it was, but he waited a minute or two to see if any other adult was going to put a stop to it. Quickly figuring out that there were no other adults in the house, he put aside his book and stood up.

I was on my stomach, sighting down on the can (I hadn't hit it once) when the gun suddenly flew out of my hands. I had no warning from Will, who had either been looking the other way or been struck dumb with fear at the sight of Grandpa bearing down on us. He stood over me, leaning on his cane, my gun in his other hand.

I got ready for a lecture. I had never been lectured by Grandpa before, but I had an idea that he was capable of delivering one worse than any my parents could dish out. I had learned in school what he did to General MacArthur, so I braced myself for a real chewing out.

Time stood still. He didn't say a word, but just glared at me. Then, abruptly, he turned on his heel and left the room, taking my gun with him. I wouldn't see it again for about twenty-five years.

I found out later that silence had been one of his best weapons as a father. My grandmother, who uttered barely a peep in public, could raise the roof in private. But my grandfather, who spent his life giving speeches and press conferences, turned stone-cold silent when someone close to him disappointed him. It was an effective tactic. He hadn't uttered a word, but I knew I was never again going to fire another toy gun in the house.

Those guns got us in trouble outside the house, too. The Secret Service command post across the street—which had so alertly picked us up on the roof—was a small house, the front room of which looked like the bridge of a battleship. They had a couple of radios, telephones, speakers, and two video monitors hooked up to the rooftop cameras. From there they could watch the entire house and grounds.

Will and I were playing in the backyard one evening after dinner, near dusk. The visibility was getting murky, and we were chasing each other through the shadows in the backyard, firing red bullets at each other and ducking behind bushes for cover. Our parents and grandparents were in the study, talking. Vietta was in the kitchen, doing the dishes and keeping half an eye on us through the window.

The agents across the street had to have seen us, but apparently they didn't notice the guns. A few minutes later, one of them glanced up at the monitor and saw what he thought was the barrel of an M-16 rifle poking around the northeast corner of the house.

I was crouched at the corner of the house, at the edge of a

small, unused brick patio beneath the back porch, when I heard the unmistakable sound of someone running toward me. Brandishing my gun, I leaped out, yelled, and sent a red plastic bullet sailing toward what I thought was my brother. Imagine my surprise when my target turned out to be two Secret Service agents running at me with their guns drawn. My little bullet bounced on the grass in front of them and skipped off into a bush.

All three of us screeched to halt and stared at each other for a long moment. Then one of them smiled and threw up his hands.

"Okay, you got us," he said. "Don't shoot."

The last time my grandparents ever came to see us in New York was during the summer of 1968.

As a younger man, my grandfather had loved to travel. He liked nothing better to get in a car and go. It's not a surprise that some of the best roads Jackson County, Missouri, ever had were built in the 1920s and 1930s, during his tenure as a county judge. (The title was "judge," but the responsibilities were those of a county commissioner.) He was so eager to get back on the open road after leaving the presidency that not long after he got home he went on a cross-country trip to Washington, D.C., without considering the consequences. He and my grandmother slowed traffic on the interstates as motorists recognized them and paused to beep a hello. Police departments and hotels along the way went nuts trying to keep them safe.

After that, they stuck to trains and planes. I think they flew to New York on that last 1968 trip. When we picked them up at the airport, we took them not to Manhattan but up to Westchester County, where we were spending the summer.

Starting when I was very young, my parents rented houses outside New York during the summer. This was done entirely for the benefit of me and my brothers, so we would have some fresh air for a couple of months and a pool to swim in. I remember those days as some of the best times of my life. Because we hardly ever stayed in the same place twice, there was the novelty of each new home. And having bushes to hide in, trees to climb, and a lawn to run across was beautiful. In Central Park we were always on a short leash. In Westchester Mom just turned us out the back door in the morning.

Without schoolwork to fight over, I, at least, got along better with Dad during the summers. He didn't seem to be as authoritarian; he mellowed, as he did on vacations. He also was wasn't around as much, having to commute to his job in the city.

The summer when I was six, my grandparents visited us at a house we had rented in Tuxedo Park, New York. The house had an oblong circular pool, a garden, and at least one snake, which Dad had to kill after it ambushed me and Will on the garden steps. That was also the summer Dad taught me to swim.

Dad and Grandpa were alike in that they seemed to dislike exercise in every form except two: walking and swimming. Dad walks everywhere he goes—if Mom will let him—and until he was about eighty, he swam on a somewhat regular basis. During summers on Fire Island, I would often look up from my beach towel to see my father in the ocean, gliding back and forth outside the breakers in an easy freestyle.

Grandpa, of course, was a legendary walker. "After age forty, it's the only kind of exercise that does a man any good," he would say. Yet he liked to swim, too. Otherwise, the Navy wouldn't have had to truck that sand into the Key West naval base to build a beach for him.

Where Dad favored the freestyle or "crawl" stroke, Grandpa swam sidestroke. He did this for one reason: to keep his glasses dry. His natural eyesight was awful, and he rarely did anything—except sleep—without them perched on his nose. And he was as ardent as a man can be about protecting them. When he was a senator, he and my mother and grandmother got into a car accident. Their car rolled over, throwing them and every bit of their luggage all over creation. Fortunately no one was hurt. My grandfather's glasses came off without a scratch. He had thrown them out the window when he saw the accident coming.

Gammy and Grandpa were both about eighty when they came to visit us in Tuxedo Park. But age didn't stop Grandpa from swimming. The second day of his visit, Grandpa donned his trunks and a terry-cloth jacket and sauntered down to the round pool, where Will and I were yelping and splashing in the shallow end. Doffing the jacket, he walked into the pool and glided away from us before we had really noticed he was there.

I don't know what we were thinking, Maybe it was that since Grandpa was in the pool, he was fair game. Maybe it was that since we were having so much fun splashing each other, we figured Grandpa would like it, too. Whatever it was, after he pushed off, we lay in wait for him. As he sidestroked back from the deep end of the pool, we let him have it with both barrels.

Mom, who was sitting by the pool, reading, was up from her chair in a flash. "Oh, no, boys!" she said. "You mustn't get Grandpa's glasses wet. He doesn't like that."

Boy, he certainly did not. Grandpa swam to the edge of the pool for his towel and wiped his glasses dry. Then he turned, simply glared at us, and shoved off again.

The only other time I remember my grandparents visiting us during the summer was the year we rented the Prince house in Bedford, New York, when I was ten. Usually, when a family left, all we rented was their house and their furniture. But the Prince family left a little something extra behind—a little something gray, yappy, and slobbery—their Bedlington terrier, Tiffany. The family was traveling and didn't want to shut her up in a kennel all summer, so they asked my parents if they would keep her at the house. My mother agreed, against her better judgment. Mom professes to hate dogs, and we were never allowed to have one in New York. "It's cruel to keep a dog in a city," she would say, or "I'll end up walking it and feeding it."

Mom didn't have to walk Tiffany, just turn her out the back door every morning as she did with me and Will. Will and I loved the dog because she was so playful, chasing us around the yard and pouncing on us. She followed my brother and me everywhere, as if she had always belonged to us. For Mom, who fed her and had to discipline her, she was a pain.

Mom would not know just how much of a pain Tiffany could be

until one night during my grandparents' visit, when *The New York Times'* publisher Arthur Ochs "Punch" Sulzberger and Mrs. Sulzberger came to dinner. This was a nerve-racking experience for my mother, who had to entertain not only her husband's boss and his wife but also her own father, who had a known distaste for people in her husband's boss's profession. Dad was late coming home from New York, and the guests arrived before he did. While waiting for him, the adults had drinks on the brick patio under a huge, beautiful oak tree. No one saw the kitten until after Tiffany did, and by then it was too late.

The kitten had managed to get loose from a neighbor's house and came sneaking through the backyard. Though Tiffany knew every squirrel and chipmunk on the property, she was not acquainted with the kitten, so she greeted it by chasing the little cat at top speed while barking furiously and snapping at its hindquarters. The kitten, reacting violently, climbed the nearest tall thing, which happened to be the oak tree.

"Oh, no! The poor kitten," I said.

"We have to save it!" Will said.

"Damn cat," Mom said.

If ever there was assembled a committee appropriate to saving a kitten, we had it there that night, a former president and first lady, the publisher of one of the most powerful and influential newspapers in the world, and a soprano-actress-writer-mother. Strike that last one. Mom would have left the cat in the tree.

Grandpa fell quickly into the role of chief executive. He gave orders from his lawn chair, punctuating them by stabbing his cane in the air.

"The first thing to do is get a ladder," he said. "And somebody get that dog away from the tree."

Ever since the cat escaped from her, Tiffany had been barking hysterically and throwing herself against the base of the tree. At Grandpa's order, Mom came up behind her, hooked a finger in her collar, and hauled her off to the house, muttering under her breath.

The ladder was brought out.

"That's it. Put it right there," Grandpa said, pointing to the base of the tree with his cane. "Now all we need is someone to go up."

The kitten had perched itself near the crotch of two great branches and was mewing at the assembly below, its tiny paws hugging the bark. His rescuer was to be Mr. Sulzberger, who, come to think of it, was the only man under eighty among us, if you don't count me and Will. I don't know how the decision was made, but Mr. Sulzberger probably offered, then insisted. Who knows, it may have been that my grandfather sent him, reasoning that publishers were expendable.

In any case, my mother came out of the house and saw her life flash before her eyes. There went her husband's boss, up a tree after a cat, his jacket off and his shirtsleeves rolled to the elbows.

"Here, kitty, kitty. Nice kitty."

Grandpa sat on the patio, waving his cane in the air and giving directions. If it had occurred to him, he could have stood up, hooked the base of the ladder with his cane, and pulled it out from under Mr. Sulzberger. But Grandpa didn't have to do the publisher harm. The kitten did that for him. Mr. Sulzberger had no sooner reached for the kitten than the little animal sank its teeth into his thumb. Mr. Sulzberger winced and recoiled. My mother nearly fainted. Grimly the publisher lunged again and this time scooped up his quarry. Then he backed down the ladder, the ungrateful kitten under his arm, a trail of blood running from his thumb to his elbow.

Grandpa seemed satisfied, though he must have known Mr. Sulzberger's sacrifice had been in vain. There's an old saying in the fire department: You never see any cat skeletons in trees.

5

The Johnson Years

As long as Lyndon Baines Johnson was in the White House, my family had more than its fair share of the spotlight. The Republicans occasionally invited us to come around, especially while Gerald Ford was in office, but during the Johnson administration, we saw the inside of the White House frequently.

Our first official visit back to Washington after the 1965 inauguration took place on April 18, 1968, when Lady Bird Johnson wanted to unveil a portrait of my grandmother, which was to hang in the White House. As they had with the inauguration, my grandparents declined the invitation to be there themselves. My grandmother, in fact, wanted no part of it. She thought having her portrait in the White House was a silly idea. Though it is a beautiful painting, she couldn't see the sense in it and wasn't planning to fly all the way from Independence to look at it. She had never been fond of the spotlight.

So, once again, the Daniels were dispatched in the Trumans' stead. And, as we had the first time, by dint of friends in high places, we went first-class. When Arthur Sulzberger heard his managing editor, the ex-president's son-in-law, had been invited to the White House, he called him up and offered him the use of the company jet.

A few days later, a limousine took us out to Teterboro, an airport for private planes in New Jersey. There we boarded the *Times* plane, a small jet that looked to me more like a spaceship. The cabin had eight big, cushy seats that swiveled like barber chairs, and there was a wet bar stocked with scotch, bourbon, gin, vodka, all in decanters with pumps on the tops to prevent people from spilling should they hit turbulence in the middle of mixing a scotch and soda.

All parents flying with small children should have it so good. The cabin was beyond comfortable, and since the plane was at our disposal, there was no worry about making the return flight on time. In the air there were no other passengers around who might not like having their hair pulled or their pants crayoned. In fact, once we were up, Dad could just let the bunch of us out of our seats to roam the cabin at will.

This was especially good for Harrison, my second-youngest brother. Harrison is a bit different from the rest of us. He was born prematurely and spent about a month of his life in an incubator, so he thinks and does things in his own way and in his own time. He was the most sweet-natured of all of us. He was five on that trip to Washington.

On April 18, 1968, Harrison was well into his button-pushing phase. This phase lasted several years, during which he would push, flick, or pull any kind of switch he came across. He loved to climb up on furniture and turn light switches on and off, and he often did it when Will and I were in the den watching television.

His favorite "buppumn," as he called them, was the one that opened and closed the garage door at that house we rented in Bedford, New York, the one that came with the Bedlington terrier. It was the perfect button for Harrison because there was such a clatter when he pushed it. That's what he liked best—making something happen. He paid no attention to the buttons on his play sets because they didn't do anything.

But every time he pushed the garage-door button, there was a loud whirring sound, and the door rattled up. The first few times he did it, he squealed and laughed with delight. It got so that we couldn't go anywhere without letting him push that button. If anyone else did it, there was hell to pay. On the *Times* corporate jet, Harrison found a button that was almost as good.

Not long after we took off from Teterboro, Dad undid Harrison's seat belt and let him go. Then he settled back into his own chair and unfolded *The New York Times.* This was the life, reading the paper on the plane without a care in the world. There was noplace the kids could go (the door was locked) and nothing they could get into. He was beginning to think he had it made when his senses were bombarded by the unmistakable, overpowering aroma of bourbon.

He swung around toward the bar, and there was Harrison with a great big smile on his face, happily mashing the pump top of the bourbon bottle over and over. Bourbon was running in rivers all over the bar and dripping onto the carpet. The whole cabin reeked. Dad snatched Harrison away from the bottle, but not before half the contents were out. When we were met at Washington's National Airport by the White House limousine, the driver must have thought the lot of us had a severe drinking problem.

At the White House, Lady Bird Johnson greeted us in the East Room downstairs.

It's been years since I've been in the White House and seen the East Room, and I remember it from that day as being all sunlight and gold trim. The East Room was furnished with aluminum folding chairs for the guests. It did not, however, contain President Johnson, who was off somewhere. But it had something even better, no offense to the president—Vice President Hubert Humphrey.

Mr. Humphrey was one of our family's favorite people. As far as my mother was concerned, he could do no wrong. And that's saying something, because she seems to have a strong opinion, often bad, of almost everyone in Washington. That's why she writes those murder mysteries; so she can kill them all off, one at a time.

Mr. Humphrey was the best adult I knew. As historians often say about my grandfather and General George Marshall, he had that knack of being able to talk to kids without making them feel like they were being talked down to. Whenever we saw him, he got down on our level and talked to us face-to-face. He made me feel like I was the only other person in the world.

He was a heck of a baby-sitter, too. During the ceremony for the portrait unveiling, my mother was trying to give an interview. She had Thomas, not quite one year old, in her arms, and he was wriggling and fussing to get down. But Mom didn't want to let him loose, knowing he might creep into the Red Room or the Blue Room and wipe out two hundred years of history with one swipe of his hand.

Mr. Humphrey saw she was in trouble, walked up, said, "Give him to me," and took off. He greeted other guests, making sure to introduce Thomas to several of the notables present; then the two of them headed toward the "Singing Strings" of the United States Marine Band. The Marines, dressed in red uniforms and armed with violins, were the musical entertainment for the reception following the ceremony.

I didn't notice the Marines. My attention was focused on the chocolate eclairs at the end of the buffet table. It's funny how your mind fixes on certain things. Here I was in the White House, surrounded by some of the most influential people in the world, serenaded by a Marine band, and all I noticed was the eclairs. In fact, until I started to put the pieces of my sometimes addled memory down on paper, really started concentrating, they were the only thing I remembered about that trip. They obviously must have been really, really good.

Thomas and Mr. Humphrey were too much on the go to weigh themselves down with sweets. After a quick stop at the buffet table for a saltine, the baby and the vice president made a beeline for the band. Mr. Humphrey figured Thomas would quickly become bored with drab gray dignitaries, so he headed for the red uniforms.

In no time, Thomas and the vice president had become fast friends with the Marines. Part of this may have been due to the fact that the Marines viewed Thomas as a comrade, since he also wore a uniform of sorts. Mom had dressed him in a crisp white linen suit for the occasion. The Marines were very impressed. Thomas's military bearing wasn't in the least harmed by the bulge of a full diaper. One Marine even gave Thomas his violin bow to use as a baton so he could take a stab at conducting. But Thomas wasn't ready for the big time. He just stood there, uncertain, bow in one hand and cracker in the other, looking like a tiny, lumpy Leonard Bernstein.

After the reception, another limousine took us from the White House back to the airport and the *Times* plane for the trip home. Though I had fixated only on the eclairs, Will had apparently been paying close attention to the pomp, circumstance, and sheer expense of the entire trip. Always aware of the value of a dollar, he was very conscious that we had been living beyond our means all day. Finally, in the plane on the way home, he turned to my father and said, "Dad, it seems to me we're getting richer."

"No," Dad said. "We just have some rich friends."

Then he made sure the bourbon was locked up safely in the bar.

The next and last official trip we took during the Johnson administration was to Norway late in 1968 for the funeral of Trygve Lie, the first secretary-general of the United Nations. Mr. Lie had served during my grandfather's administration and was a friend of the family. His daughter, Guri Lie Zeckendorf, was one of my mother's friends. Her sons, William and Arthur, went to St. Bernard's School with Will and me. Mom had arranged for them to travel with us to their grandfather's funeral.

On a cold, wet December day, we flew to Oslo on *Air Force II* with Vice President Humphrey, who was going as President Johnson's representative. This was not only our swan song with the Johnson administration but also Mr. Humphrey's swan song as vice president. The month before, he had lost the presidential race to Richard Nixon.

We had held a mock election at school, and I had campaigned hard for Mr. Humphrey. It was the first and last time I campaigned personally for a politician, and it was especially important for me to do a good job because I liked him so much. I don't know how much of it was my doing, but Mr. Humphrey easily won the school election. Alas, the world didn't turn the same way as St. Bernard's, so we headed off to Norway on what would probably be his last official use of the vice-presidential plane.

At the end of the trip, when the plane was being towed off to the hangar, Mr. Humphrey watched it go, then turned to my mother. "Well," he said, laughing, "I guess it's back to old Northwest Airlines."

If Mr. Humphrey was down in the mouth on the trip, you would never have known it from watching him. For the seven-hour flight, he seemed to be in an unending good mood. He walked up and down the plane during the flight, chatting with passengers, most of whom were government personnel. He stopped to talk to my mother. He even sat with us four kids, and not for just a quick chat. He pulled up a chair and stayed for about forty-five minutes, during which, in the time-honored Truman tradition, we played several hands of poker.

Our stakes were not quite as high as Grandpa would have liked. We were playing for hard candy. Mr. Humphrey was staked to about ten pieces, including some lemon drops, cinnamon swirls, and fireballs. For a while, he did pretty well. But Will and the Zeckendorf boys were more than a match for him. He finally bowed out when he was down to two pieces of butterscotch. Then he walked back up the plane, eating what was left of his stake.

In Oslo, the only time I remember seeing him again was at a banquet given for our party at the Oslo museum where they keep the *Kon Tiki*. I remember less of Mr. Humphrey than the *Kon Tiki*, which was the balsa-wood raft that explorer Thor Heyerdahl used to re-create the ocean voyage South Americans might have taken to Polynesia. It sat in a pool of light in the center of a vast exhibition hall. I was fascinated by it and was allowed to buy a *Kon Tiki* model. When I got it home, I found it wasn't something you could snap together. You had to cut the balsa wood logs with an X-acto knife and string the rigging yourself. I never finished it. My father refused to help me. He had already had enough with the anatomically correct *Tyrannosaurus rex* skeleton I brought home from the Museum of Natural History.

But beyond the *Kon Tiki*, the museum itself was fascinating to me—not as a place to browse and learn but as a place to play. Will, Arthur, William, and I had the *Kon Tiki*—and the entire museum—to ourselves that night. We were up from the table after supper and gone, on an hour-long game of hide-and-seek through the cavernous, empty halls.

The museum was only half-lit, so there were hundreds of shadows in which to hide. And if you stepped into a pool of light by mistake, there were long, dark halls down which you could escape. Outside, the sun never set. That night, when we were playing in the museum and, later, when we were going to bed in the hotel, it was never night outside. It was the same every night at that time of year. The sky, gray and often filled with snow, would just dim down at the end of the day as the sun skirted the horizon.

When it got to be bedtime, my argument to my mother was "Why do we have to go to sleep if it isn't going to get dark?" Her response was to pull the shades.

Our hotel was old, the rooms finished in dark wood with nine- or ten-foot ceilings and enormous windows that stretched nearly as high. Our room was furnished with two enormous, deep feather beds. I had never seen or slept in anything like them. The mattresses were more like giant down quilts than mattresses. When I slipped over the side and under the sheets, I sank into the thing like I was going under in a pool of marshmallow or into a warm snowbank.

The beds were not the only wonder to be discovered in an Oslo hotel room. In the bathroom, we found the usual accoutrements, plus a strange extra device neither Will nor had ever seen before. It looked like the toilet, which sat next to it, but it had a decidedly untoilety character. It flushed in reverse, sending up a geyser of warm water whenever you pushed the pedal. Will and I looked at it from several different angles and spritzed it a few times, but couldn't figure out for the life of us what it was for, so of course we called in our mother.

"It's, uh . . . ladies wash their, you know . . . after they use the toilet," she said.

Will got the idea instantly. He was always kind of a devil where Mom was concerned. He loved to tease her. On airplanes, knowing they scared her, he would look out the window and point out what he swore were loose rivets on the wing flaps. In Oslo, the instant he realized what the bidet was for, he got a really good reaction out of her by turning it on and yelling, "Look, it's a water fountain!" He'd almost gotten his lips on the stream before Mom screamed and yanked him away from it.

On the way back from Oslo, we took a side trip to Copenhagen for one night so Mr. Humphrey could pay an official visit to the Danish prime minister. I remember only one thing about that trip.

There was a crowd of protesters in front of the American embassy when we arrived. I can't for the life of me remember what they were protesting, though it might have been United States involvement in Vietnam. In any case, it was not a big crowd. I have a mental picture of them, pacing back and forth in the snow outside the embassy gates, their heads lost under caps, their faces hidden by thick scarves. It was bitterly cold that night, and they held their placards in mittened hands. As they chanted and shouted, their breath came in heavy plumes, like smoke from an engine.

Though the crowd was small, the American military contingent at the embassy was ready for World War III. After dinner, some of the guards asked if Will and I and Arthur and William would like to see the command center at the back of the building, which seemed like a fine idea. Sitting at the elbows of adults all evening with no place to run or play, we were wasting away with boredom.

Following the guards, we walked outside and around the embassy, listening to the protesters' chants fade away behind us. At the back, down a short flight of stairs, was a small heavy door leading to what looked like a dungeon. An almost overpowering wave of heat hit me when the guard opened the door. It was all the more striking for the biting cold outside. With the blast of heat came the heavy, musty scent of people and animals in close quarters. As my eyes adjusted to the low light, I could see that the room was crammed with soldiers. At the ends of chains and leather leashes that looked more like barbers' strops, there was a pack of some of the most foul-tempered Dobermans and German shepherds on earth.

The instant we opened the door, the dogs started snarling and snapping and straining at their leashes as if they'd gone bonkers. It was only after several severe rebukes from their handlers that they calmed down. All of them looked like they wanted to make a snack of the four of us.

I don't know what happens inside a child's mind—mine in particular—when he sees an animal. Even after what I had just seen, I couldn't get it in my head that these dogs were dangerous, that they had been trained to kill. They snapped and growled and even lunged at me, yet the instant they calmed down, I assumed they would suddenly be friendly. Without thinking, I reached out to pet the closest shepherd.

Since its handler had brought it to heel, the dog had been sitting still as stone, watching all of us intently. But when I reached for him, he came off the floor like a fanged jack-in-the-box, jaws snapping at my outstretched arm. It was so sudden and vicious that I felt like I had been jolted out of my skin. I can't remember whether I pulled back myself or whether a guard yanked my arm away. Either way, it was close. A step farther and I might have had my hand torn off.

Later, as we were walking back into the embassy, I wanted to trot over to the protesters and say, "Hey, let me tell you about this big dog they've got back there . . ."

6

The End of December

By December 26, 1972, I had known for several weeks that Grandpa Truman probably wasn't going to live much longer—had known it but not known it. My mind turned to other things when I thought about it. The idea of his dying did not seem real; he had been there all my life—out of reach, mostly, but always there, like a distant star. And it seemed to me that stars rarely died.

I had felt almost nothing when Grandpa Daniel died seven years earlier. He had been dearer to me than my grandfather Truman. We had gone fishing together. At his house, I had pulled worms from the dirt, dangled my fingers in the bait pond behind the garage, and scooped up armloads of pecans under the old tree in the backyard. I had loved the smell of his pipe. But I was young when he died, and though I had a well of wonderful memories of him, it was a shallow well. At his viewing, I felt nothing but apprehension and morbid fascination at the sight of him in his coffin, his lips and cheeks rouged.

Though I was just as empty seven years later, my mother was not. On Christmas Day, she came down the stairs in our apartment, crying, a tissue pressed to her nose. They had told her on the phone that Grandpa Truman had slipped into a coma and was not expected to live. He had been in the hospital since early December.

This was only the third time in my life I'd seen her cry. To this day, I think it was the last. The first time was the day John F. Kennedy was killed. I walked into the library in our apartment that day to find my mother staring at the television screen, grainy images of reporters, cars, and people running. She had a hand pressed over her nose and mouth, and there were tears running down her face. All she said was "Oh, my God." It scared me to see her that way. It was the first time I had ever seen her lose control.

The second time I saw her cry it was my fault, mine and Will's. On April Fool's Day, when we were about eight and six, Will hid, and we told her he'd fallen and broken his arm. I didn't expect her to cry. I thought she would be hopping mad instead. When her face twisted up and she said, "Oh, my God! Which hospital did they take him to?" I felt sick to my stomach. Will ran out from the library, holding up both arms and yelling, "I'm okay, Mom! See? I'm okay!"

I don't know if my mother cried the morning of December 26, 1972, the day my grandfather Truman died in an Independence hospital. The last time I had seen her with tears in her eyes was in New York on that Christmas Day, the day Grandpa went into a coma. I was home from prep school, where I was a sophomore. Will, who was thirteen, was still in school in New York. When Mom came down from taking the doctor's call, we were sitting in the dining room, finishing breakfast, at the same table where my grandfather had ordered me to get back on my hobby horse after I had tipped it over.

"Your grandfather's in a coma," she said. "They're not sure he's going to live. I have to fly out to Independence."

Hearing the news and seeing her like that left me feeling sick, unsteady. I can't honestly say I was shaken by the idea of my grandfather's dying; we had not known each other very well. But I did sense that I was losing a part of myself, a part that I would miss in other ways.

Grandpa died early the next morning, without ever regaining consciousness.

When Mom called from Missouri, she was back in control. For us, my father and my brothers and me, there were travel arrangements to be made, people to call, suitcases to pack. At the time, I thought it was odd that Mom should have been so upset when

Grandpa had seemed about to die and so controlled when it actually came to pass. But by then the reality had sunk in. When you're an ex-president's daughter, funeral plans are complicated, and people, hundreds of people, want to see you, to touch you, to say they're sorry. So by the time Grandpa died, I think Mom had put on her public face.

We departed New York for Kansas City the afternoon of December 26. We went quietly, as we always did when left to our own devices. The reporters and the agents and the police only followed us around when Gammy and Grandpa were nearby. We had packed quickly, throwing a couple of days' worth of clothes into duffle bags and suitcases and shaking the dust off dark blazers and gray slacks we hardly ever wore. We were met in Kansas City and driven out to Independence. Little was said during the trip.

That day, being in the limelight changed. It soured somehow. The photographers and reporters became intruders. When we arrived, and for two days after, they were strung out along the iron fence that surrounds the house and grounds in Independence, hurling questions and snapping pictures. At our mother's request, Will and I stayed as far away from them as we could. When we weren't in the house, we holed up in the back corner of the yard, between the garage and the house belonging to my aunt May Wallace.

Aunt May, whom the family called "Beufie," pronounced "Boofie," was my grandmother Truman's sister-in-law. She lived in a one-story house next door to my grandparents. Her house wasn't technically part of the Truman property, but it, the big house, and the garage formed a sort of family compound. Aunt Beufie had been married to Gammy's brother, George Wallace, who died when I was very young. Before she became a Wallace, she was a Southern, daughter of Colonel William Southern, editor of the *Independence Examiner*.

By the time I met her, Aunt Beufie was a rambunctious senior citizen, more energetic than most children I knew, a world traveler and as good-natured as anyone could be. For me and Will, she was one of the best reasons to visit Independence. She liked to joke, she didn't order us around, and she seemed to delight in everything we did, whether or not it was strictly delightful. That day Will and I had climbed out onto the roof as children, we saw Aunt Beufie coming across the yard from her house and yelled down to her. From almost the same spot where my grandmother would stand minutes later with a scowl on her face, Aunt Beufie smiled and waved as if she were in a parade.

Her good nature was how she got her nickname. She was always teasing my mother when Mom was a child, so Mom told people, "Aunt May's spoofing me." The "spoofing me" became "Beufie."

Will and I stayed with Aunt Beufie while we were in Independence for Grandpa's funeral. There wasn't room in the big house; there were too many people and too much going on. But that was fine with me and Will; we were comfortable with Aunt Beufie. In her house and small side yard, we had a refuge from the press, who were forbidden by the Secret Service from coming down the alley behind the garage. At the iron gate that surrounded the house, they couldn't get closer than about forty yards.

At one point, though, a photographer sneaked through the yard of the house next to Aunt Beufie's and started taking pictures over her back fence, about twenty feet away. I had just cocked my arm to throw Will a football when I noticed him and glared. The picture in the next day's paper was captioned something like: "Truman's grandsons having a game of catch." If the photographer had taken one more frame, he would have had an ugly picture on his hands.

Will and I kept one newspaper picture from the funeral. It arrived by mail a few days after we got back to New York and was a photo of the two of us with our family at the gravesite. Both of us still had long hair and would have for years to come, something that apparently aggravated the letter writer. With a black marker, the writer had outlined our hair and scrawled across the margin: "To appear at your grandfather's funeral with such God-awful hair is disrespectful, sick and sad. No wonder your grandmother stayed at home."

The writer was referring to the public viewing in the entrance hall of the Truman Library, which my grandmother had not attended. But the picture was taken at the private graveside service the next day, which my grandmother did attend. The clipping was unsigned and there was no return address. A coward. My grandfather would certainly have agreed with the message, but he would have had nothing but contempt for the messenger. Will and I pinned the scrawled clipping up on the bulletin board, showed it to visiting friends, and had a lot of good laughs over it.

On December 27, Grandpa's casket lay in state in the entrance hall of the Truman Library. During that day and into the next, thousands of people filed by to pay their respects. President Richard Nixon and former president Lyndon Johnson were among the mourners. Originally Mr. Nixon had planned to attend the funeral the next day, but my grandmother wanted the hullabaloo kept to a minimum. It took less planning and required fewer soldiers for the president to attend the lying in state and lay a wreath at my grandfather's flag-draped casket. Dad made the final decision, after the White House tracked him down at La Guardia Airport in New York, while all of us were on our way to Kansas City.

Directly after they left the library, Mr. and Mrs. Nixon came to the house to pay their respects to my grandmother. On his way in, he was waylaid by my youngest brother, Thomas, who was six. Thomas started yanking the president's pants leg. Mr. Nixon seemed not to feel a thing, and I got the impression, perhaps wrongly, that he was ignoring Thomas. In any case, my father called the president's attention to the assault on his pants.

"Mr. President, I think Thomas has something to say to you."

"Oh, excuse me," Mr. Nixon said, bending down. "What is it, Thomas."

"Mr. President, where are your boys?" Thomas said, apparently looking for someone to play with.

"Oh, I don't have any boys," the president said. "But I have two lovely girls, and maybe when they grow up and get married, they'll give me some grandsons."

This didn't help Thomas at all. He wanted someone to play with immediately. It was not in his plan to wait for love, marriage, conception, and childbirth to run their course. Disappointed, he wandered off to see if any of the other adults in the room had children his age.

Later that afternoon, Mr. Johnson arrived with Mrs. Johnson and their two daughters, which, again, didn't do Thomas any good. As the former president came in the door, I was sad to see that he looked thin and very tired. I remembered him as such a strong, robust man from that day just eight years earlier that he had invited us up to the White House living quarters.

"What's wrong with Mr. Johnson?" I asked my father.

"He's very sick, Clifton," Dad said. "He's had heart trouble for some time now."

Owing to his health, Mr. Johnson's stay was brief. Looking back on it and knowing how sick he was, it was above and beyond the call of duty for him to come at all. During the entire visit, Lady Bird Johnson stayed at his side, much the same way my mother would stay by my grandmother at the funeral service for Grandpa the next day. Weeks later, when I was back at school, I happened to poke my head into the television room of my dorm just in time to catch the news of President Johnson's death.

The morning of Grandpa's funeral the next day, Will and I were rooting around in his desk in the second-floor hall. I always thought it was odd that my grandparents kept a desk out in the hall like that, pressed up against the stair rail. Like every other piece of furniture in their house, it was chockablock with keepsakes—photos, a lamp, books, papers, and desk-type knickknacks such as an inkwell and letter openers, pens, and pencils. The drawers were similarly stuffed, and it was through them that Will and I were rooting.

I found what I was looking for, pulled them out, and stuck them quickly into my pocket. Then Will and I walked downstairs and headed over to Aunt Beufie's. Once inside her house, we checked to see that she wasn't home, then ducked down into the small basement. There I brought out the two small packs of cigarettes I'd taken from the desk in the big house.

They were from an airline, I can't remember which one. My grandfather must have picked them up during a trip, but I can't imagine why; he never smoked. When I was nine, I got a similar pack of airline cigarettes from a friend and decided to try one out in the closet of my parents' library.

I got in there with the cigarettes and a box of kitchen matches and tried to light one. I struck match after match, but the tobacco wouldn't catch. I was in the middle of my umpteenth try when I heard my mother calling me, and I panicked. Instead of staying put until she was gone, I ran right out, a small sulfurous cloud in my wake. I can't remember what Mom said, but it wasn't good. The reason I hadn't been able to get the cigarette lit was that, being afraid to inhale, I blew out, snuffing every match.

The packs we took from Grandpa's upstairs desk held four cigarettes each—and they were old and very, very stale. The first drag I took burned my throat and brought on a coughing fit that I thought was going to summon every adult in town. William fared even worse than I did. By that point, I had been smoking for more than a year, sneaking cigarettes behind the dorms at school or during day trips into Boston on Saturdays. Will had never had a cigarette in his life and would end up being miserable for most of the funeral that day.

At the service for my grandfather in the Truman Library auditorium, my grandmother and my parents and my brothers and I sat on the stage, behind a curtain that let us see but not be seen. My grandmother understood the need to include my grandfather's many friends and colleagues in the service, but she was not up to facing the two hundred and fifty people in the auditorium that day. It was just as well for Will. He was sick to his stomach the whole time, even to the point of plotting which stage exit he would have to use to escape to a bathroom.

The lying in state had gone on until the morning of the funeral. When they finally closed the library doors, there was still a long line of people waiting to pay their last respects. During the service in the auditorium and the short graveside service afterward in the library courtyard, I was numb—just going through the motions. The ceremonies ran together for me in drumrolls and rifle volleys.

The day was bitterly cold. The start of the service was signaled by a twenty-one-gun salute fired by a battery of howitzers lined up in the shallow valley below the front entrance to the library. Thomas jammed his fingers into his ears, counting to twenty-one as the guns roared. Riflemen later fired another salute at the end of the service in the library courtyard. None of us were prepared for that second salute, which was so loud it cracked the largest plate-glass window in the library.

Before my grandfather's casket was lowered into the ground, soldiers neatly and respectfully folded the flag that had been draped over it, never letting it touch the ground. One of them handed the tight, triangular package to my mother, who gave it to my grandmother. All the press cameras were relegated to the roof of the library so they could shoot down on the courtyard.

On television and in the papers the next day was a picture of my father leaning over to talk to Thomas. "What are they going to do with the flag," he had asked as the soldiers folded it slowly, end over end.

"They're going to give it Gammy," Dad said.

Thomas watched as the soldiers presented the flag to Mom and Gammy.

"I wish I had a nice flag like that," he said.

Late that afternoon it began to snow. That night, Will and I used the new-fallen snow to cool a pan of Aunt Beufie's chocolate fudge.

About a month later, I was walking down the corridor of my dorm at Milton Academy when one of my friends stuck his head out his door. He had his stereo on; the strains of rock music were coming from his room.

"Hey, Clifton. Come here and listen to this!" he said. "Hurry up!"

"What's up?" I asked.

"Check this out," he said, nodding to his stereo to indicate the song.

"Who is it?" I asked.

"Chicago."

I was not a fan of Chicago, so I shrugged.

"So?"

He looked at me like I wasn't getting the point, which I wasn't.

"Listen to the words, man. They're singing about your grandfather."

It was then that I caught the first strains of "America loves you, Harry Truman . . . America, needs you, Harry Truman."

I was dumbstruck. A rock band was singing about my grandfather. I didn't know it then, but from that point on, things were going to be different. Up until that moment, being Harry Truman's grandson had been almost a private thing. Few people knew, and those who did—close friends and family—made little of it. But with his death, his popularity began to soar. Books were published. There were television specials and magazine articles. People, often people I didn't know, began to make the connection between my name and his.

While Grandpa was alive, it would never have occurred to me to mention to anyone that I was his grandson—any more than it would have occurred to me to say I was Elbert Clifton Daniel's grandson. My parents would have been beside themselves if I had put on airs like that. But now I did not have to put on airs; the connection was brought up to me. Even my peers, none of whom had been alive when he was president, seemed to know and have respect for who my grandfather had been and what he had done.

All of this left me struggling with my feelings. I was a teenager trying to find my own identity. I came from a home where that identity had been bruised somewhat in my parents' quest for normalcy. So when Grandpa's fame grew, I both reveled in and reviled it. I loved the attention because it was something I could never have at home. Yet there was a part of me that resented it because it wasn't due to anything I had done on my own.

Worst of all, I had the nagging feeling, which vaguely persists to this day, that I was unworthy of the attention I got because of him. I wondered whether I would ever be able to do anything myself that would win for me the respect and admiration that people had felt for Harry Truman.

7

School, Batman, Slingshots

For the grandson of a man who enjoyed knowledge with something approaching gluttony, I have had a checkered academic career.

I was late for my first day of kindergarten at Brick Church School, which was actually my mother's fault. But I aggravated this breach of the rules by getting into my first fight about five minutes after she left.

Our classroom was a rectangle, a *big* rectangle. I guess if I went back there today, it would look small to me. To a five-year-old it was huge. Up and down its length, there were children playing. Some were in the kitchen corner, playing house; some were putting together cabins and forts with Lincoln Logs; and others were at a table, drawing.

"What would you like to do?" asked the teacher.

I looked around the room, and my eyes fell on two children playing with what we called "big blocks" in the center of the room. They had piled up the hollow, wooden boxes into a castle. On a throne in the center of the castle sat the most beautiful five-year-old girl I had ever seen. For some reason, I have never suffered from this problem little boys have about not liking little girls. I always liked girls. I was certainly not afraid of catching cooties from them.

The name of the little girl in the castle was Holly Kegg. I know that not because I remembered it all the way from age five but because I met Holly years later, when we were both about fifteen, and she told me a story about her first day at kindergarten.

Seems there was this little boy who came in late. He stood by the door with the teacher for a few minutes after his mother left. It was her fault that he was late. Then he pointed right at Holly and her playmate, John O. McGinnis, who was playing the knight in shining armor who guarded the castle. The teacher took the new boy over to the shelves at the side of the room, by the windows, and Holly, reminded of her game, lost track of him for a few minutes.

When she saw him again, he was standing nearly in front of her, wearing a suit of armor.

"Holly, John, this is Clifton," the teacher said. "He'd like to play with you."

The little boy looked unsure of himself.

The teacher left, and the three of them stared at each other in silence for a few moments. Then the new boy turned to John and said something to the effect of "Stand aside, varlet!"

John sized him up. Having gotten to school on time, he was wearing the better suit of armor—shining tin, nary a dent in it, with a full yellow plume flowing from the top of the helmet. The new kid had on the secondhand armor—green tin and covered with scratches and dents. The plume was nothing but a red stub.

For John, the only thing to do was treat this lumpy knight as the enemy. "Ha and odds bodkins!" John yelled, or something to that effect. "On guard, knave!" And the two clashed in mortal combat.

The fight lasted about three seconds, for John, splendid as he looked in his silvery breastplate and helmet, was possessed of a thin tin sword that wobbled and flapped as he swung it. The green knight, on the other hand, held a plastic gladiator's sword that, while it didn't match his armor, was nonetheless good and heavy.

Princess Holly watched from her throne as the green knight brought the sword down hard on her protector's helmet and cleaved unto it a right deep dent.

"Aaaaaaaahhh!" yelled John, the helmet now crimped around his ears like a bottle cap. "Aaaaaaaaaaaarrrggghhhhh!"

Moments later, overwhelmed by superior forces, the interloping green knight was disarmed and led away to the corner of the room. John O. McGinnis, by the way, went on to become a brilliant student and is now probably a nuclear physicist or billionaire software inventor.

I am a newspaper reporter.

For the first few years I was in school, my parents sent me uptown on a private bus. I'm sure it was very nice and comfortable, but I don't remember a thing about it. For as long as I can remember, I rode the Madison Avenue bus to school.

From the first through eighth grades, I attended St. Bernard's School on East 98th Street. The private boys' school was housed in two adjacent four-story buildings between Madison and Fifth avenues, about twenty city blocks uptown from our apartment. Looking around New York today, I wouldn't let my kids open the front door without supervision, let alone cross that distance on a city bus. But things were different in the mid-1960s. Besides that, I wasn't really alone. Each morning when I went out in my short pants, kneesocks, and blue school blazer, there were at least five other kids at the bus stop dressed exactly the same way, all of us carrying little brown briefcases to boot. We looked like an undergrown board of directors meeting.

That's not to say that every ride passed without incident. One morning, running late, I missed the rest of my board meeting and went by myself on the bus alone. Well, I wasn't alone, but the adults on the bus, like all New Yorkers, were pretending not to see one another, so I might as well have been alone. When the bus drew near my stop, I got up and yanked the bell cord that ran along over the windows. It was supposed to ring a bell next to the driver's head, alerting him that a passenger wanted to de-bus. But that day, I pulled a bell cord that had not been properly maintained. I yanked and yanked, but nothing happened. The driver, unaware of my wish to get off, cruised past my stop at 98th and Madison and sailed on up toward Harlem, just ten blocks away.

I was not raised a racist, but I just couldn't see being put out in

Harlem in short pants and kneesocks, not to mention a little blue blazer with a red-and-gold emblem on the pocket. So when the bell pull wouldn't work and the bus flew past my stop, I panicked and ran toward the driver.

"Stop the bus!" I yelled. "You missed my stop."

The driver looked me up and down and decided he was both unimpressed and unconcerned that I was being taken to my doom. "So, you'll get off at the next one," he said with a shrug.

For three blocks, I stared out at a landscape that was changing before my eyes, becoming more alien with every storefront that glided past. Not long before, I had seen a short movie called *The Red Balloon,* about a little boy who had been chased down by a gang of thugs who popped his big red balloon with rocks. When I stepped off the bus in my kneesocks and blazer, I felt like a big red balloon, bobbing there on the pavement like a target. I thought I saw shadows in every doorway and imagined a gang of kids chasing me, the way they had hunted down the balloon in the movie. I had three blocks to run and never has a small child moved faster, brief-case cutting the air like a scythe, one hand clamped over the little school beanie I forgot to mention I was wearing.

First grade was about the last time I did anything nice for for my brother, Will—if you can call someone teaching you to read when you're three years old "nice." In the afternoons, when I was home from school, we would sit together and pore over my early readers. Looking back on it, I probably didn't so much offer to teach him as react to his asking. He was always the most intelligent and curious among us. His first day in kindergarten, after we had spent weeks reading together, he stunned the teacher by sitting on the floor in a semicircle of kids, a book open on his lap, and declaring: "See Dick run. Run, Dick, run!"

I don't suppose my relationship with Will was much different from that of any other two brothers. We could be close when we wanted to be, usually at Christmas, but the rest of the year we seemed barely able to tolerate each other. Our relationship went downhill from the day he came home from the hospital, when I was not quite two years old. That day, I bit him out of jealousy, then bit my mother for bringing him home. When he was a toddler, I used to snatch his favorite toy from his hands and let him chase me until he was out of breath. Then I would stop and punch him in the stomach. No wonder we talk so little these days.

In fact, Will has never been a great talker. I'll run my mouth until people start nodding off; he was always more content to watch and listen. As a toddler, he talked so little that Mom thought he might be a little slow. But it wasn't that. It was just that I was yapping so much Will never got a word in edgewise.

Before I started school, Mom came to us about noon every day and asked, "What do you want for lunch?" "Peanut butter and jelly," I would say. "And Will wants tuna fish." (I had become his official spokesman.)

The first few times she didn't trust me. "Is that really what you want?" she would ask Will. And he would look at her and nod. Never said a thing.

Every day it was the same. "What do you want for lunch?" And Will never uttered a blessed word. Finally, about noon the day she dropped me off late at kindergarten to cave in John O. McGinnis's helmet, she walked into the library and started to ask Will what he wanted for lunch. But she caught herself and said, "Oh, never mind. You can't talk. I know what you want anyway—a tuna fish sandwich." She was turning to leave when he said, with exquisite diction, "No, I'd like a peanut butter and jelly sandwich, please."

Mom almost tripped over her lower jaw. Will has never said much, but when he does talk, it usually has an effect.

Will would go on to have very little trouble in school. He has said it was never easy, but that didn't stop him from getting A's and B's. I, on the other hand, got one A in my entire academic career—for handwriting. For the rest of my schooling, I wouldn't be able to tell a square root from a dangling participle, but my teachers would always be able to read clearly where I went wrong.

All this mess started in third grade. I have come to find out that in third grade schoolwork gets serious. It is pretty much fun-and-games up to that point, and I had been able to fudge my way through first and second grade. But in third grade you are expected to start producing.

I remember it as the year they taught fractions, which came to symbolize the entire year for me. There were no more comfortable, familiar whole numbers. Everything was broken down into little bits, and you had to figure out how to put it back together again. Interestingly enough, at St. Bernard's, third grade was also the cut-off point for female teachers. There were no skirts to hide behind or feminine sympathies to play upon above the second floor; third grade was a place for men.

Third grade was, if not quite my Waterloo, at least the beginning of a four-lane highway leading there. It was also the start of a long souring of relations between me and my father.

I simply wouldn't do the work. I don't know any other way to explain it. It wasn't that I couldn't do the work. With a gun to my head, I could conjugate and multiply with the best of them. But without the threat of lost privileges, I was content to stare out the window and daydream.

My fantasy life was as rich as my school career was arid. Alone, in the quiet of my room, I created intricate worlds with their own laws and populations. At night, while everyone around me slept, I would lie awake and live other lives. I craved that escape so much that, to this day, I do not fall asleep quickly. Some of those fanciful places I created as a child are clearer to me than actual memories.

The stuff of my dreams came mostly from television, to which I was slavishly devoted. There wasn't a waking moment I didn't spend watching, or thinking about watching, television. I can still be mesmerized. I go slack-jawed and bug-eyed. A tree limb could come through the roof and I wouldn't flinch.

Nothing so well illustrates the effect fantasy and television had on my life and my relationship with my father as the years-long war we had over the TV series *Batman.* I was fascinated by the show, so much so that I would do anything to be able to see it—

even my homework. When my father became aware of how much I loved watching Adam West run around in purple tights, the rule was no *Batman* until after the homework was done.

I did my best to find ways around the rule. Dad usually came home tired from *The New York Times* and wanted nothing more than to have a scotch and soda, eat some dinner, and relax. Keeping after a few dozen reporters all day, then coming home and trying to keep track of my homework as well, was sometimes too much for him. More than a few times he forgot to ask if I had done it. Or he would make a mistake and trust me.

"Have you done your homework?" he would ask.

"Yep," I would lie through my teeth.

"Good. You may go watch *Batman.*"

Later, I would do my homework sitting on the toilet in my bathroom with the clothes hamper pulled in front of me like a desk. If my mother or father knocked on the door, wondering what I was up to, I'd dump the books in the hamper and yell, "Excuse me! Can't a guy have a little privacy?"

But more often than not, I simply didn't do my homework. I can remember so many dawns that I dreaded going to school because I didn't have the math homework or I hadn't done the reading. All day, I sweated through classes, wondering if the teacher was going to call on me. Looking back, it wasn't worth it. I could have saved myself years of anguish if I had simply taken a half hour or an hour every night and done the work. But back then I couldn't see it. There was some immutable force separating my nose and the grindstone.

I would like to have been able to blame my problems in school on my parents and teachers. I've wondered what would have happened if both had taken more time with me or been a little freer with praise when I did something right. I grew up in a family, and a school, where praise was in relatively short supply. You were expected to do your schoolwork without needing a pat on the back.

That may work out for some children, but until I got older and had children of my own, I hadn't considered that nature might play as big a role as nurture in determining your outlook on school.

When it comes to schoolwork, my daughter, Aimee, could be my twin. She dreads it. And no matter how much I try both praise and threats, she would rather stare out the window or play with a toy at her desk while everyone else around her is hard at work.

It's gotten so the fear of school has even invaded her dreams. I happened to be up early one Sunday morning recently, and as I passed Aimee's room, I saw she was out of the covers, curled up like a ball. When I moved her to get her under the covers, she woke up.

"Is it Sunday or Monday?" she asked sleepily.

"Sunday," I said.

"Oh, good. We didn't miss it."

She wasn't talking about some outing or a television program—or even Christmas Day; she had nothing special to do that Sunday. It was just that she didn't want to miss a day off from school.

I have no idea what I did to infect her with my loathing for schoolwork—or even if it was anything I did. Maybe the both of us were just born lazy. But now, like my father, I'm engaged in a war with my child. It's gotten to the point that she loses toys and privileges if she doesn't pay attention in class. If that doesn't work, I'll try something else. I'm determined to spare her the feelings of failure that still dog me. I still want to dawdle and cut corners. It's a constant battle to discipline myself to get things done on time.

Right or wrong, I attribute some of my failures as a student and as a human being to the way my parents raised me. I don't think it was only them, but the way in which people in our social circles raised kids in general. Some of my childhood friends have life histories similar to my own, though I don't know if any of them went on to screw up as thoroughly as I did. Our parents were busy people with high-powered careers. Dad was always at the newspaper. And if he wasn't actively working on it, he was reading it at home. It was our job to fit into their lives, not their job to fit into ours.

My parents—and now I am psychoanalyzing them without benefit of a degree—are both only children. It has always been my feeling that, as only children, they were used to having all the attention that made it difficult for them later in life to spare attention for us.

As products of an earlier and more reserved generation, my parents were also not physically affectionate or demonstrative. We have a tough time saying "I love you" in our family. Hugging occurs, but rarely, and very quickly when it does. I wrestle around on the floor with my kids, even though someone usually gets bruised. Often it's me. But I do it not only because the kids and I enjoy it but also because Dad never did it with me and my brothers. He just wasn't the type to wrestle. I felt I missed a lot not having physical contact with him, and I don't want my kids to go without that touch.

My parents have also always had a tough time letting us do things on our own. If we had trouble tying a shoe or doing a math problem, they were always ready to wade in and grab the laces or the pencil. Whenever I actually did my homework, Dad often corrected it so thoroughly that I began to get the idea that I could never have done it on my own. That left me, as I said earlier, afraid to try for fear of not doing a good enough job. Years later, I would find that my fear of failure could only be erased by alcohol.

I spent a miserable last five years in grade school, putting more energy into my excuses than my work. I was small, in addition to being dense, so I was a target as well. The other kids used to get a kick out of feeding me the wrong answers in class. I didn't help my own case by daydreaming. During math class one day, the teacher was doing one of those exercises in which he would lead us through a series of calculations—take five, multiply by two, subtract one, divide by three, etc. At the end of one long set, he turned to me and said, ". . . subtract four and what do you get, Daniel?" I, of course, had been staring out the window, so all I could say was: "The answer, sir."

What saved me from being a total washout in school was my friendship with Paul Lowerre, one of the most popular kids at St. Bernard's, and a four-inch growth spurt the summer I turned thirteen. When I went back to school that fall, I was still a lousy student, but big enough that people thought twice about feeding me bogus answers.

Being Harry Truman's grandson meant little at St. Bernard's. I was in school with the children of high-powered executives and financiers. Chip Cronkite, Walter's son, was a classmate, so the last thing I could do was claim superiority by dint of money or lineage. About the only thing I had going for me, besides Paul, was athletic ability. Even that didn't start to show up until I was about twelve.

St. Bernard's was modeled on an English boys' school, complete with heavy emphasis on athletics and sportsmanship. We had recess daily in the gym or in a walled concrete courtyard behind the building, where I skinned my knees about once a year. On fall afternoons, we played soccer in the park. In the spring, it was baseball. Football was unheard of, and basketball didn't arrive until after I left.

Grandpa Truman hadn't been much of an athlete as a child because of his eyes; he was extremely nearsighted. Any athletic prowess I have I got from my grandmother, who, it was said, threw a baseball like a boy, only a lot harder.

Clark Clifford once told me a story about a dinner party he went to at the White House when he was one of my grandfather's advisers. He and Mrs. Clifford and several other guests were talking about sports when Grandpa smiled and looked sideways at Gammy. "Well, you know Bess was a champion athlete," he told their guests.

"Not now, Harry," she said.

"Was she really?" Mr. Clifford asked politely.

"Yes indeed," my grandfather said with a grin.

"Harry," my grandmother warned.

But it was too late. The other guests were beyond curious, and Grandpa wasn't about to let her off the hook.

"What sport did you play, Mrs. Truman?" someone asked.

It was the cue Grandpa had been waiting for, and as my grandmother shot him a withering glance, he said proudly: "Why, Bess was the high school shot-put champion."

He made the most of the moment, because he knew he was going to get killed later.

I started out like Grandpa—not much good at sports—and wound up more like Gammy. I was a scrawny kid. But as I grew, I magically became coordinated. At St. Bernard's, I managed to turn myself into a halfway decent soccer player and played center half-back my last year for the varsity, called the "first team." I also made starting pitcher for the baseball team that year.

But once again, my grades interfered. My work in math that spring was so poor that the headmaster, Mr. Westgate, took me off the team and announced that he was going to set me straight in math by tutoring me every afternoon in Latin, his best subject. Mr. Westgate apparently couldn't do math any better than I could. He punctuated his threat by hitting me across the knuckles with a ruler.

After one tutoring session, he forgot all about me, and I sneaked back out to the park in the afternoons and joined the softball team. I spent the rest of the spring watching my former varsity baseball teammates playing on the next field.

Let me make an abrupt about-face and head back to third grade for a minute. It was at that time that my parents tried to mold me a little better by exposing me to two extracurricular activities—music and the military. Both of those things had done much for my grandfather Truman.

When I was eight, Mom signed me up for piano lessons with St. Bernard's music teacher, Charles Morris. My grandfather had loved piano lessons. In fact, he liked playing the piano so much that he once said that if things had turned out a little differently, he might have made a heck of a dance-hall musician. For me, piano lessons were hell. Most of my friends, including Paul, took them before school on weekday mornings. I had them at 2 P.M. Saturdays, right smack in the middle of every pickup ballgame I wanted to play or gory Saturday afternoon movie I wanted to watch.

Mr. Morris was a very nice, gentle, patient man, but I used to hope he would have an accident on the way to our apartment every Saturday. To be fair, he might have hoped that I would have an accident before he got there, because teaching me was actually harder than getting hit by a bus. The strongest image I have of Mr. Morris is seeing him sitting at the piano, groaning. "No, no, no. Have you looked at this at all?"

I hated practicing, so I rarely did it, and I never learned to read music. This may have been partly due to Mr. Morris's gleeful assertion that the notes on the treble and bass clefs—A, C, E, G and G, B, D, F, A—stood for "All Cliftons Eat Goobers" and "Great Big Daniel Fools Around." To avoid ever having to learn to read music, I often called upon my mother, who could read music as fast as most people read an eye chart.

"Mom, can you play this for me?" I'd say. "I'm having a little trouble."

Taking pity on me, she would play the whole piece perfectly, and I would watch her fingers.

It was on one of the few Saturdays I had off from a piano lesson, possibly during a vacation, that I made one of the biggest blunders of my life. I turned my mother down when she asked me if I would like to go to lunch with her.

My mother was forever going to lunch, either to visit with friends or meet with agents. I can't remember what her purpose was that day, but whatever it was, it was obviously something she didn't mind sharing with her twelve-year-old son. I was the only one in the house besides her, Will and Dad and Harrison and Thomas having gone off somewhere, either alone or together. With no impending piano lesson to dread, I was happily glued to the television late that morning when Mom walked into the library.

"Do you want to go to lunch with me?" she asked.

"Where are you going?" I asked, keeping one eye on Johnny Quest.

"Sardi's."

That got my attention. I liked Sardi's. In fact, I liked being taken out to eat, period. I still do. There's the thrill of strange, new food, sweet butter and thick rolls, the little scraper the waiter uses to scoop the crumbs from the table, and the dessert cart! But even Sardi's wasn't enough to pull me from the tube, especially since there was a special episode of *Star Trek* coming on that afternoon.

"No thanks, Mom," I said. "I want to stay here. Is that okay?"

"You're going to throw me over and pass up lunch at Sardi's to watch *Star Trek?*" she asked.

I just grinned at her and nodded.

"Well, suit yourself," she said. A few minutes later, I heard her key in the lock.

For the next two hours, I was in heaven. I couldn't imagine anything better than watching the morning cartoons until they ran out, which was usually around twelve thirty or one, then having an episode of *Star Trek* to soak up for a whole hour. The show, which was still in its original run, usually came on at eight or nine at night, which was past my bedtime. Being able to sit, with the whole house to yourself and no interruptions, was unbelievable. Phasers on stun! "Beam me up, Scotty!" "Damn it, Jim! I'm a doctor, not a . . ."

But I had unknowingly chosen an hour of happiness over fifteen minutes of ecstasy. Not long after *Star Trek* ended that afternoon, Mom came home and stood in the library doorway wearing a very smug expression.

"You should have come to lunch," she said.

"Why?" I asked, still warm from the glow of an hour of transporters and bug-eyed aliens.

"Well, you never know who you're going to meet when you go to lunch," she said. "Guess who came over and had a drink with me after lunch?"

I was unfazed. Whenever she played this game, it was usually after she'd met some politician or artist whose reputation spanned the globe and everyone on it, except for twelve-year-olds. She had yet to impress me with any of her conquests.

"Who?" I asked, waiting to hear a name that would mean nothing to me.

Mom smiled as if she knew what I was thinking, knew that I was smugly waiting for a name I would find monumentally unimpressive. Then she drew the name out slowly, like pulling a sword from a wound.

"William Shatner."

I was stunned. My mouth dropped open. I had chosen to watch an episode of *Star Trek* I could see in reruns for the rest of my life while passing up my only chance ever to meet the leading man, the commander of the USS *Enterprise,* Capt. James T. Kirk.

Days later, after deciding not to kill myself, after all, I vowed never, *never*, to turn down lunch with my mother again.

At about the same time Mom signed me up for piano lessons, she also signed me up for the Knickerbocker Greys, a fancy paramilitary group for Park Avenue kids run by an Army Reserve colonel named William Warrick. Colonel Warrick also owned the camp I went to, Adirondack Camp on Lake George in upstate New York.

A quick aside about camp: The first year, when I was ten, my parents sent me off to live in the woods for a month with only one pair of underpants. Since laundry was only done once a week, that pair saw more than its fair share of action. By the time my parents showed up for the midsummer parents' weekend with replacements, the old pair had been carted off by the local hazardous waste disposal team.

Underwear aside, I loved camp—and also the Knickerbocker Greys. As teenagers, Grandpa Truman and some of his friends had formed a junior militia in Independence. They drilled, fired toy cannons every Fourth of July, and dreamed of fighting in the Spanish-American War. The Knickerbocker Greys was a little more organized than that, but basically the same idea. Grandpa was delighted that I had been pressed into service by my mother. The military was where he had discovered his natural ability as a leader.

The Knickerbocker Greys got the name "Knickerbocker" from the fictitious Dutch author of a history of New York written by Washington Irving and the "Greys" from the fatigue uniforms we wore, which were made of heavy gray wool. Descendants of the original Dutch settlers of New York were called "Knickerbockers" and, for a time, so were all New Yorkers. On the days we drilled, we had to wear the uniforms to school, which not only made us hot and itchy, but also signaled to other kids on the street that you were some sort of weenie.

Every Tuesday and Friday afternoon after school, we would go to the 7th Regiment Armory on 66th Street and Park Avenue to drill. There were eight companies, each with about twenty kids. Alone and in groups, we forward-marched and left-flanked, right-flanked and to-the-rear marched. We right-shouldered arms and left-shouldered arms using toy M-1 rifles with wooden bullets in the chambers. We stood at attention and at ease.

Twice a year, the parents shoehorned us kids into stiff collars, blue tunics, and white pants for a dress review so we could show off our flanking and shouldering. During these reviews, there was always a first-aid station at the back of the armory for kids who passed out. You couldn't breathe while wearing those stiff collars.

The ranks went from buck private to cadet colonel. There were no cadet generals. You couldn't have a thirteen-year-old general when the man who ran the whole show was a sixty-year-old colonel. Each year, there were three "competitions," as they were called, during which you drilled. If you drilled well—that is, if you saluted just so and held your rifle very straight—then you got promoted.

I made private first class at the end of my first year, when I was eight years old. The second year, I made corporal, then sergeant. Sergeant was great, because I got to carry a sword instead of a gun. My third year I made lieutenant, which meant I got to chuck the sword for a saber, which was even better. I was promoted to captain my fourth year. When I left at the end of my fifth year, I was a major.

The Greys gave me a sense of pride I didn't have at school. In the Greys I was an officer, not the class joke. When I gave orders, they were followed. And I was taught not to abuse the privilege. Colonel Warrick led by example. He was a gentle, humorous man who went out of his way to encourage me and the other cadets.

One of the stories we used to love to tell about Colonel Warrick was about his trick for making sure he knew the name of every Greys cadet and Adirondack camper. If he forgot your name, he would sidle up to you and clap his hand on your back. "Well, hello there, Mr. . . ." he would say while pausing to flip back the collar of your shirt so he could read your name tag. ". . . Daniel. How are you, son?"

The summer after my last year in the Greys, when I was thirteen, Colonel Warrick approached me at camp (he did not have to read my name tag by this time) and told me I was going to be cadet colonel that fall. I was very surprised to hear that. There were three other majors, all of them, I thought, better qualified than I to be cadet colonel. On top of that, I thought I had shown considerable un-colonel-like behavior that spring by being officially reprimanded for dancing the Funky Chicken in front of my company during parade drill.

Still, I thought long and hard about Colonel Warrick's offer. Cadet colonel was, after all, what most of us in the organization aspired to be. But I had changed since joining the Greys at age eight. There were lots of reasons I didn't take the job, the greatest of which was a wish to fit in with my peers at school.

Each year, the Greys had an annual parade down Park Avenue. During the parade that spring, in 1970, we had been picketed by a handful of protesters carrying signs, calling us little warmongers. I didn't have strong feelings about Vietnam, but being in the Greys suddenly seemed unpopular. I wanted to be on the other side, the side that had the long hair, the bell-bottoms, and the buckskin jackets. Like almost everyone else at thirteen, I wanted to rebel, to be different from my parents. And I think that was the reason I chucked the Greys, which had given me more pride in myself than anything else—because it had been my parents' idea, not mine.

The piano lessons lasted one more year, both for me and for Will. He actually fared better both with the piano lessons and the Greys. The minute I gave them up, he was allowed to give them up as well. Because of the difference of nearly two years between us, he took both only about half as long as I did. With the Greys, that didn't bother me, but I wanted him to have two more years of piano.

Before my adolescent rebellion began, my father had begun to try to prepare me for the next step in my disastrous school career. At the end of my seventh-grade year at St. Bernard's, he began taking me around for interviews at prep schools. This was an annual ritual among many seventh-graders in New York's private boys' schools.

At every campus we went to, there was at least one other father-son team just like us waiting outside the admissions office or walking around campus like a couple of shoppers. As for my father and myself, neither of us were very enthusiastic shoppers. The interview process seemed fruitless in light of my dismal grades.

That spring I was interviewed at some of the biggies in the prep school pantheon—Choate, Hotchkiss, Groton, Taft, St. Mark's, and Milton Academy—all of which, save one, went by in a monotony of ivy-covered walls, manicured lawns, and buildings that smelled of chalk and wood polish. The only one that stood out was the venerable Milton Academy—and then only because it was the worst place I had ever seen.

I came to find out later that Milton Academy was, and is, one of the best prep schools there is, if I may be so bold to say. Each year, a big chunk of the graduating class goes on to Harvard, which is conveniently located just fifteen miles away in Boston. The school, midsize by prep-school standards, has been sitting out there in the Boston suburbs, in Milton, Massachusetts, since the late eighteenth century, turning out lawyers, doctors, politicians, and such notables as T. S. Eliot and James Taylor. Deval Patrick, chosen by President Bill Clinton to head the Civil Rights Division of the Justice Department, graduated from Milton in 1974.

So I don't know what it was that gave me the willies when I visited Milton that spring of 1970. When I got there, the place just had an air of secondhandedness about it. Part of my feeling along those lines was due to rumors I had heard at St. Bernard's that Milton would take kids with borderline grades that larger, better-known schools passed over. If ever there was a kid with borderline grades, it was me. It didn't help Milton's image that our guide for the campus tour was a kid who wore his hair down in his face and walked around with a pair of moccasins half off the backs of his feet. He looked just like the kind of dangerous, drug-taking thug I had been warned about at St. Bernard's.

Needless to say, I was appalled when Milton turned out to be the only school that would take me.

During my last year at St. Bernard's, the staff got it into their heads to teach classes on the evils of marijuana and other drugs. This was, no doubt, to prepare us to resist the temptations we were likely to face at boarding school. For the task, they picked a teacher with the very appropriate name of Ted Skull. He was so good at his job that I headed into the spring of my eighth-grade year having nightmares that the following fall, kids at Milton would push me to smoke pot. If I refused, I feared that they would lace my food with something stronger.

As strong as those fears were, they all vanished that summer, in the sand under the yacht club at Point o' Woods, Fire Island.

Point o' Woods was the summer place my parents discovered after the luster of Bedford had waned. The private community sits about halfway down Fire Island, off Long Island's eastern shore. It is bordered by a fence with a gate, locking all nonmembers out and creating a place where, in my day, anyway, you didn't have to lock your doors at night. Houses there come in all shapes, from Victorian to modern, and in all sizes. There are cottages and houses that look like cottages pretending to be mansions. Most are secluded from each other by screens of thick, low-growing pine, holly, and other sorts of prickly bushes. I know they're prickly, because I've been in them often after leaving the seat of my bicycle. In addition to bushes, Point o' Woods has a grocery-candy store, a club, a casino (for dancing, not gambling), and the yacht club, which is a grand name for a place to park Sunfishes and fiberglass bathtubs called Mercurys.

I went under the yacht club that first summer, when I was fourteen, with two friends and a dusty, half-full bottle of scotch we had found in the attic of the house my parents had rented for the summer. We took our cigarettes with us. Smoking was another charming habit I picked up that summer.

I don't know how to describe what happened as we sat in the dark and smoked and drank, except to say I fell in love. Being drunk was like being in another world, another body, even. Insecurity vanished. I was fearless. I was, if only in my own mind, the coolest thing on earth, a handsome devil, a devastating wit, a philosopher.

I tried out my newfound coolness that night on a friend of mine, Carey Smoot, one of the most desirable baby-sitters on the island. Paul Lowerre had seen her on a visit earlier that summer and also fallen in love, dubbing her simply the "Girl in the Blue Bikini." Nothing more needed to be said. I had had a crush on Carey since that day.

So when she happened by the yacht club that night, I decided to declare my love for her, thinking that she would, of course, reciprocate. But I declared my love so loudly and with such foulness of breath that it was all she could do to keep from bashing me in the chops. It didn't help that one of my two drinking buddies was loudly and foully declaring his love alongside me. The pair of us became so unruly that Carey had to ask the third of our little trio, who was older and wiser and less plastered, to pull us off her.

I woke up remembering nothing of this, but was later told that, having been spurned by Carey, I went around kissing the yacht club lampposts. My friend and rival suitor wandered into some bushes, where he was found and borne home by two of his older stepsisters.

With an episode or two like that under my belt by fall, Milton suddenly seemed tame. Far from being fearful that my food would be drugged, the first thing I did was sneak out to the cemetery to smoke pot.

The cemetery was across the street from the school, a place with a lovely pond and park at its center where students went to smoke cigarettes. Only one teacher, Mr. Duncan, went in there regularly. Evenings and weekends, he often strolled the lanes between the headstones in full Highland regalia, including a kilt and kneesocks, playing his bagpipe. I thought his mournful Scottish dirges were very good, especially since I could hear him coming from a mile away.

That first night I went into the cemetery with three or four new friends, we headed not for the pond but for the rows of white headstones, where we sat on someone's grave and passed around a double-stemmed pipe. What we didn't know was that both bowls were filled with oregano, courtesy of the kids who invited us out there and took our money. I didn't feel a thing, did an awful lot of coughing, and wondered afterward why my mouth tasted like pizza. I didn't actually get stoned until months later, when several of us finally got hold of some real marijuana.

As it had been at St. Bernard's, I was not Milton Academy's model student. When I wasn't trying to get stoned, I was breaking windows. Within weeks of the start of school, I had taken a friend's "wrist rocket" slingshot and a handful of pennies and put out several panes of glass in the upper story of my dorm.

Slingshots have always gotten me in trouble. When Paul and I were about twelve and he was staying the night, we took a slingshot into my bathroom and took turns firing wads of wet toilet paper across the street at passersby. Many of our friends engaged in the same weekend sport, only most of them lived on higher floors, so they simply dropped the toilet-paper wads out the window onto people's heads. Since my family lived on the first floor, we had to fire horizontally. It was the first time such a stunt had been tried. Unfortunately it was doomed to failure.

That night we posted Will by the bathroom door to watch for my parents. Paul and I grabbed the slingshot and took turns at the window. The one who wasn't shooting sat on the toilet, the idea being that if we were caught in the bathroom together, one would say he had to go and the other was just keeping him company. At the time it didn't sound at all stupid.

Posting Will as lookout had been a mistake. By not including him, we doomed ourselves. He got bored and quickly fell asleep. When my father peeked into the room a few minutes later, he found Will fast asleep in front of the bathroom door.

I was in midshot when my father burst into the bathroom and yelled, "What in God's name are you doing?" Paul was sitting on the toilet and, at that second, might have actually had to use it. He jumped a foot when the door swung open.

"Give me that thing," my father snapped, jerking the slingshot out of my hand. Then he turned to Will, who was standing at the door, fully awake and terrified. "William, go downstairs and get me the *big kitchen knife.*"

Paul saw his life flash before his eyes. He was sure the reason my father wanted the big kitchen knife was to kill him for being part of this horrible fiasco. He prayed that if he lived, he would never, ever, accept an invitation to spend the night at my house again. He was still sitting on the toilet, frozen like a deer caught in the headlights of a speeding truck, when Will brought the knife to Dad. Paul prayed silently as Dad brandished the knife in the air and with one deft motion cut the rubber bands of my slingshot in half, rendering it useless forever.

"There!" he said, handing it back to me. "Now, go to bed!"

Dad was the one who bought me that slingshot when he and Mom visited me at camp one summer. Mom had strongly advised him against it.

Having put the other slingshot episode behind me at Milton, I got on with the business of being as bad a student there as I had been at St. Bernard's. As the report cards rolled in, each more or less as dismal as the last, my parents despaired. They threatened, they cajoled, they pleaded, but there really wasn't much they could do. My mother tried shame. During Sunday lunch at the Club at Point o' Woods that summer, she was talking to a summer neighbor, a prominent New York businessman, when I walked up. "This is my oldest son, Clifton," she said, introducing me.

"How do you do, young man," he said. "And where are you in school this year?"

"Milton Academy," I said.

"Ah, yes. A fine place. Do you enjoy it."

Before I could answer, my mother cut in with: "Yes, but he's not doing very well."

Though she would tell a near-total stranger that my grades were awful, she never told my grandparents, both of whom went to their graves without every knowing how badly I had done in school. My father said he didn't want to burden Gammy and Grandpa with that information since it wasn't their problem, but mine and his. My parents didn't even tell my grandmother when she came to visit us for Christmas the year after Grandpa died.

By that time, my sophomore year at Milton, we were living in Washington, D.C., where my father had taken over the Washington bureau of *The New York Times.* The *Times* had a devil of a time getting my mother to move back to Washington and wound up having to buy her a Mercedes as a bribe.

It was Christmas of my sophomore year that Gammy spent a week with us in Washington. I remember nothing of her visit save one thing.

The house we had rented in Wesley Heights had a dining alcove in the kitchen. Gammy was sitting there, by the window one Sunday morning, when I came down to breakfast. My mother was at the stove, making scrambled eggs for one of my brothers. By that point, my hair had grown well past my shoulders. I had it in a ponytail when I sat down next to Gammy with a bowl of Cheerios and the Sunday funnies. After a second or two of bending my head toward the funnies, the rubber band began to yank the hair at the nape of my neck, so I took it out. Watching my hair fall down over my shoulders, she said simply: "You know, you have beautiful hair."

I nearly choked on my Cheerios. My mother, who caught the comment from across the room, almost dropped the frying pan full of scrambled eggs.

"My God, Mother! Don't tell him that!" she all but screamed. "He'll never get it cut."

She was right. Having Bess Truman's blessing meant my hair would get progressively longer over the next few years, to the point I could tuck it into my shirt-front pocket. As my parents had warned, it made me look like a girl—one girl in particular. At Milton one afternoon, the father of a friend of mine saw me walk by and started chuckling to himself.

"What's so funny, Dad?" my friend asked.

"Oh, it's nothing," his father said. "It's just that that kid looks like Margaret Truman."

I wonder if my grandmother said what she did that day in the kitchen simply to tweak my mother. For years after that incident, I thought she really liked my hair. But in the summer of 1994, I was given a present by Dr. Ben Zobrist and the staff of the Truman Library. It was a letter mailed April 17, 1972, by my grandmother to a friend, Mary Bostian of Independence.

"I am really sorry Nellie Post has to contend with all those hippies," Gammy wrote on page two. "It does seem time something was done about them. When I saw my two big grandsons with long hair at Christmas time I almost expired. But they were clean and had on decent clothes."

Even with decent clothes, I was not to make it back into the White House again until I was nineteen and my hair was shorter. But in 1973, when I was sixteen, Will and I did make it back into Blair House with our father as tour guide.

He took us there as a history lesson, to refresh our memories of when we had been there last, during President Johnson's 1965 inauguration. He had made arrangements for a guided tour, but when we got there, we found the staff in something of a flap over the arrival of Soviet president Leonid Brezhnev and Foreign Minister Andrei Gromyko.

The Russians had made camp in Blair House, turning the front waiting room, presided over by a portrait of Abraham Lincoln, into an office. They had carted in filing cabinets and plugged in two clunky-looking, green Soviet-made phones connected directly to the Russian embassy switchboard. Each phone had a nameplate printed in Russian, which none of the Blair House staff could read. Dad, who had picked up more than a smattering of the language from living in Russia in the mid-1950s, slipped on his reading glasses and peered at the phone labels.

"One says Brezhnev and the other says Gromyko," he said.

Grateful—and extremely busy—the Blair House staff let us poke around the house on our own for about half an hour. Dad showed us through both Blair and Lee houses, including the rooms where our mother had lived—and where we had stayed as children. On the way out, he wanted to show us the bedroom where he had slept on a 1964 trip to Washington with Grandpa Truman.

As we came to the threshold of his old room, we found three people inside. One of them was obviously an American, slim and well-dressed. The other two looked just like the Russian villains from the James Bond movies I had seen. They were human chunks of granite, barely contained by their ill-fitting dark suits. As we stepped into the doorway, both were peering under my father's former bed, presumably looking for electronic bugs or bombs.

We might have tiptoed quietly out, but Dad walked boldly in, followed by us. Both guys peering under the bed nearly bashed their heads on the box springs when he cheerfully called "Good morning" to them in perfect Russian. They stiffened and stared at us, slack-jawed and suspicious, and I thought they were going to reach into their coats, pull out of couple of automatics, and march us to the basement for questioning. But after a moment they both just nodded, said "good morning" back, and we were on our way. Dad didn't think a thing of it, but I was sure we were followed home.

I think it was that same day that the three of us stopped off for about ten minutes to watch what became known as the Watergate hearings. These were the Senate hearings into the break-in at Democratic National Committee Headquarters at the Watergate complex in Washington that ultimately led to President Richard Nixon's resignation. Sorry to say, the hearings did not make a huge impression on me. The only reason I know I was there is that the Truman Library has a photo of it.

I did not stay in Washington much while our family lived there. Right after Christmas every year, I usually made my way back to New York to stay with friends and make the rounds of holiday parties and bars. New York had a subculture of "preppy bars" that were lax in checking identification. On any given holiday night, you could find the places bulging with teenagers.

Back at school, I threw myself less into study and more into rock bands and experimenting with drugs. The first and last time I did acid I was fifteen and, with some friends, stayed up all night in a vacant floor master's apartment watching tables tilt at odd angles and books wiggle as if they were under water. Acid is very overrated as a recreational drug. I had no revelations, no insights, did not see God. And it wore real thin the next day at breakfast when my fried eggs kept moving around on my plate.

We had started the night before trying to get in backstage at an Allman Brothers concert at Boston Garden. It was while waiting around in the lobby that I met Caroline Kennedy. My girlfriend, J.J. McCulloch, had been to school with Caroline in New York. Caroline and I said hi, the only word I've ever spoken to her, and she and J.J. fell to catching up with each other while I stood off to one side. It was then that I noticed an odd-looking hippy standing in the center of the lobby.

He was wearing bell-bottom jeans, sandals, a white T-shirt, and a buckskin vest. His hair was brown, straight, and held in place by a green headband. He was just standing there, looking from side to side, as though he had lost someone. Something about the guy bothered me, but I couldn't figure out what it was until he faced me head-on and I noticed his hair was longer on one side than the other. He turned out to be a Secret Service agent in a wig, there to protect Caroline. She was fifteen and would have about one more year of Secret Service protection, which lasts for ex-presidents' kids until their sixteenth birthday. I had half a mind to walk up to the guy and ask him if he knew anybody on the Truman detail.

Caroline went on to enjoy the concert. We had no tickets and were deserted by the friend of a friend who was supposed to get us in backstage. We wound up getting chased out of the garden, along with the rest of the milling, ticketless crowd, by Boston police with German shepherds. While we were all sprinting away from the dogs, the guy in front of me ran right through a plate-glass door. In a strange twist, I met him on Fire Island a few years later. Nice guy. Not a scratch on him.

With such a sterling extracurricular life, my grades showed little improvement. By the end of the first semester of my senior year, the headmaster, David Wicks, called me into his office.

"Clifton," he said, tamping tobacco into his pipe, "students at Milton are allowed no more than five grades below a C during the entire four years they are here. More than that and they don't graduate. You have most of a year to go and you already have five D's to your credit. Of course, that's not counting this report card," he added, tapping the card, which was on his desk.

I waited while he lit his pipe. I knew there was worse news coming. My grades for the first semester were two C's and three D's, which was three more than I could afford.

"Now, we've asked your father to speak at your graduation this spring," Mr. Wicks continued, the smoke rising above him. "The question is: Are you going to be there?"

I went back to my dorm wondering the same thing. To turn three D's into three C's, I would have to get at least B's during the next semester, a phenomenon for which there was no precedent in my life. As it turned out, Dad was not sold on the idea of speaking at Milton, but he did it anyway, hoping to inspire me in some way. I don't think he knew the inspiration would be fear.

It's amazing what fear can do. I didn't get B's that last semester. I got straight A's. I raised my average for the year to straight B's. My parents and teachers were stunned—and annoyed that I had apparently always had this ability. Both they and I were at a loss to explain why it was hardly ever brought into play. I went on to astonish everyone by getting into almost all the colleges to which I applied, among them Syracuse University and the University of North Carolina at Chapel Hill, my father's alma mater.

When I was accepted at Chapel Hill, which had been my first choice, I delighted another UNC alumnus, who happened to be a Milton English teacher. He was so delighted, in fact, that he invited me up to his room and gave me a sample of North Carolina culture, a bourbon and ginger ale. I chose Chapel Hill not because I liked it particularly or thought it offered what I needed but because I thought going there was what my parents expected me to do. I had no compass of my own.

My father gave the commencement address at Milton that spring, following valedictorian Sandy Cardin, who, by virtue of a wise mouth and a straight-A average, was a tough act to follow.

Dad launched into his speech by saying, "I'm going to take some advice given by Susan Ford to her father, President Gerald Ford, when he gave the commencement address at her school recently. She told him not to talk too long, not to tell any jokes, and not to talk about her."

I couldn't imagine where this was leading.

"Well, I'm not going to talk too long," Dad said. "I can't tell any jokes because your valedictorian has stolen them all from me, and I am certainly not going to talk about . . ."

And he was looking right at me as I waited for the other shoe to drop.

". . . Susan Ford."

All my classmates bellowed. I was sitting next to Mike Clasby, a football player and one of the biggest, most rocklike kids at Milton.

"Hey, your old man's pretty funny," he yelled at me, and elbowed me hard enough that I thought I heard a rib snap. Chip Counihan, who was sitting on my other side, did the same thing at the same time. Thank God he wasn't as big as Mike. I might have been crushed.

At the close of the ceremony, my father and I both got a special privilege. Mr. Wicks let him hand me my diploma and shake my hand. I stepped off the podium wearing a goofy grin and waved the diploma above my head. My mother, sitting in the front row, kept gesturing to me and mouthing, "Stop that. Stop that."

The last time my parents saw me that afternoon, I was walking across campus with a cigarette in one hand and a bottle of cheap champagne in the other. I stayed on in the town of Milton for three days of parties before taking the train home to New York.

8

The Secret Handshake

During summer school at the University of North Carolina in 1977, I took a course, Geology 11, nicknamed "Rocks for Jocks." It was the simplest of courses, rumored to be the number-one choice of varsity athletes. I was no varsity athlete, but the course had also been endorsed by people like me, who had flunked out of their freshman year and needed a couple of credits to get back in.

Like the foam on a glass of flat beer, my freshman year had disappeared. I spent more time at fraternity mixers, on road trips, and in bars than I did in classrooms. As a result, my grade-point average was a 1.3, .2 below what I needed to squeak into the sophomore class. So that summer I signed up for a freshman English course and Rocks for Jocks. I had to get at least a C in each to get back into school.

About the third week of summer school, I and my Rocks for Jocks classmates went on a field trip to a nearby quarry to look at, what else, rocks—in their natural habitat. Our route out of town took us down the row of fraternity houses near the heart of campus. Mansion after columned mansion glided by outside our window. I missed this stately parade because I was squished in the back of the station wagon we were riding in. I didn't realize it when we came abreast of the Delta Kappa Epsilon fraternity house, but several of the girls in the car had a better view.

"Look at that!" one of them said, disgust dripping from her voice. "They are such animals!"

I craned my neck, and the front lawn of the house came into view. It had been gouged down the middle and filled with water so that it looked like nothing so much as a big bog. About half a dozen fraternity brothers were taking running starts and flinging themselves, backsides first, along the slimy ground. Shouts of "Yee-hah!" issued from their lips. They were unrecognizable from the coats of mud they wore.

Around them the grounds were blighted with beer cans, crushed plastic cups, toilet paper, and what looked like bits of underwear. The grass, what little was left, was scarred with brown, muddy skid marks. Around the mud slide, the fraternity had placed what looked like most of its living-room furniture. Arranged on a couple of leather armchairs were a handful of girls, drinking beer, talking, and half watching the sliders.

Near them on a couch was a lone casualty, passed out cold on his back with his mouth wide open. He had apparently drunk enough to anesthetize himself completely, because someone had been able to sneak up with a ballpoint pen and draw an intricate pattern of curlicued lines all over his face. Flies were landing on him absolutely fearlessly.

Now, this kind of sight was not uncommon along the UNC fraternity row on any given evening. However, it did seem a little stunning at eight o'clock in the morning.

"What fraternity is that?" asked another of the girls in our car.

"Delta Kappa Epsilon. The Dekes," said the first girl.

"What are they doing?"

"They call it an early morning mixer," I said. "They've been drinking bloody marys and screwdrivers since breakfast. Some of them have probably been up all night."

"How do you know?"

I shrugged. "They do it all the time."

"God, what a bunch of assholes!" the first girl said. "Just look at them!"

I did, somewhat longingly. I knew and liked every one of them, including Andy, the guy passed out on the couch who now looked like a Maori tribesman dead on the battlefield. Were it not for a little self-control, I might have been lying next to him. I had been invited to the party, though I kept it a secret from my Rocks for Jocks buddies that day. I was, after all, a dues-paying assh . . . uh, member of the Deke house.

My grandfather Truman had practically educated himself. Though his schooling in Independence was very good, he inhaled information on his own as well. As an adolescent, he read and read and read, soaking up multivolume histories and historical biographies two inches thick. Though he did not go to college, he took correspondence courses, never getting a grade lower than somewhere in the high eighties.

I went to Chapel Hill full of hope that I would change, become more like him. The last semester at Milton, when I had made straight A's for the first time in my life, had seemed a good omen. Despite my terrible scholastic track record, I wasn't resigned to being a failure at school. I kept thinking I would do better once I had licked whatever it was in my nature that that made studying abhorrent. I was always starting fresh, making resolutions. Somewhere in me a quiet little voice kept telling me I could be better than I was. Unfortunately, a loud, obnoxious voice kept yelling: "Go on, drink another beer!"

At Chapel Hill I listened to the louder voice, joining a fraternity that seemed to thrive on an air of lawlessness. The Dekes had a reputation for wildness, which some of us worked very hard to maintain. For example, coming back to the house from class one afternoon, I found two of my brothers on the roof of a side porch. The house, a brick mansion with white columns, supported two side porches. These guys, dressed in cardigans and golf shoes, were on the porch that faced a parking lot between the Sigma Alpha Epsilon house next door and a deserted frat house behind the SAEs'. They were up there with a six-pack and a bucket of golf balls, smacking drives into the windows of the deserted house.

Another example: When I came back from New York the next year, I found a huge party in full swing on the front porch. I got out of the taxi across the street just in time to see the Coke machine from the second floor inching out the bathroom window. This was one of those old-style Coke machines that had a big red-and-white front door and was filled with bottles, like a refrigerator. Not that modern drink machines are lightweight, but this thing was to one of them like a 1955 Cadillac is to a 1994 Nissan. As the machine edged its way over the lip of the window, the crowd below seemed to sense it was in danger and divided just in time to let the machine flip over once in midair and land on its back on the porch with a horrendous crash. A moment later the crowd surged back over it. People sat on it as if it were a couch dragged out from the living room.

Then there was the night I was sleeping off a party on the couch in the fraternity house president's room when we heard what sounded like a brawl taking place on the first floor—things crashing against walls, people yelling. The fraternity president and I ran downstairs in our boxer shorts and sprinted down the hall to the kitchen, the source of the racket. Halfway there, we both slipped and slid about twenty feet in a slick of blue cheese, ranch, and Thousand Island salad dressing. Two of our fraternity brothers and two sorority girls had gotten plastered and absolutely trashed the kitchen and the dining room.

To be fair, the members of Delta Kappa Epsilon were no wilder than many other fraternity boys. Most of them made it to class, whether or not they had a hangover. Most graduated, on time, and went on to have successful careers. I, however, did not have my grandfather's self-discipline. I was not ready to be let loose on a campus where no one checked up on you or cared if you came to class and where the inclination to drink to excess was seen as a positive trait.

The first outing I had with the Dekes was going tubing on the Haw River. Tubing is an uncomplicated sport requiring only a bathing suit—which is actually optional—an inner tube, and a couple of six-packs of beer. The object is simple: to dangle your bottom through the inner tube, float with the current, and get drunk.

I had only one reservation about the tubing trip—poisonous snakes. I was a city boy, and despite four summers at camp, I

Here I am with Will, ages five and three, greeting Grandpa as he arrives in New York the day after his seventy-eighth birthday. I can't remember who brought the cake, but I do know who ate most of it. (*Courtesy Wide World Photos*)

Taken off the coast of Duck Key, Florida, in 1963, I think by my father. Note that the fish is (*a*) dead and (*b*) very close to the cooler. That hand-on-hip bravado is all show. I was scared to death.

Will and I pose in our dress uniforms before a parade with the Knickerbocker Greys, the paramilitary group we belonged to in New York City. Mom thought being in the Greys would make us tidier children. It didn't work. Those stiff collars we're wearing were murder.

Such a happy group this is—posing in the summer of 1965 at the house we'd rented in suburban Westchester County, New York. It looks like we've all just had a huge fight, probably over putting on coats and ties and posing. Dad and Mom may have also been thinking about the cat that chewed up *The New York Times* publisher Arthur "Punch" Sulzberger at our house that summer. Mom and Dad are in back. Will and I, ages six and eight, are in the middle, and Gammy and Grandpa are in front. Grandpa is holding Harrison, obviously the only one who knew where the camera was.

The family went out to the airport to meet Gammy and Grandpa when they arrived in New York City for Christmas in 1965. I like this picture because it shows me and Gammy together. We're being trailed by Dad and Grandpa. I was eight years old.

Above, left: Harrison, age four, is standing outside my grandparents' house during a snowy Christmas visit in 1967. *Above, right:* Will and Thomas, ages eight and one, pose behind my grandparents' house during that same Christmas 1967 visit. Over Will's shoulder is the back porch of the house where, on pretty days, Gammy played bridge and Grandpa read the morning papers. That corner of the house is also the one I was peeking around when I almost got shot by the Secret Service.

My grandparents' house at 219 North Delaware Street in Independence. It's now a historic site administered by the National Park Service.

Will and I pose outside the Little White House on the Navy base in Key West. This was taken in 1968, when we were eight and ten.

This photo was taken in the *Apollo* spacecraft simulator at the Kennedy Space Center in Florida in 1968. That's Robert Spottswood, son of Senator John Spottswood, on the left, Will, and me. Behind us is *Gemini* astronaut Tom Stafford, nice guy and tour guide.

Here's the family in April 1968 at the White House unveiling of Greta Kempton's portrait of Gammy. Lady Bird Johnson and Vice President Hubert Humphrey hit it off very well with the children, especially Harrison, who's getting the handshake. He was five, Thomas was two, Will was nine, and I was eleven.

Seconds later, Mr. Humphrey scooped up Thomas and headed off to the reception that followed the unveiling.

Eventually Thomas decided to try out for the Marine band that played at the reception. The Marine at left offered his bow and violin for practice, while another tried to give Thomas a quick lesson. My brother then figured that running up and down the long, carpeted halls of the White House was much more fun. When it was time to leave, Dad had to catch him.

My classmate, Charlie Kothe, me, Will, and his classmate, Ross Boylan, pose onstage at the *Ed Sullivan Show* late in 1968. Mr. Sullivan asked us all, including my father, to stand up in the audience at the beginning of the show. The hats say YOUR FATHER'S MOUSTACHE.

In Copenhagen in early 1969, when we were on our way back from the Norway funeral of Trygve Lie, secretary general of the United Nations while Grandpa was in office. William and Arther Zeckendorf, Mr. Lie's grandsons, are second and fourth from left. Will and I are third and last from left, ages nine and eleven. I have completely forgotten who the other two kids are. The guy in back is a nice man with whom we played poker on the flight over.

shared my mother's disinclination to bond with nature, especially with poisonous snakes. There are four varieties native to North Carolina, by the way, including the cottonmouth, which spends a lot of its time in rivers, waiting for tubers, or so I had heard. I tried to confirm this information with one of the Dekes, John Adler, who was driving several of us to the river in his truck.

John was easygoing and likable, an aspiring writer and serious outdoorsman who hunted with a bow and arrow. He had an almost—but not quite—cherubic face, thinning blond hair, muttonchop sideburns, and a thick southern accent. He seemed to know everything there was to know about nature.

"Aren't there poisonous snakes in the rivers around here, like cottonmouths or something?" I asked.

John laughed. "Aw, you don't have to worry about snakes, Clifton. There ain't any in the Haw River. It's too cold for 'em. Besides, they can't bite under water."

"Why not?"

"Well, think about it. If they open their mouths to bite you, they'd drown, wouldn't they?"

This seemed to make perfect sense to a New Yorker who, at age five, had let two pet turtles die because he didn't know they needed food. I went the rest of the ride confident that I would not have to worry about having my backside ventilated by a cottonmouth.

But when we got to the river, John Adler turned out to be a bald-faced liar—or at least not as wise about the ways of nature as I had thought. I was just about to put my tube in the water when I looked down and chanced to see a small snake swimming along, under water, with a catfish in its mouth. It was, according to witnesses, a cottonmouth.

"I thought you said they can't bite under water," I yelled at Adler. "What'd he do, wait until the fish jumped out and bite him in midair?"

John was unfazed. "Oh, quit bein' a sissy and get in the water. That little snake isn't gonna bother you. He's already got a fish."

"What about the ones that don't have a fish?"

"Oh, go on. Get in!"

It was only because there were twenty people watching and jeering that I got into the tube and pushed off from shore. As I floated away, I tensed my buttocks muscles, bracing for a puncture wound.

Our little armada floated out into the middle of the Haw, accompanied by hoots and hollers and the *pffft-pffft-pffft* of beer cans being opened. It was a beautiful late-August day, sunny and hot. With all that ice-cold beer on our hands, we were in heaven, bobbing along, yelling at each other and laughing. A couple of brothers had even wedged a cooler full of beer into an inner tube and tethered it to their own tubes, like a floating bar. These days, I hear, people stick a whole keg in a tube and everyone just glides by to tank up.

As the beer went to my head, I relaxed about the snakes. In fact, I had pretty much forgotten about them when I felt something jab me in the leg.

"What the hell was that?" I yelled, trying to hop out of the tube and walk on water.

"It was a damn rock," someone else said. "They're scraping my legs."

I caught my toe on another jagged edge the instant he said it.

"So what, are we just going through a rough spot?" I asked.

"No. Shit! I was afraid this was going to happen," John Adler said. The rocks, while preferable to snakes, were nonetheless worrisome. "The river's too low. We're going to have to get out before someone gets cut up."

One by one, we kicked and paddled our way to the bank and tried to regroup, dragging our inner tubes and our beer with us. The original plan had been for us to float down to a boat landing where we had left another truck. But as it was, we were strung out all over the place, people climbing out of the water wherever they could get ashore. We managed to find all but two of our party, which was very annoying to legendary UNC basketball coach Dean Smith. One of the two we misplaced was one of his players, who, with a sorority girl, had to spend the night in the woods.

Being Harry Truman's grandson meant little at college. I found this out because I had gotten into the habit of trying to work the fact into the conversation whenever I could. The recognition was like a high, a short glow. To carry the analogy a step further, name dropping was just about as cheap and useless as taking drugs. The feeling was fleeting, unproductive, and unearned. But I did it anyway.

Most of my fraternity brothers regarded my heritage as mildly amusing. Some occasionally called me "Harry S." Older people in North Carolina generally recognized Clifton Daniel as my father's name more often than they associated it with Grandpa. This was, after all, my father's country. He had been born and raised in Zebulon, about an hour and a half away, and had graduated from Chapel Hill in 1933. So now I could try to embarrass Dad's side of the family directly.

I did a pretty good job—drinking half the night, ducking classes. Biology was my only class on Fridays during my first semester, at eight o'clock in the morning. One of the only times I made it was after one of those early-morning mixers, during which people dig mud holes and pass out on the lawn.

During Hell Week, I stumbled into psychology class wearing a three-day-old shirt and ashes caked in my hair. How the ashes got there or why, I can't remember.

Hell Week is a quaint DKE institution crafted to bond the pledges to one another for life. In the case of our freshman class, it didn't work. None of us keep in touch with each other today. That's probably because we would be reminded of being kept up most of the night for three days in a row, having to clean the toilets with toothbrushes and being grilled on Deke history while having obscenities screamed at us in the basement of the house.

The older Dekes would push our hands into the urinals and flush cold water over them while making us stare at a sixty-watt lightbulb.

"What does the lightbulb say?" they would yell.

And you would squint and strain until you could read aloud, "General Electric, sixty watts."

"Wrong, you moron! Lightbulbs can't talk!"

We were required to eat a raw egg before every meal.

I was exhausted, but I didn't dare go back to the dorm to sleep. The Dekes were patrolling the dorms between classes to make sure the pledges stayed awake. During the psychology lecture, I fell dead asleep, and my head smacked the desktop with a crack that made everybody in the class spin around.

"Mr. Daniel, are you all right?" the psych professor asked.

"Yes, I'm fine," I said, rubbing my forehead. "I'm just a little tired."

She looked at me for a second, took in the hair and the shirt, the bags under the eyes, and the loud tie I'd been made to wear—and then she smiled.

"You joined a fraternity, didn't you?"

One of my classmates, Carson Joyner, also smiled. She knew what fraternity houses could be like. Later that year, Carson and I went on a double date with one of my fraternity brothers, Tom Hackney, and his date, Lucy Credle. Our first stop was the pig pickin' at the Deke house. If you've never seen a pig pickin', it is like it sounds. A whole pig is slow-roasted all night long, then cut up and served with barbecue sauce and beer the next afternoon. Though plates of barbecued pork are passed around, most people stand at the pig and pick at it, hence the name.

The night before the pig pickin', the Dekes had held the annual Martini Chug. The object of this colorful event was to drink as many martinis as you could between the hours of ten and midnight. I drank three, then headed to the Shack, the local beer-and-pinball emporium, for some beers to wash the nasty taste of the gin out of my mouth. The winner stayed at the house and drank nine martinis and didn't even have to be taken to the hospital.

Three of my fraternity brothers did go to the emergency room that night. Two were released, and one was kept for observation. When he was taken to the hospital, he insulted the doctors and made a grab for every nurse within reach of his wheelchair. When they let him out the next day, he came to the pig pickin', got drunk all over again, and threw a half-full, half-crushed beer can at another brother. Said brother ducked, and the can caught me in the head for five stitches. I spent the first half of my date with Carson at the hospital.

I didn't date often at college my first year because I had a steady girlfriend, Marti Carioty, who was at Concordia College in upstate New York. I only got to see her once during that school year, at Thanksgiving, when I invited her to Washington. It was a short but memorable visit.

That was the last of the three years my family lived in Washington. My father, who was Washington bureau chief of *The New York Times,* was being transferred back to New York City pending his retirement. I was eighteen, and Gerald Ford was in office.

It was Dad's continual interest in educating me, despite my lack of interest in the project, that caused him to arrange a tour of the White House the second day Marti was in Washington. This was actually more for Marti's benefit than mine, since I had already been to the White House. The night before, we had stayed out late for dinner and drinks in Georgetown, so it was with bleary eyes that we arrived at the White House gate a little before nine the next morning.

This was to be a no-frills affair. Dad sent us on the regular public tour. There was to be no hoopla, no Truman's-grandson shtick. Marti and I got in line with everybody else. But as much as Dad thought he and Mom had an agreement about having their children maintain a low profile, he could never count on Mom to play along.

I had just walked past the guard at the White House gate when he called out my name.

"Mr. Daniel, could you come back here for a minute, sir?"

By dint of my lifestyle, I was conditioned to expect authority figures to question my every move. I didn't doubt that I had broken some sort of law. I just couldn't figure out which one. But the guard was smiling as I walked toward him.

"I'm sorry, sir," he said. "Would you please step over there and see the sergeant-at-arms?"

People were staring as Marti and I walked over. I couldn't

imagine what I had done to get arrested at the White House. Marti was beginning to wonder if coming with me had been a good idea. I approached the sergeant, who was standing by a small side door, away from the main gate.

"Excuse me. I'm Clifton Daniel. The guard said you wanted to see me."

He looked me up and down for a second and said, "Wait right here, please." Then he stuck his head in the door and said something to someone inside. Then, nodding to whoever it was, he stepped aside and held the door open for us.

"Please see Mr. Farrell down the hall, sir."

Marti was now truly nervous. As we walked down the hall, she tugged at my sleeve.

"What's going on?"

"I don't know. I didn't do anything . . . I don't think."

As we approached an office door, a man stepped out to meet us.

"Clifton, hi," he said, shaking my hand. "Michael Farrell. I'm the director of the visitor's office for the White House. The last time I saw you, you were about this high." He held his hand about three feet off the floor. I guessed he had been at the White House during the Johnson administration.

"Hi, Mr. Farrell," I said, and introduced Marti. "Is something wrong?"

"Oh, no," he said quickly. "Not a thing. It's just that your mother called and she wants you to call back."

I stopped and looked at him, then at Marti, whose mouth had dropped open as wide as mine, then back at Mr. Farrell.

"My mother called?"

"Yes," he said, handing me a slip of paper with my own phone number on it. "I think she wants you both to meet her for lunch."

He directed me to a small room off the corridor which contained a control panel more complicated than the one I had seen in the *Apollo* simulator at Cape Kennedy. I assumed I was looking at the White House switchboard. With all the lights and wires, that thing could have handled every call in North America. Mr. Farrell flicked a switch somewhere in the middle of the mess and handed me a receiver. I dialed my home number and got Mom on the second ring.

"Mom, what the hell are you doing calling me at the White House?" I said.

She was offended by the question.

"Well, why shouldn't I call you at the White House. I used to live there," she said. "I can call anytime I want. All I wanted to do was tell you both to meet us for lunch."

The last time my mother had actually slept in the White House was for one night early in John F. Kennedy's administration.

Mr. Kennedy had thrown a formal dinner party for my grandfather. Grandpa was a fellow Democrat and former president—and about forty percent of the people in the Kennedy administration had also been in the Truman administration. There were about sixty people at the dinner, including my mother and father and a number of my grandfather's friends and former associates. Mom was seated between the president and the attorney general, Bobby Kennedy.

The main course that night was grouse, and Mrs. Kennedy had high hopes for both it and the man who had prepared it, her new French chef. One of the things the former first lady is remembered for is bringing a sense of style to the Kennedy administration. She had done a lot to refine and redecorate the White House, and *monsieur le chef* was part of the overhaul. Alas, he and the grouse did not get along.

Grouse doesn't have to be cooked long, only about fifteen minutes. The chef knew that, but what he or someone working for him didn't know is that once cooked, a grouse can't be reheated. To keep the grouse toasty for sixty people, it was cooked and put under warming lights for an hour or so.

When the grouse was put in front of my mother, she picked up a knife, one of the same knives she had used a decade earlier, and dug in. The blade did not sink in, but was instantly repelled, like a sword glancing off a shield. The grouse, baking under the warming lights, had turned to stone. Mom wasn't the only one having trouble. Up and down the table, she could hear sharp clinks as people's knives slid off their birds and cracked against their plates.

Someone said, "Oh, my!" as a particularly strong assault sent a grouse skittering to the floor. Two more grouse followed closely. Some guests carried gamely on, finally wrestling away hard-won slivers of tough bird. Others, having been repulsed, simply shrugged and made light of it.

Not the president. His expression remained as hard as the grouse.

Mom finally gave up, threw down her knife, and turned to Bobby Kennedy. "These gold knives never could cut butter, anyway," she said.

This comment elicited such a peal of laughter from Mr. Kennedy that it alarmed people at the table who knew him well. Apparently the attorney general was not given to such fits of gaiety. Several of his acquaintances came up to my mother afterward to ask, "What on earth did you say to Bobby?"

Mrs. Kennedy was so sensitive about the evening's troubles that she was somewhat put out the next day to find that her houseguests had left early. This was no reflection on her or the grouse, or even the French chef. My grandfather had simply gotten up at the crack of dawn, as usual, and had everyone in his party fed and on their way by eight thirty, while the Kennedys were still sleeping. Mr. Kennedy knew this and had said good night the night before. He had apparently forgotten to tell Mrs. Kennedy.

A little after nine in the morning, the phone rang in my parents' room at the Mayflower Hotel. "Margaret," said a plaintive voice. "Where are you?" It was the first lady calling to find out why her guests had sneaked off.

Whether my mother intended it or not, the White House was on alert the day Marti and I visited that a member of the presidential progeny was on the premises. We were put on a smaller, private tour numbering about eight people.

"This is nice," Marti said as we walked through the Blue Room, the Red Room, and the Green Room. "I'm glad your mother called."

As we traipsed around, it looked like we had the White House to ourselves, save for one other group that kept crossing our path. And they're weren't your ordinary tourists. They were traffic stoppers: fifteen of the tallest Chinese women I have ever seen in my life, all of them wearing dark blue Mao suits. They were gliding along, huddled around an interpreter about half their size and staring at the crystal chandeliers—which looked to be only about an inch or two above their heads.

"That's the Chinese women's basketball team," our guide informed us. "They're here for a tour and a special ceremony with President Ford."

As the team moved off in front of us, Mr. Farrell appeared. "If you'd like, we can get you into the Rose Garden to watch the ceremony," he said.

"Thank you," I said, then added in a masterpiece of understatement, "That would be really nice."

"Good. I'll come get you when it's time."

It was at about this time that I noticed the woman from Texas. I had not, heretofore, paid much attention to the other members of our group. They seemed a nice, diverse group, mostly well-to-do. There wasn't anyone outstanding, until the woman from Texas started talking. Now, here was a grouse.

I don't know where I got the idea she was from Texas, unless I heard it said. There wasn't anything about her accent that might suggest it, and there were no longhorn steer appliqués on her dress. She was bird-thin, with a dark bouffant hair-do and a tiny handbag slung over her arm, and she was walking with a friend near the front of our little band. My chief complaint about her was that she seemed to have an opinion on everything the guide was saying. The portraits weren't very well executed, she opined. To her mind, the White House furniture and the wallpaper were just so tacky.

Her running disparagement was nothing more than an annoyance, something to listen to and snicker at, until it fell upon my grandparents. We were passing through the China Room, which is on the basement level, next to the Diplomatic Reception Room, when the guide paused in front of the cabinet containing my grandparents' presidential china.

As the guide moved off, the Texas woman shot a last glance at the china and said: "Hmmph. It's plain . . . like the Trumans."

I was absolutely tongue-tied. I had no idea what to say—or if I should say anything. I tried coming up with something snappy, but my brain felt as if it were tied in a knot. You know the feeling. You always think of the perfect comeback ten minutes later, when it's too late. I didn't want to just tap this woman on the shoulder and stammer something like "So there. Nyah."

Plus, I am, by nature, a diplomat. I like people to like each other and, more important, to like me. Fear of confrontation used to actually make me sweat—even occasionally as a journalist, especially when I approached people cold for an opinion, a man-in-the-street interview. Most people are very nice about allowing you to probe their brains in the middle of a mall, but there are a few who will look at you as if you're something they found on their shoe and say, haughtily: "I don't talk to reporters."

To be fair, some of them have had a bad experience with the press; perhaps they've been misquoted. Others don't like what they read in the papers, or they may think it's fashionable to dislike reporters, so they act like petulant movie stars. You can't say anything. They can be mean to you all they like, but if you sass them back, they'll break their rule about talking to the press and talk to your editor.

The best comeback never used by a reporter came from Kirsten Brown Mitchell at the *Wilmington Morning Star.* She was sent to cover a celebrity auction in which a dinner with newsman and Wilmington native David Brinkley was auctioned off for about two thousand dollars. At the end of the auction, Kirsten approached the woman who made the high bid. "Excuse me," Kirsten said, introducing herself. "Can I ask you a question or two?"

The woman gave her a condescending glare. "I don't talk to the press," she said, waving Kirsten away.

"Well, thanks, anyway," Kirsten said graciously. Then, when the woman was out of earshot, she muttered: "If you don't talk to the press, what the hell are you going to do with David Brinkley all evening?"

At the White House, I thought I might have revenge of sorts. Mr. Farrell walked up moments after the Texas woman had bad-mouthed my grandparents and said, loud enough for the group to hear: "We'll go out to the Rose Garden now."

As I walked off, I saw the woman staring questioningly at us. Maybe someone would tell her who I was and she would be embarrassed.

Nah.

Mr. Farrell showed us out to the Rose Garden and stood us behind a group of reporters and photographers, opposite the Oval Office. The Chinese women's basketball team was arranging itself on the steps outside the office itself.

"This is great," Marti said, smiling from ear to ear.

In a few minutes, President Ford emerged from the Oval Office and strode over to greet the team. He's a big, square-shouldered man, but those basketball players made him look like a munchkin.

He said something like: "I'm very glad to welcome you to the White House, and I hope that our two countries can continue in this spirit of cooperation, etc., etc., etc."

Marti and I were both having a good time, enjoying this piece of presidential protocol and feeling somewhat privileged. While all this was going on, Mr. Farrell walked up to us again. It was beginning to appear that he was stalking us, but only in the nicest sense of the word.

"When we get close to the end of the ceremony, we'll walk behind them to the Oval Office and have you meet the president."

That's when Marti's jaw dropped open.

I thought she was going to be delighted. Instead, she said, in a very loud, panicky whisper, "What? I can't meet the president of the United States! Look at me! My hair's not brushed, I'm not wearing any makeup! I'm wearing blue jeans, for god's sake!!"

She looked better than I did. I hadn't gotten up in time for a shower that morning, so I had bad hair. Thinking I was just going on the two-dollar tour, I had thrown on sneakers, jeans, and a dirty shirt, the last of which I covered with a sweater and a corduroy jacket. Still, I was doing better than Marti in the panic department.

"You look fine," I said. "We're just going to shake his hand and say hi."

"Oh, that's easy for you to say!" she snapped. "You've done this before!"

"Hey, maybe I should slip him the secret handshake."

"What?"

"He and I are fraternity brothers. He was a Deke at the University of Michigan."

"So?"

"So there's a secret handshake all Dekes are supposed to know. Let me see if I can remember how they taught us to do it."

And I turned my hand over and wiggled my middle finger in midair.

"Clifton, don't you *dare!*" Marti hissed. "He'll think you're crazy. We'll both be arrested!"

"They won't arrest us. I think you're supposed to slide your fingers across the other guy's palm like this," I said, experimenting on my own left hand. "No, that's not it."

"Oh, my God," Marti moaned.

But there was no time for her to plead with me further. Suddenly Mr. Farrell had sneaked up on us again, and we were following him, walking behind the president and the Chinese women, who blotted out the sun. He took us to the door of the Oval Office and stood with us while the ceremony wrapped up. He and I chatted amiably. Marti went silent.

Within a minute or two, President Ford finished the ceremony and walked toward us. Mr. Farrell stepped forward. "Mr. President, this is Clifton Truman Daniel, Mr. Truman's grandson, and his friend Marti Carioty."

We shook hands all around. I don't remember exactly what was said, but I'm sure we traded the usual chitchat.

"It's nice to meet you, Mr. President."

"It's nice to have you at the White House, Clifton. How are your parents?"

"They're fine, thank you. Heard from Mr. Nixon lately?"

Blah, blah, blah.

The president was so gracious, warm, and approachable that I liked him immediately. I liked him so much, in fact, that the following November, on the occasion of voting in my first presidential election, I flew in the face of family tradition and voted for him, a Republican.

Not that it did him any good.

While our meeting was going on, the White House photographer was snapping away. My parents have a copy of the print he sent them. President Ford and I are in the foreground, shaking hands.

As our brief encounter with the president concluded, I brought up the one thing he and I had in common. "Mr. President, you and I are fraternity brothers."

"Oh, really?"

I could feel Marti tense up.

"Yes sir, I just pledged Delta Kappa Epsilon at the University of North Carolina."

And Marti was standing there, thinking: Oh, God. He's going to do it. He's going to slip the president of the United States that stupid handshake, and the Secret Service is going to tackle us and we're going to jail.

Much to her relief, the president did not scream out for the Secret Service.

"Well, that's great" was all he said. "It's a good house." And with a final good-bye, he disappeared into the Oval Office.

Marti thought we were free and clear. But as we were on our way out, Mr. Farrell had one more surprise for us.

"Mrs. Ford would like to say hello on your way out," he said.

"Oh, good!" I said. "I wonder if Mrs. Ford knows the secret handshake."

"Oh, my God," Marti muttered.

9

Into the Abyss

"You're out of school when?"

"Just about now, Dad," I said into the phone. "Exams end in two days. I'm out of here May fourth."

It was the end of my freshman year at Chapel Hill, and I was standing in the corridor of the Deke house talking to my father on the wall phone outside the upstairs bathroom. It had been a revelation to me that summer vacation began more than a month earlier in college than it did in high school.

"What are you planning to do?" Dad asked.

"I don't know. Maybe go see some friends, hang around. Richard Barbour mentioned visiting him in Milton."

"I see."

Dad certainly did see. He saw that I was planning to spend yet another summer without a job. I had not had a summer job since being sexton for the church at Point o' Woods two years earlier. I was seventeen that summer and spent the whole two months dusting the pews, running a vacuum cleaner over the burgundy carpet, sanding and repainting the church's white trim, and hauling wagons full of fairly rank seaweed from the bay beaches to mulch the flower beds. I also got to ring the bell on Sunday mornings.

"What are you going to do in Milton?" Dad asked.

"Richard's parents are selling the house, so they need to have it painted. They're going to pay me and Richard to do it, plus feed us."

"Good. When do you start?"

"Early June."

"What are you going to do until then?"

"Like I said, go visiting, maybe stay with Meacham or Tony in New York."

"I see," Dad said. The thought of having his oldest, least self-disciplined son loose for more than a month with nothing but time on his hands was troublesome.

The summer I had worked as sexton, I spent the time between the end of school and the beginning of summer as an intern in Senator Hubert Humphrey's Washington office. The job wasn't glamorous (it didn't even come with a paycheck), but it was one of the nicest experiences I've ever had. I did a lot of filing, but I also got to eat lunch, at least once, with the boss in the Senate Dining Room, ride the underground train between the Senate Office Building and the Capitol, and help answer mail and write legislation.

The legislation was simply a proposal by Senator Humphrey for some new statues for the corridors of the Senate. I think I started off with something like "When in the course of human events, it becomes necessary to put up a bust . . ."

The mail was routine correspondence. If you got a letter from Senator Humphrey in the last two weeks of June 1974, it might have been written by me. I hope I didn't promise you anything outrageous.

Both assignments were small potatoes to Senator Humphrey and his staff, I suppose, but they left me feeling ten feet tall. As far as I could tell, they seemed to think I was smart enough and sensible enough to answer a senator's letters, erudite enough to compose legislation, however minor.

That was a new feeling.

But I wasn't thinking of Senator Humphrey or self-esteem during that conversation with my father on the Deke house phone two years later. I just wanted to get out and party, and my father knew it.

"Let me make a suggestion, since you're going to have some time on your hands before we go out to Point o' Woods," he said. "Your mother is going to Missouri to celebrate what would have been your grandfather's ninetieth birthday this May eighth. On that date, she is also going to preside over the presentation of the Truman Scholarships at the Truman Library.

"She is also going to help dedicate a statue of your grandfather in front of the Jackson County Courthouse in Independence. Your old fraternity brother, President Gerald Ford, will be there.

"Let me suggest that you go with your mother. It would be nice for her to have some company. I can't go because of one thing and another at the office, but you can. It would also give you a chance to see your grandmother."

Since I really didn't have any plans, I agreed. Not that I was such a considerate son or grandson, but I knew a trip to Independence involved hobnobbing with the president and other forms of deferential treatment, which my ego seemed to need more and more.

"When you come back from Independence," my father continued, "maybe you'll consider going to Greece with both your mother and me."

My father, it turned out, had been engaged by General Foods to brief their American executives living in Europe on the upcoming election between President Ford and Jimmy Carter and what the outcome might do to business. The deal included all expenses, plus a fee. Dad was proposing to have General Foods waive the fee and take me along.

"Gee, Dad," I said. "Twist my arm."

So the first month of my summer vacation was taken care of. I had yet to figure out what to do with the rest of of it, not to mention the whole next year. That day on the phone, I didn't bother telling my father I had flunked out of college.

I remember only one thing about the ceremony at the Jackson County Courthouse—that I had a spiffy new pale green seersucker suit I had bought in Chapel Hill from Maurice Julian, father of soon-to-be famed designer Alexander Julian. I also got to shake hands with Mr. Ford again, but again, I did not try to slip him the secret Deke handshake.

At the ceremony for the Truman Scholars, I was introduced by John Snyder, Grandpa's former secretary of the Treasury, as "the daughter of the son of Harry S. Truman." And by that point my hair wasn't even long anymore. It must have been that suit.

Later, making chitchat with the scholars, I found myself feeling both superior because of my lineage and inferior because I had just butchered my freshman year. Mentally I took the low road, thinking of the scholars as geeks and pencil pushers. It wasn't until years later that I realized I had been the only geek in the room.

I did not spend much time with my grandmother during the trip. We were out a lot at ceremonies and whatnot, and she was not inclined to go with us. In those days she spent much of her time reading in the living room. Her yellow chair near the front door was practically walled in by teetering piles of paperbacks.

At night I slept in the bedroom across the hall from Gammy's. Mom slept in what used to be Grandmother Wallace's old room, the biggest one upstairs. All three of us were guarded throughout the night by a man who sat downstairs with a shotgun.

You have never slept well until you have stayed in a home protected by the Secret Service. The headquarters of the detail protecting my grandmother was across the street, in a small house on the corner. It had been a good vantage point for years, with two cameras covering the house and grounds and several panic buttons at various places inside my grandmother's home.

But after my grandfather died and my grandmother became more frail, the Secret Service no longer felt watching the house was enough. So they sent an agent in every night to sit downstairs. His job was as much to listen for my grandmother as to keep intruders at bay. He came in every night at about ten o'clock and sat in the music room or living room until dawn.

When I first met him, I was watching television in the music room. This was my only entertainment that week in Independence. After Mom and Gammy had gone to bed, I sat there for several hours each night drinking beer and smoking. When the Secret Service agent walked in, the whole house took on the aura of a gangster movie.

"Do you mind if I watch TV with you?" he asked after introducing himself.

"No, not at all," I said. "Pull up a chair."

He was built like a bear and carried a small leather case, which he set on the floor next to the chair he carried from Grandpa's study. Unzipping the case, he removed a shotgun, its barrels and stock sawed off, and placed it gingerly on top of the case.

"Would you like a beer?" I asked, thinking he probably couldn't drink on duty.

"Sure," he said.

As I went to the kitchen, I wondered about the wisdom of giving a beer to a man with a sawed-off shotgun.

"Thanks. What's on?" he asked.

"Carson's about the only thing I can get on these old sets. Is that all right with you?"

"Fine. That's pretty much what I watch every night."

My grandmother had two television sets—one upstairs, in Grandmother Wallace's bedroom, and the one we were watching in the music room. My grandmother and grandfather never had much use for television, so both of the sets were decrepit. The rabbit ears on top of each pulled in two channels—one for each ear and both of them fuzzy.

"You're in here all night?" I asked.

"Yep."

And we sat and drank beer and watched Carson. The agent had exactly two beers, no more. And I went up to bed and slept like a baby.

I wound up doing the Secret Service's job for them just once during that visit, one night when my grandmother fell in her bedroom. She was ninety-two and still sleeping in the upstairs bedroom she shared with my grandfather for fifty-three years. It would be a couple of more years before age and negotiating the staircase forced her to sleep in the ground-floor bedroom off the living room.

The night she fell, I had just gotten upstairs from watching

Carson with my shotgun-toting friend. It must have been about midnight, which is when the *Tonight* show ends in the Midwest. I was settled into bed with a magazine when I thought I heard someone calling my name. The voice was so faint I thought I had imagined it. But I had not had that much to drink, so when I heard it again, I got up and went to the door of my room. Across the hall my mother was doing exactly the same thing.

"Did you hear something?" she asked.

"Someone called me," I said. "I thought it was you."

"Wasn't me," she said, shaking her head.

Just then we heard it again, only this time the call was for my mother.

"Margaret."

The voice was neither fearful nor did it seem the owner was in pain, but the instant Mom and I realized it was coming from Gammy's room, we both fell all over ourselves to get to the door. But as we rounded her threshold, all we saw was the chair and dresser and the twin beds, one of them turned neatly down for the night. Gammy was nowhere in sight.

"Mother?" Mom said.

"I'm over here, behind the bed."

We scooted across the room and found my grandmother lying on the floor between her bed and the wall, holding on to the bedspread with one hand.

"I slipped coming back from the bathroom," she said. She may have been slightly embarrassed, but more than anything, she seemed to be angry at the indignity.

"Are you all right?" Mom asked.

"Yes, I'm fine. I just can't get up."

"Clifton . . ." Mom said.

I was already putting one arm behind Gammy's shoulders and the other under her knees. I wasn't sure I could lift her, so I tensed every muscle I owned, especially the ones in my back and legs. But Gammy was a lot lighter than I had thought. It was like bracing to lift a case full of milk cartons and finding someone's come along and drunk most of it. I nearly flung her across the room.

"Put her on the bed," Mom said, unfurling the covers a little farther.

I laid Gammy on the bed and took a step or two back. Mom pulled the covers up.

"Mother, are you sure you're all right?" she asked. "Nothing's broken?"

"No."

"Do you want me to call the doctor?"

"No, no, no. I'm fine. I just slipped."

I said good night and walked back across the hall to my bedroom and my magazine. Mom told me the next day that Gammy had been very impressed by my muscles.

"He's so strong," she told Mom. "He just lifted me up like I was nothing."

Hearing that felt good. I don't know that the one incident was enough to inspire me to become the physical fitness nut I am today, but I did make a mental note then to keep up with my push-ups. I thought it best not to tell my grandmother she had nearly been airborne.

I went from Independence straight to Athens, Greece. Mom and Dad did what they usually did and flew in separate planes. This was in case one of the planes crashed. They wanted to be sure there would be at least one parent left to nag the children. Very admirable, but that's why I have to laugh whenever my mother looks at me with a straight face and tells me flying is safe.

Dad flew by himself, leaving Mom and me, the two cowards, on our own. We compensated by sitting in first-class and eating filet mignon for lunch. After that, Mom did what she always does on long flights. She fell fast asleep. I headed to the bar and drank steadily for the entire seven-hour flight, though I did take a break to watch the in-flight movie, *Give 'Em Hell, Harry.*

Mom had seen this filmed performance of Sam Gallu's stage play umpteen times, but I was fascinated. There were times when actor James Whitmore turned a certain way that I swore I was looking at Grandpa. These days Kevin McCarthy plays the role. You may remember him as the man running from the pod people in the original 1950s version of *Invasion of the Body Snatchers.* I had dinner with Mr. McCarthy in Wilmington in October 1994. He's a wonderful man and full of great stories. Though we talked a lot about the play, I've yet to see him do it. Mom likes his version of Grandpa. She says it's truer than Mr. Whitmore's, which was more fiery and combative than she thought Grandpa really was.

After the movie, I made friends with the first-class stewardess, Bunny, since she had the key to the liquor cabinet. She was in her forties, had a son my age, and was very nice to me. Maybe she shouldn't have been so nice, because I drank pretty much her entire stock of alcohol. I started with the beer, then worked my way through the wine and ended up drinking the green crème de menthe.

When we landed in Athens, I was a basket case—very loud, very talkative, very soppy. Everything was funny, and everybody was my best friend. It was all my mother could do to keep me from hugging the Greek customs agents and loudly declaring my underwear as being duty-free.

My father was also a basket case when he arrived, but not from drinking. He had come down with a dandy head cold and went nearly straightaway to his hotel room to recuperate before giving his speech a few days later. This, I thought, would free me to act like an animal, but I didn't count on the General Foods executives of Europe.

Far from being the party animals I was hoping for, those executives and their wives were in their forties and fifties, and most of them had children my age, so I wound up with about ten sets of surrogate parents. It didn't matter that my parents missed most of the sightseeing trips around the beaches and ruins and the day trips to the islands. I had plenty of supervision.

"Don't smoke so much."

"You've had enough beer, young man."

"No, you will not go out after hours with the tour bus driver."

My father, who lost his voice and had to conduct his seminar in a whisper, recovered in time to take over for the last three days, which the three of us spent in Athens. As the guests of General Foods, we had been staying at a beach resort outside the city. This last three days was our time, paid for by my parents. While we were there, we had dinner with broadcast journalist Cokie Roberts, whose husband, Steve, was then *The New York Times* bureau chief in Beirut. Mr. Roberts kept Mrs. Roberts and their children in Athens because it was a hell of a lot safer than Beirut.

In Athens, we also had lunch with the American ambassador to Greece, which wound up reminding me of that story about the Kennedys' overcooked grouse. The ambassador's chef didn't overcook the game birds he served us in Athens that day, but he had a startling way of presenting them. They came out, nestled against the slopes of a huge rice pilaf, with their little cooked heads tacked back on with toothpicks. *Bon appétit!*

We came home to Washington and a revelation more startling than the pilaf-*avec*-bird-head presentation. We had left the country without telling Will. He called from Phillips Academy in Andover, Massachusetts, not long after we left, looking for some cash so he could take a trip with some friends when school ended.

"Hi, Eulalee, is Mom or Dad there?" he asked when the housekeeper answered.

"No, Will. They've gone to Greece."

There was a long silence at the other end of the line.

"They've gone to Greece?"

"That's right."

"What, you mean like Greece, New York? Greece, Indiana? Greece where?"

"No, Greece, Greece. They went to Athens, Greece. Clifton, too."

There was another long pause.

"Clifton went, too? They just all left the country and went to Greece?"

"That's right."

Another long pause.

"Okay, fine. Thanks."

When we got home, Eulalee told us he called twice more to make sure what he'd heard was right.

My parents still do this, by the way. Sometimes when I call for a handout or just to check up on them, I, too, get the housekeeper.

"Hi, Grace. Mom and Dad home?"

"No, they're on the Kirghiz steppe."

"Really. Doing what?"

"Your father is speaking to nomadic yak herders on the breakup of the Soviet Union and how that's likely to affect the yak business."

"Fine. Please tell them I called."

Dad isn't the only one in the family who can pull down a paid vacation. I called once and found they had weighed anchor for Australia, with both giving shipboard lectures to pay their passage. Mom is a switch hitter in this regard. She can either talk about the Truman presidency and her life in the White House, or she can discuss any number of ways to bump off philandering senators, embezzling congressmen, or morally bankrupt generals.

I came back from Athens wearing a string of blue worry beads as a necklace and spent the rest of that summer living with Richard Barbour and his family in Milton, Massachusetts. By day we painted Richard's parents' house. By night—actually, by weekend—I played drums for a rock band, and Richard helped haul around amplifiers.

When my parents went out to Fire Island, I started dividing my time between Massachusetts and New York, making the five-hour train ride to Boston from New York every weekend to rehearse and play a party or club. It was while waiting in Penn Station for my train one afternoon that I got my only close-up look at presidential candidate Jimmy Carter.

He was in the middle of the second of two groups of reporters that burst from a track entrance at one end of the concourse. The first group was moving like gangbusters, yammering about where to set up cameras and whether or not they had time to make phone calls. The second surrounded Mr. Carter like drone bees buzzing around a queen, their microphones thrust in his face. All heads in the station turned to watch the group buzz past.

My grandfather's press coverage was less frenetic. *New York*

Times photographer George Tames ran out of film at the start of a press conference in the Oval Office one day. He dropped to one knee behind the throng of reporters and started reloading. He didn't realize it, but he looked like he was in a complete panic. He was making all sorts of noise, knocking film canisters around and rattling his equipment. Suddenly he noticed the room had gone completely silent. When he looked up, he found the pool of reporters in front of him had parted and my grandfather was squatting down in front of him.

"What the hell are you doing, George?" Grandpa asked. "Take it easy. We'll wait."

Grandpa would always wait for a photographer to get set up. Not only that, he was accommodating enough to stand still. When visiting heads of state came calling at the White House, he often gave them directions on how to pose for the photographers.

"I'm the president of the United States, commander in chief of the most powerful nation on earth," Mr. Tames occasionally overheard him telling visitors. "I don't take orders from anyone in the world—except the photographers."

Some of the visitors didn't seem to know whether Grandpa was kidding.

I finished out that summer with the band, then had to figure out what I was going to do for the year before summer school started and I had a chance to raise my academic average. I was nineteen, and I had declared to my parents that I wanted to take the year off to find myself. I don't know if I ever told them I flunked out.

Dad didn't think I could find myself with both hands and a mirror. And he wasn't going to let me sit at home for nine months strumming a guitar and writing poetry. So he got me an interview for a desk assistant's job at CBS News, home office of our family friend Walter Cronkite. My interview was with news director Larry Doyle.

"The job stinks. You'll be underpaid. People will yell at you," he said, or something like that.

"Sounds perfect. I'll take it," I said. "My father will kill me if I don't."

"Sound reasoning. Welcome aboard."

Except for the fact that Marti and I went through a protracted breakup, that was a great year. CBS was hardly the evil place that Larry Doyle portrayed it to be. True, I worked midnight to eight in the morning on weekends, but otherwise, the job was a lot of fun. My coworkers were good people.

Aside from the other desk assistants, the one I knew best, perhaps, was Dave Jackson, one of the journalists who gave the hourly radio reports. Dave and I got into a short-lived habit of going to a pub across the street for a couple of beers after we finished our all-night shift. We would sit there and swap stories and sometimes get pie-eyed. I once came home so drunk that I swore at my mother when she woke me up a little later to let a workman fix something in my bathroom. I didn't even remember talking to her.

Still, I thought my drinking was under control. I never missed a day of work because of a hangover.

I had a salary, plus income from trust funds created by both my Daniel and Truman grandparents. I lived at home, paid no rent, and was well fed. On any of my nights off, I could afford to take a date to an expensive restaurant and a Broadway show. During Thanksgiving and Christmas holidays, I rented a white tie and tails and escorted a friend, Courtney Pyles, to several debutante balls at the Plaza Hotel. I began to develop a taste for nightlife and for living beyond my means and my station in life.

That June, I went to the first summer session at Chapel Hill and qualified for readmission, doing just well enough to squeak my grade-point average up above 1.5. Proud of my accomplishment, I promptly took off the end of July and most of August to loaf on Fire Island.

That half a summer was one of the last carefree times I enjoyed before things got crazy. I had gotten back into school, and despite my scholastic track record, I was hopeful, once again, that I would do better my sophomore year.

But my second year at Chapel Hill was even worse than my first. Not only did I skip classes, but I didn't even make it to two of my end-of-year exams, preferring to get stoned and go to a movie instead. By summer I was living a lie, having told my parents I had done well and intended to return to college that fall. I stayed in Chapel Hill, working as a waiter and living in a log hunting lodge outside town with three fraternity brothers.

When school started, I had no classes to go to, no job, and no prospects. The highlight of the fall was a drunken road trip—I should say airplane flight—to Arizona to see Marti for a stab at reconciliation. The trip turned out so well that she came to see me two weeks later. But we weren't alone, as we had been in Arizona. When she saw me around my drinking buddies, she was so dismayed at what I had become—loud and abrasive—that she hardly spoke to me the rest of her stay. I don't think we've spoken since.

I lasted just two months at Chapel Hill that fall before throwing in the towel for good. A week before I left, I was standing on the Deke house porch with a fraternity brother, David Zuck. I don't know about him, but I was dead drunk. And I was moaning about how much I hated college and rationalizing a mile a minute about why I was such a failure at it.

After listening politely for several minutes, David said simply. "Hey, college isn't for everybody."

That was all I needed to hear. This was validation. David, who had a grade-point average close to his own shoe size, had meant there were other ways to get an education. But in my haze and delusion, I took him to mean that maybe I didn't need an education. So I left Chapel Hill for good and headed to New York. I had no background in theater, save a bit part in *A Midsummer Night's Dream* in grade school, so it seemed to me the wisest and truest course I could pursue would be to become an actor.

10

Acting the Part

I did not choose to take a stab at an acting career because I loved the craft. I chose acting because I wanted to be recognized and fussed over whenever I walked into a room. I was tired of people standing in front of me at parties and saying, "Gee, your grandfather was such a great guy. You must be so proud." More than that, I was tired of feeling like a second-class citizen in my own house. I had spent about twenty years being told that I was not the important one—Grandpa was.

I wanted to be recognized for myself, in a completely selfish sort of way. For those who knew me, this was not news.

"You'll get a bit part in some soap opera. You'll play a pizza delivery boy or something," Paul Lowerre said when I told him I was going to study acting. "The day it airs, you'll go out and stand under a street lamp half the night to see if anyone recognizes you."

He was only half right. I would certainly not have stood out there half the night. I would have stood out there all night, if that's what it took.

Aside from the fame, acting also seemed to be a way I could make a lot of money. Money had always been very important to me. I wasn't interested in it so much for security or status, but because it had the power to buy friends. Whether they meant to or not, my parents had taught me to equate money with affection—or, rather, to substitute money for affection. It always seemed easier for my parents to buy us a present than hug us or tell us they loved us. I have been the same way with my own children. At the time I was thinking of becoming an actor, money, I thought, could buy me love.

After I left the University of North Carolina in the winter of 1978, I went back to New York and moved in with Paul, whose life seemed to be in an orbit similar to my own. He had flunked out of Franklin College in Lugano, Switzerland, and was on the run from a very bad living situation at the University of Vermont. To wit: He lived in an apartment over his favorite bar.

In New York, we chose a fourth-floor walkup on East 81st Street and filled it with cast-off furniture from college and home, including a tiny black-and-white TV that got two or three grainy channels and reminded me of my grandparents' television sets in Independence. We were by no means the only living things in the apartment, which is why we threw a sign up on the door: WILD BACHELOR PAD AND COCKROACH FARM.

While watching TV, Paul and I often passed the time by snacking on melba toast with sweet butter. We hit on this little delicacy because (a) it seemed to help our hangovers and (b) neither of us could cook anything more nutritious. In fact, we ignored our kitchen so thoroughly that there were fuzzy little organisms growing in the out-of-date containers of sour cream and pimiento spread.

Not surprisingly, both of us got fat, myself especially. Watching television one afternoon, I dropped a few melba toast crumbs onto the lap of my boxer shorts. That's a nice picture, isn't it? Two supposedly educated young men from good families sitting around in their boxers, eating melba toast with sweet butter and staring at a nearly useless television set. Anyway, when I looked down, I noticed a series of red streaks running down the insides of both thighs.

"Oh, my God," I stammered over a mouthful of melba toast. "I've got some kind of horrible rash. Look at this!"

Paul glanced over casually and said, "That's no rash, you moron. Those are stretch marks."

They sure were. And the ghosts of them are with me to this day, despite a thrice-weekly six-mile run and a weightlifting program. The good news is, you can barely see them—and then only when you look close, which you will never do because, frankly, I don't know you that well.

When Paul and I were not eating melba toast, we were supposedly making great inroads into academia. At least that is the huge lie we were telling our families and ourselves. I had enrolled in acting classes at HB Studio, a well-known drama school in Greenwich Village. Paul took classes in international banking at New York University.

What we did best, however, was sit in the bars along Third Avenue and drink until we ran out of either money or time. Occasionally we put on suits and strayed into a disco, where we sat in dark corners and drank fifteen-dollar rum punches or ten-dollar beers. No matter where we went, we hardly ever came home before dawn.

Paul and I lived in cycles. We would wake up from an all-night binge, feeling sick and sick of ourselves, for a day or two. The next day, we would feel driven and go back to classes. Ambition and hope would be renewed. Two days later, we would begin to feel so good about ourselves that a drink was in order—and the whole cycle would start over. It was like falling into a hole, getting hurt, climbing out, then, forgetting that the hole was there, turning around and falling right back in again.

When the city bored us, we took to the road. We hopped in Paul's canvas-topped Jeep and drove six hours to get plastered with Paul's friends at the University of Vermont in Burlington. Occasionally we stayed with his parents, who lived in Manchester. We ate psychedelic mushrooms at Skidmore College in upstate New York (apparently I lied about only tripping once, as a teenager) and once woke up on the floor of a waitresses' dormitory on Fire Island. We took an overnight train to the University of Virginia just so we could get drunk for three days with friends. On the way, I caught the flu and holed up in a hotel room, watching cartoons.

We would go anywhere. Anybody who would have us was a port in our storm. All we needed was gas, a little cash, three or four six-packs, and a couple of packs of cigarettes.

It truly is a wonder we survived. I once drove to the University of Vermont with a friend to meet Paul, who had gone up earlier. We took along a case of beer, keeping it cool in the trunk. It was the dead of winter. There was snow and ice on the roads. When we had drunk about a six-pack each, I convinced her to let me drive—at night, in the snow and ice. I had not had a valid driver's license for a year. I drove so fast that the car often left the road when I crested a small hill. The two of us thought it was hilarious.

When we weren't actively trying to kill ourselves, it seemed Paul and I were intentionally letting our lives go down the drain. Drunk, we gabbed about our great hopes for the future and came up with a half a dozen harebrained schemes to get rich, including a ludicrous Pet Rock–style gimmick that seemed really exciting—to drunks. At one point, I spent months considering the romantic notion of becoming a salvage diver in Fiji—I even made plane reservations one night when I was plastered. Never mind that I had never been within arm's length of a scuba tank.

It wasn't as if I didn't have chances to make something of myself as an actor. Early on, I met Andy Warhol at a party, and he put my picture in his magazine, *Interview*—"Harry Truman's grandson, the up-and-coming young actor." Warhol's minions even dressed me head to toe in Armani fashions for the photo. My parents also arranged for me to meet comedian-producer Alan King and theatrical producer Joseph Papp, both of whom made time to talk to me and might have helped me had I been willing to start at the bottom and do some work. In fact, Mr. Papp was all set to give me a job as a stagehand. I, however, wanted a crack at playing Hamlet right off the bat. I needed instant stardom.

In theater, you take a lot of minor roles before you ever get to play the lead. These small roles are often jokingly referred to as "spear carriers," because directors casting classical works, like some Shakespeare and certain operas, often needed lots of extra soldiers (spear carriers) to pad out the cast. These small roles are an honest way to learn the craft, but I couldn't wait. I guess it's because with a high-profile grandfather and high-profile parents, I had often felt like a spear carrier in my own family.

If I wanted instant stardom, I was not going about it the right way. While I was in New York, I was a client of three different theatrical agents, all of them good, who sent me on a variety of auditions. But I couldn't stay sober enough to make anything good come of the auditions or attend the acting classes they enrolled me in.

One audition I remember was for the Army, back in the days when they were running those commercials where the fresh-faced kid leaves a job interview dejected and says: "No experience, no job. But I can do that job!" Then they show him jumping out of airplanes and throwing himself over barbed wire, getting oodles of job experience. That might have been me—if I had shown up for the audition with my hair combed and without two-inch bags under my eyes. I was not fresh-faced, and I did not look like I wanted a job very badly.

After a disastrous audition for another agent—during which it became apparent that I hadn't learned my lines or given an ounce of thought to character development—the agent angrily sat me down and said, "Look, you've just wasted my time and yours. I think you need to give some serious thought to what you want to do with your life."

I felt bad for about two days. Then I got together with some friends, got drunk, and forgot all about the agent and his advice.

I set myself up for each failure, because each failure fed my self-image. Each time I didn't get a part in a commercial or a show, it confirmed my belief that I was worthless. With each defeat, it became easier not to try. Of course, that's not what I was thinking at the time. At the time, I thought all the people who didn't hire me were idiots. To spare my ego, I cultivated an image of myself as a happy-go-lucky ne'er-do-well. I told myself I just hadn't found my niche. I would drink and go to parties and hope that someday my ship would come in.

My parents had no idea how to help me. They would not—or could not—sit me down and tell me I had a problem. I think they were afraid they would drive me even further away. When I was a teenager, I had gotten into the habit of telling them to butt out of my business whenever they made suggestions. Actually, most of the time I just listened politely to their advice, then ignored it. So they weren't hopeful that I would suddenly start hanging on their every word,

When I was floundering in New York, my father tried to help as best he knew how by putting me in touch with all those people who might help me, including Mr. Papp and Mr. King. But he couldn't help change our relationship so that I might listen to him. My mother, at least publicly, preferred to pretend there was nothing wrong with me. To friends, she even denied that I had a problem. In private, she lay awake at night wondering if she would see me alive again the next day.

By that point, I had pretty much shut my parents out of my life. I treated them as if they were my landlords, a nice older couple I knew and sometimes went to dinner with. I did not confide in them. I don't remember that we fought. For more than four years, we just trod carefully around each other, being polite.

Paul and I lived together until early in the summer of 1979, when we accepted an invitation to a party at the massive Long Island estate of one of Paul's chums from the University of Vermont. The invitation fit in well with our plans, since we were on our way to visit friends in Montauk, at the tip of Long Island. Staying overnight at a huge estate seemed a very nice way to get to Montauk.

I don't recall a thing about the party, including where we slept that night. All I remember is that someone we met had a movie theater in his basement and that we went joy riding in the host's jet-black Trans Am. The Trans Am part is significant because it points up the important element in this particular story line: They had plenty of gasoline.

This was 1979, and there was an oil shortage. All that summer, there had often been no gas at the pumps. There certainly wasn't any to be had the morning after that party. When Paul and I staggered out to his Jeep, we found the gauge was on empty. We would have been stranded save for the estate's private supply. The lawn was so huge that the family was allowed to have its own agricultural gas pump to fuel its fleet of mowers.

So, gassed up, we headed for Montauk and the apartment of a

friend of mine from Fire Island, Christie Field, who was working in Montauk for the summer. We had nothing planned except to drink and visit and possibly lie on the beach. We were also planning to sleep on Christie's floor and would have except for Dede Gentile. We met Dede at Christie's the first night we were there, and she took pity on us and invited us to stay at her father's summer house outside town. Her father was conveniently away.

Paul actually knew Dede by proxy. Her older sister, Ursula, had been his schoolmate at Franklin College in Lugano, Switzerland. She had not thought much of him at first, chiefly because he drove everywhere at ninety miles an hour in a Fiat Spider with a bottle of Chivas Regal in his hand. This had earned him the scornful nickname Chivas.

Ursula still remembers the day she first saw the name "Paul Lowerre." It was stenciled on the trunk that came roped to hers off the ship from America a couple of weeks into the first semester.

"Maybe he's a nice guy and he'll help carry my trunk to the apartment for me," Ursula told her friend Elizabeth Peabody.

"You don't know who that is, do you?" Elizabeth asked.

"No. Who is it?"

"That's Chivas."

Appalled, Ursula unbound her trunk from Paul's and hauled it away before he could appear and somehow get a toehold in her life.

Her opinion of him changed dramatically some months later when she was forced to talk to him in Venice. She and Elizabeth were having a drink at an outdoor café when Paul strolled by. He had gotten bored and wandered off from an art history class tour. When he spotted Ursula and Elizabeth and asked to join them, Ursula was sure she was in for a horrible conversation with a drunken maniac. But Paul turned out to be well spoken, funny, and cultured—in short, not nearly the maniac she had thought.

At the moment Dede was leading us to her father's house in Montauk, Ursula was at home in Bronxville, New York, preparing to come out the next day. She hoped to spend a quiet couple of days with her friend Ellen Griffiths soaking up sun and reading good books.

Paul has said that he owed his life and his happiness to the Ayatollah Khomeini, because without that gas shortage, he and I would have been long gone the next day when Ursula and Ellen arrived. As it was, they showed up to find the porch of the house draped with our bodies, the both of us in physical agony. The house itself was trashed.

Paul might have done what I did, which was sit there with a dumb look on my face and mutter, "Oops, sorry. Nice to meet you." But he had been smitten. Despite the hangover, he found the energy to help Ursula clean up the house, thereby causing her to cast a favorable eye upon him. So favorable was her attitude, in fact, that she accepted his invitation to dinner in town that night on the condition that Ellen go along. I, the porch slug, was left out of the equation.

I remember being hurt and jealous. I did not want my party pal to fall in love and go off and live a normal life, which is exactly what happened.

The old Paul Lowerre dropped off the face of the earth after that. Ursula had fallen in love, but she wasn't going to spend the rest of her life with a man whose only skills were Jeep driving and beer drinking. So Paul became a man with a mission. Commuting to the University of Vermont every week, he cleared up the academic hash he had created out of his record there, then finished his degree at Marymount Manhattan College in New York. Not long after, he was hired as development director for the Seamen's Church Institute near the Battery at the tip of Manhattan. When he came to my parents' apartment one day to introduce them to Ursula, my mother took in the story of his miraculous transformation with thinly disguised envy.

"Ursula," she asked sweetly, "are there any more at home like you for Clifton?"

Yes, there was, but Dede knew me all too well by that point.

Paul and Ursula's wedding on June 27, 1981, was magnificent. In keeping with the occasion, I went through it with the grandest hangover I've ever had in my life. I was the best man. Since the initial snub when Paul went to dinner with Ursula in Montauk, he and she had been taking great pains to include me in their life. I went to Montauk with them on weekends; they invited me to parties. While Paul was commuting back and forth to Vermont, Ursula often gave me the job of escort, and we became good friends. There was a time we could talk on the phone, about absolutely nothing, for more than an hour.

The night before their wedding, I left the rehearsal dinner and headed for the bars with several of the groomsmen, including a couple of our wilder friends from Vermont. We were out all night chiefly because, by this point, I had discovered the fortification of cocaine. I could now drink more, stay awake longer, and act like more of a jerk than ever before.

Having done so until five o'clock the morning of the wedding, I was in no mood to be awakened at nine, which was exactly when Paul woke me up.

"Hey, get up! All of you!" he snapped as he barged into my bedroom.

Three or four of us were draped haphazardly over the beds and cots, knuckles on the floor, faces pressed against the night tables. Our clothes, all of them reeking of beer and smoke, adorned the furniture.

"Kill him," someone suggested politely.

"What the hell are you waking us up for?" I whined, my head splitting. "We haven't been asleep for more than about four hours."

"I need Lou's stroller."

He was in a panic. Lou was his soon-to-be father-in-law, Louis A. Gentile, a Bronxville, New York, surgeon, the man whose house we had trashed in Montauk.

"What does he need it now for?" I moaned. "You're not getting married until four."

"He's not going to get married at all if he doesn't shut up and get out of here," someone grumbled from under a pile of sheets.

"He wants it now. He wants to make sure it fits."

The damage had been done. All of us in that room felt so horrible that once awake, we couldn't go back to sleep. Seth Mann, one of Paul's oldest buddies from Vermont, was so shaky he nearly cut his throat shaving. The blood spilled over the collar of his white shirt, making a stain that would be visible at the back of a huge cathedral, let alone the back of the Fifth Avenue Church, where Paul was getting married.

"Okay, who'll head down to Brooks Brothers and get me a plain white dress shirt," he croaked, waving a fifty-dollar bill around. "Take you half an hour and you can keep the change."

I almost took him up on it. In those days, a Brooks Brothers dress shirt was about thirty bucks, so I stood to make twenty for a half hour's work. Dad, however, saved me the trip by making Seth's stain disappear with a liberal coating of Wite-Out.

At three thirty that afternoon, Paul and I were at the church, St. Thomas, cooling our heels in the rector's study. I have never seen Paul happier or more nervous. He was so nervous he could barely talk to me, which was fine, since I could barely talk myself. He spent most of the time staring blankly at some wooden tablets on the wall.

"What are you reading?" I asked.

"These tablets," he said.

"They're in Latin," I said, looking.

"Yep."

"So what do they say."

He turned and gave me a bewildered stare. "I haven't the foggiest."

At the start of the ceremony, we both found that we had paid absolutely no attention during the rehearsal the previous afternoon. We took what we thought were our proper places at the foot of the altar steps and waited for the procession to begin. I looked down the aisle to see Ursula and her father headed right toward me, not Paul. I was in the hot seat, standing smack in the aisle next to the enormously imposing Dickensian vicar who was performing the ceremony. Paul was beside me in the best-man slot, smiling goofily. Quickly I grabbed him by the shoudlers and switched places—to a lot of twittering from the front rows.

The altar was almost my Waterloo. The hangover had become

so bad that I could have easily fainted or gotten sick. I was afraid of doing either, or both, so I kept an eye on the door leading to the vestry as a means of quick escape.

I made it through the ceremony, but when the priest asked for the rings, my hand was shaking so badly I had serious doubts I could get them from my vest pocket to the prayer book without dropping them. He and Paul and Ursula had their own doubts, because when I looked up at them, all three were staring at me with great apprehension. Before I dropped the rings onto the Bible, they were rattling around in my hand like the clappers of a bell.

The reception at Dr. Gentile's house in Bronxville was a painful blur. By then my hangover was so bad that I couldn't even drink it away, though I tried two or three times. That night I wound up going home early for the first time in years. I was in such bad shape, in fact, that I let a skinny caterer in a powder-blue leisure suit and white patent-leather shoes push me around at the reception.

He was shooing groomsmen and other guests away from the bride's table, and everybody listened to him except for Seth, who figured that as a member of the wedding party, he could pretty much sit where he wanted. Seth is also about six-two and built like a linebacker.

"No, no, no, no, no," the caterer scolded when Seth eased into a chair. "That's the bride's table. You can't sit there."

"I'll sit where I want," Seth said.

"No, you won't," the caterer said, and made the mistake of trying to pull Seth up by the arm. It was like watching a chimp try to move a rhinoceros. Seth grabbed him by his powder-blue lapels.

"Listen, white shoes," he said, his teeth inches from the caterer's nose. "Touch me again and I'll bust up your head."

At least someone with a hangover stood up to that bully of a caterer.

After Paul and Ursula's wedding, my life went pretty much straight downhill. I continued to study acting halfheartedly, though I had long ago left HB Studios. I did stick with a series of evening acting classes taught by an actor friend of mine, Hal Sherman, but that was easy for me. We almost always went out for a drink afterward, so I had that to look forward to.

The one time I got a part in a play, an off-off-Broadway production of *Peer Gynt,* it was after I stayed sober for two weeks. Staying sober made me very, very focused, painfully aware of everything about my life and the people around me, which was why I got the part. More than anything else, being sober brought up anger. I was mad for two weeks. Talk to me and I'd snap, as if I were withdrawing from cigarettes or heroin. But it wasn't like being irritable from the effects of withdrawal. It was almost a good feeling, a restless feeling, like I wanted badly to do something, say something, make a statement, create something. Unfortunately, the feeling was totally unfocused and, ultimately, uncomfortable. I started drinking again the minute I got the part, to celebrate an achievement. About two months later, I wound up getting kicked out of the production after missing too many rehearsals and forgoing the formality of learning my lines.

Somewhere along in there I also flunked an audition as a waiter at a very popular Greenwich Village restaurant. So not only was I a dud as an actor; I couldn't even make it as a waiter wanting to be an actor.

Feeling that acting might not be my thing, after all, I went to Marymount Manhattan College to study advertising and quit after my first assignment was criticized. I also worked part-time for Tiffany in the summer of 1981 and again that Christmas, selling monogrammed playing cards to Japanese tourists.

During my first Tiffany Period, I got it into my head to be a jewelry designer but gave up when it was pointed out that I would have to spend years learning art and metallurgy. Instead, I spent weekends on Fire Island, lying on the beach and drinking beer. My actors' union, the American Federation of Television and Radio Actors, was on strike that summer, so when anyone suggested that I spend my weekends auditioning, I could smile and say: "I'm on strike." Truth be told, I didn't even know what we were striking about.

I had been living at home almost since the day Paul met Ursula in Montauk. For a time during the summer I worked at Tiffany, I also shared my old bedroom with my brother Will.

I have often said that if we had not been born brothers, Will and I would have nothing to do with each other. In a family short on affection, we grew up competitors and, occasionally, reluctant allies. Because of that, our conversations are guarded to this day. Even so, we can't make small talk. Our discussions almost always center on the family. We talk about Mom and Dad and why we turned out the way we did. We can't discuss the weather or current events. We always want to know how the other is dealing with his life or if the other's experiences can help shed light on our own. Until recently we almost always met only when both of us were drinking. Otherwise, it seemed, we couldn't tolerate each other.

The summer I worked at Tiffany, Will and I went out together on a scalding hot afternoon, one of the countless days I skipped work. We both had vicious hangovers and wanted nothing more than to sit in a cool movie theater and drink ice-cold colas. We planned to watch about four movies, but stopped at two. Will had a beer between the first and second, after which the second movie turned out to be kind of a dud, which put a damper on our enthusiasm. Still, I remember it as one of the nicest afternoons we spent together, simply because I wanted so badly to have a normal relationship with him.

During the summer of 1982, I started seeing a psychotherapist. Looking back, it seems I went solely so I could sit for forty-five minutes and heap bile on my parents, to rage about how cold and demanding they had been, how they had put themselves first. I quit after four or five sessions because the therapy was expensive and didn't seem to be getting anywhere. More to the point, I think I remember that the therapist had the temerity to suggest that my parents might not be my only problem and that I might want to do something about my drinking and drug taking.

By that time, that is to say, my last two years in New York, my partying had reached epic proportions. When I was out, I was *out*—sometimes for forty-eight hours at a time, drunk and pumped up on cocaine. I would start off with dinner at a restaurant, then hit the bars until four in the morning, then go to an after-hours club until well after daylight. Then I stumbled home to crash. Sometimes, though, I stayed out, spending the day at the apartment of a like-minded nutcase, continuing to drink and snort cocaine. When evening rolled around, I would start all over again.

Sometimes I led the dregs of my little group home to my parents' apartment, where we would park ourselves in the library and smoke and snort lines off the coffee table while I trotted out my Harry S. Truman scrapbooks. I always liked taking home someone I hadn't met before so I could show off. Occasionally we overstayed our welcome. I still cringe at the memory of my mother coming downstairs at eight o'clock in the morning to find her library awash in a cigarette haze and two or three pairs of manic, red-rimmed eyes staring at her.

She never said a thing except to tell me quietly and sadly that she thought it was time everyone went home and that I needed some sleep. Sometimes, after she made the suggestion, I went back out.

Paul and Ursula were often in on the start of these binges, but weren't party to them. They would invite me for drinks and dinner or to a party, and I would start the evening just fine, telling myself I would have a few drinks and go home. But once I had a couple of drinks, I was on the phone, trying to rustle up a gram or two of cocaine. My friends and I made up codes so I wouldn't have to say the words *gram* or *cocaine* in front of Paul or my parents.

Searching for drugs and diversion took me from Harlem to John Belushi's after-hours bar downtown. I talked to Belushi, for about a second and a half, while he was standing by the jukebox. I was much more interested in the guy who was selling cocaine in a Winnebago in the parking lot.

At about this time, I had developed a taste for limousines to go with my taste for drugs. I figured if I couldn't be as famous as my grandfather, I could at least blow all the trust fund money he had left me to look like I was. The bigger and gaudier the limo, the better. I became such a regular with one limo company that when I ordered a town car one night, they sent me a white stretch with a sun roof. Paul hated to see me throw money away like that and used to despair when he knew I was on a toot and coming to see him.

"Oh, God. Clifton's here," he would call to Ursula from the living-room window.

"How do you know?" she would ask.

"There's a white stretch limo about half a black long parked out front."

A friend of mine, Jason Doherty, was with me during a lot of these limo adventures. He remembers them as being carefully orchestrated. Since I was paying for the car and the cocaine, I figured I could call the shots, and I usually led the group at a frenetic pace, bouncing between clubs and bars and parties just to be in the limo.

Paul was most annoyed by the habit I developed of using limousines to pick up and ferry around people I had just met and turned into instant best friends. The last straw was when I cruised by his apartment one night, having been up the entire night and day before, with a carful of complete strangers. Hauling me out of the car and dragging me up the sidewalk, he shook me hard. It was the first time he had ever laid a hand on me in anger.

"What the hell do you think you're doing? Who are those people? I've never seen any of them before," he yelled.

"They're my friends."

"Your friends? Bullshit. I'm your friend. Those people are just into you for who you are and the drugs and the limo. What's the bill on that thing up to now, anyway, about six hundred bucks?"

With that, he threw everyone out of the car, including a black-belt kung fu expert, and sent the driver and the car back to the garage.

That still wasn't enough to shake me off the course I had chosen. Paul kept on trying after that, but he was beginning to lose stamina for the fight. My friendship with Ursula was all but wiped out because she saw firsthand what my behavior was doing to Paul. He worried about me, he ranted about me, he took the plaintive calls from my mother, who would never think to approach me directly.

Finally Paul had just about reached his limit. If my parents couldn't say anything to dissuade me from the course I had chosen, he was about to.

11

Turning Point

During the time I was abusing myself in New York, my grandmother Truman was still living at 219 North Delaware in Independence. You would never have known it from talking to me. I had no contact with her save an occasional phone call, which was usually short. I remember those calls as being painful, because Gammy had become very hard of hearing and was also difficult to understand. Besides, with my life the way it was, there wasn't anything I really wanted to tell her.

I missed a great chance to know my grandmother Truman in a way few people have. In the ten years after my grandfather's death, I could have flown to Independence on any number of occasions. I could have spent two weeks at a time with her, talking, laughing, reading. I could have spent hours at the Truman Library, soaking up my family history. For many hours more, I might have sat in the library at the house and read the books my grandparents had read, to know what they liked and didn't like, to see the thoughts that shaped their lives.

My grandmother, by turns, meant everything and nothing to me. Often, I forgot she was alive, so far removed were we from each other by distance and family dynamics. My mother did not feel the need to see Gammy often. In turn, I have been told, Gammy did not necessarily want to be visited. But I often thought of her as a lonely recluse, living by herself in that enormous, empty house, cared for by nurses, unloved by her family.

I considered going to visit her on my own at one point. In the end, I gave up the idea. I thought I would be bored, that we would have nothing to say to each other. And if I went, I would have to do without my precious nightlife for a week or more, something I rarely tried. Underneath it all was a feeling that she wouldn't like having me around, that somehow I wasn't worthy.

Beyond the phone calls, the only contact I had with my grandmother in the last years of her life was the card I got from Independence every Christmas. It was one of those little cards you use to send kids money, with a little oval window for the face of the president on the bill. Every year, I could see Abraham Lincoln staring out at me. No matter my age, Gammy always sent me a five.

She died on October 16, 1982, when I was twenty-five. She was ninety-seven and had lived almost ten years longer than my grandfather. A simple service was held in Independence, at the church where my mother was married. Will and I read passages from the Bible during the service. Nancy Reagan, Rosalynn Carter, and Betty Ford sat in the front row, across the aisle from my family.

I had asked Paul and Ursula Lowerre to go with me to the funeral. Even though I lived with my family, I had become so estranged from them that I felt I needed support from someone else, someone close to me in a way my parents were not. I opened up to Paul and Ursula, something I could never do with Mom and Dad. I don't think I was completely honest with anyone during that period, including Paul and Ursula—even myself—but those two knew me better than anyone else.

I sat down with them in the dining room of my parents' apartment to ask them if they would come to the funeral. I also put the question to my family. After all, the Lowerres weren't going to go to Independence without my mother's approval. Asking them along was not only out of the ordinary, but a breach of the unwritten rule about family isolationism. Few people outside the family ever took part in Truman-related affairs. I was aware of that when I asked Paul and Ursula to go. It felt like I was committing some sort of sacrilege.

To this day, I question my motives for asking them along. On one hand, it was a simple wish to have the support of close friends in a time of tragedy. On the other hand, I may have been unconsciously trying to show my parents that I would rather have my friends' support than theirs. And I can't deny that part of me wanted attention so badly that I was anticipating the chance to show off for Paul and Ursula in front of the dignitaries and television cameras I knew would be at the funeral.

Whatever my reasons, they were moot. Both Mom and Will squashed any idea of the Lowerres attending the funeral. Will's opposition was violently vocal. In an emotional scene in our apartment dining room, he accused Paul and Ursula of being leeches, of wanting to go along just for the thrill and the publicity.

Leeches, which Paul and Ursula certainly are not, have always been a sore spot for Will. During my life, I have rarely run into anybody who wanted to be my friend simply because I am Harry Truman's grandson. And no one has ever tried to use my friendship to their advantage. But Will hates the thought of having his privacy invaded by Trumanophiles. As he puts it: "I was always made to feel like being Harry Truman's grandson was the best part of me." Consequently, "I hate people coming up to me and wanting to talk to me just because some son of a bitch was my grandfather."

Despite his feelings, Paul and Ursula might have gone, anyway, had there been time to make arrangements with the Secret Service and other government agencies involved in the funeral. My mother told them gently that there just wasn't time to make sure they would be with the family and not standing behind a barricade along the procession route.

My grandmother's death was, if not a turning point, at least the beginning of a path leading to one. The winter after she died, my behavior became more and more erratic. When I went out, I was routinely gone for days at a time with no word to my parents. If I wasn't out, I was in the basement, snorting lines off a tabletop and drinking until past dawn. I often slept off my hangovers in one of the basement bedrooms, then spent the entire day down there watching television and eating bagfuls of Oreo cookies and washing them down with quarts of whole milk.

My parents left me alone through all this, never mentioning my behavior or that fact that I seemed to have turned into a bat, sleeping in the dark basement all day, then flapping out, half-crazed, at night. I think what they were most afraid of was rocking the boat. I had been at odds with them for years, and trying to talk to me or hint to me that I might have a problem would probably have set me more resolutely against them. Not that I gave them many chances to talk to me. It seemed I planned my entrances and exits so that we hardly ever crossed paths. I didn't stay in the basement all day because I wanted company.

In defense, my father at least developed a dark sense of humor about my drinking and taking drugs. When a friend called asking for me one afternoon, my father said cheerfully, "Clifton got up at about eleven this morning, watched about an hour of television, thoroughly exhausted himself, and went back to bed. I'll be glad to tell him you called."

If I had no use for my parents, I had even less use for my sober friends, and they for me. I had no time for people other than those I drank with, and I shamefully avoided the best of them during the day. Jason Doherty, who had been on more limo rides with me than he cared to remember, was growing weary of the all-night parties and often tried to coax me out into more normal activities. The only time he succeeded, we went across the river to New Jersey to have dinner with his mother, signaling not only a normal activity but interaction with someone who didn't do drugs and stay out all night. Still, I went only after I had begged off the invitation several times.

What Jason saw in me I will never know. If you ask him directly, he will simply shrug his shoulders and say, "There just seemed to be more there." It is amazing that he saw anything under all the layers of crap.

By the spring of 1983, I could not set foot outside my door without a vial of cocaine in my pocket. If I did not have any, I could not have a couple of drinks without being overcome by the urge to go sniffing around for some. It's sick, but I did not feel whole if I wasn't carrying that little white-packed bit of plastic. It got to the point where I began to have fond feelings for bar and restaurant bathroom stalls. I was in there, a spoon up my nose, as often as I was at a table.

The people I hung out with were people who could get me the cocaine and/or those who would gladly let me share it with them. People who sold me drugs occasionally called the house. My father once called me to the phone with a pained and very angry look on his face. "There's a young woman on the phone who says you owe her six hundred dollars," he said. "I think you had better speak to her."

It turned out that one of my partying buddies had taken six hundred dollars' worth of cocaine from the woman, telling her it was for me and that I would pay for it. It took me days and several more phone calls, and a lot of sweating, to convince her that he owed her the money, not me. I just knew she was going to send some bruiser after me to collect. Worse, I was terrified of the possibility that the collector might harm my parents. After that, I never went near that particular "friend" again.

My other friends—that is to say, the ones with brains and prospects—had to give up being around me. I dragged them down, and not just because I kept them out all night. My life was like a black hole. You either got out of my orbit or got sucked in.

One by one, friends stopped calling—even some of the ones I had partied hardest with. They went back to school or moved on to new jobs and brighter futures. I was too much work for too little return. You couldn't carry on a normal relationship with me. If you were with me, you were either smashed and crazy or hungover. There was no relating beyond that.

I, in turn, shunned longtime friends. The last person I wanted to see was someone who knew me when I wasn't slack-jawed and hollow-eyed. One such old friend, Carey Smoot, the beautiful babysitter I first met on Fire Island, came by to introduce me and my parents to her fiancé. During their visit, I had to be dragged up from my burrow in the basement. Carey and I had been the closest of friends; we had few secrets. We should have been locked in conversation for hours that afternoon, catching up and happily rehashing the past. Instead our meeting was brief, strained, and uncomfortable, a blip of an encounter in the dining room not ten feet from the basement stairs. I just wanted them to be gone so I could crawl back into the dark and feel lousy all by myself.

To keep me from stewing alone like that, Paul, like Jason, kept trying to get me out during the day. I had been to see him once at his new job in the Seamen's Church Institute, a visit I thoroughly enjoyed because we were heading to a party afterward. Paul had other aims in mind that day. I remember that he showed me proudly around the office, introducing me to every coworker he could find. Looking back, it seems to me he was not so much showing off as trying to get me excited at the prospect of normalcy, the rewards of work.

In the spring of 1983, he invited me to have lunch with him at his office, still hoping that somehow the sight of his success and happiness would trigger something positive in me. He had to invite me several times. There was no party to go to afterward, so I kept putting him off, complaining that I was sick or had an audition. The last excuse was laughable. After about the third time I stood him up, Paul snapped. "You know," he said angrily over the phone that day, "someday you're going to call me and I'm just not going to be there anymore."

A few days later, I went into the library of our apartment to see my father.

"Dad," I said. "I think I need to get out of New York."

I can't honestly say whether or not it was Paul's threat alone that sent me to see Dad. But I still get a slight chill when I recall his words. And perhaps those words and the trip to his office, the sights and sounds of a normal life, had done something to drive a small wedge under the big block of misery I had crawled underneath.

Suddenly I no longer had grandiose dreams of being a screen superstar or riding in limousines. Instead, I had a picture in my head of a small town, a nice little car, a neat apartment, and a steady job. Where the hell that came from, I'll never know—but I suddenly lowered my sights—or suddenly became realistic.

"Where do you want to go?" Dad asked when I had pulled up a chair in front of him. "What do you want to do?"

"Somewhere in North Carolina," I said. "I thought maybe I could work for a small newspaper down there."

I had chosen the University of North Carolina because it had been my father's alma mater. Now I was choosing his home state and his profession. It must have been instinct, because I had no idea whether I could even write a coherent sentence. In fact, at the time I didn't see journalism as a career at all, just something to get me out of New York. Beyond that, I had no idea where I was going or what in the hell I was doing. I just knew I had to get away.

"It so happens that *The New York Times* owns a string of smaller newspapers, most of them, incidentally, in the Southeast," Dad said. "Let me make a few calls and we'll talk again.

"By the way," he added quickly and, I thought, unusually forcefully, "let me say that I think this is a good idea on your part. I think it will do you a world of good to get away from the city."

He had practically jumped up to offer that last part. My father is very reserved. It takes a lot for him to get worked up. That day, I think I had given him the opportunity he had been waiting for. After years of watching and cursing to himself and worrying, he might finally have the chance to do something to help me. I had tied his hands for so long. He had been chafing at the bit so hard that he broke from the gate like lightning. Fewer than twenty-four hours later, he called me back into the library.

"I've had a talk with Jack Harrison, who is the president of the New York Times Regional Newspaper Group, which oversees those smaller newspapers I told you that *The Times* owns. There are two papers where he feels you might do well. One of them is in Wilmington, not far from where you went to college."

I had been to Wilmington once when I was in college, on one of two visits to Wrightsville Beach, which is eight miles away. The second visit involved beer and daiquiris, plus drunken waterskiing and a trip to a water slide.

"Mr. Harrison said the paper in Wilmington, the *Star-News*, has an intern program. They're willing to take you on and train you, if you think that's what you want to do."

A week or so later, I had lunch with Paul at the Seamen's

Church Institute on my way to the airport for the flight to Wilmington. I had on a new seersucker suit my father had bought me, black socks and loafers, a white shirt and a blue tie. The rest of my clothes fitted into one suitcase. My father had to buy me the suit because nothing else I owned fit me. I was thirty pounds overweight (a hundred and eighty-five on an ectomorphic five-ten frame). For years, new clothes had not been a priority.

I was shaky and scared during lunch, hoping, as I always did when I had to fly, that a natural disaster or serious illness or a nuclear attack—anything—would intervene and save me from having to get on the plane. I wanted that lunch to go on forever.

Though my fear of flying overrode everything else, I was also scared about leaving New York. I wondered if I had made the right choice. At the same time, I had a tremendous sense of relief, of escape. I wanted to run from my demons, to leave behind the drugs and the drink, the stupid things I had said and done, the people I had said and done them to.

Still, I wasn't at all sure I was up to what I was running toward—a new town, new faces, a steady job. In a way I didn't care if the plane went down in flames on the way to Wilmington. I felt so bad about what I had done and what I had been, yet I knew I would do it all again. Maybe, I thought, it would be better if I didn't get a chance to try. Nonetheless I drank several beers during lunch because I knew I would not get up into the air without fortification.

I arrived at the *Star-News* in a grander style than most new interns. The evening I landed at New Hanover County Airport, Mr. Harrison and his wife, Mary, met me and took me straight to a restaurant on Wrightsville Beach for dinner. Afterward I spent the night at their beach condominium.

The next day, Mr. Harrison took me to the *Star-News* to show me the building and introduce me around. If anyone was resentful at having a legacy forced on them, they didn't show it. Actually resentment for legacies was probably low at that time due to Anne Silverstein, a reporter I had met at dinner with the Harrisons the night before. Anne was the daughter of Lou Silverstein, *The New*

York Times's chief layout designer. In addition to being a legacy like myself, Anne was everything Mr. Harrison hoped I would be—bright, talented, a hard worker. He actually told me, "Give me a couple of good years at the *Star-News* and there's no telling where you can go from there."

What Mr. Harrison couldn't have known was that I really didn't want to go much of anywhere in the newspaper business.

The *Star-News* managing editor at that time was Bill Coughlin, lanky and white haired, a newspaperman of the old school. He had worked everywhere my father had worked—Cairo, London, Moscow—and then some. He was a fighter pilot in World War II. His office wall was peppered with grainy black-and-white shots from a career that had begun in the 1940s. There he was, posed beside his P-38 fighter plane; holding up the head of a leopard he had bagged in Africa; pencil in hand, interviewing Eisenhower. None of those experiences prepared Bill for the task ahead of him.

"What do you mean, you can't type?" he said my first day at the office, his pipe nearly slipping from his mouth.

"I mean I can't type," I said.

"Well, you're not going to get very far in this business if you can't type. I want you to sign up for typing classes at Cape Fear Technical Institute or Miller-Motte Business School. You have got to know how to type."

The idea of typing classes, like so many other ideas, put me off. So I neglected to enroll until the classes were full and the deadlines were past. A lesser man would have wasted his time nagging me. Bill simply threw me a typing book and pointed to the "fishbowl," a glassed-in conference room in the center of the newsroom.

"Here, go sit in there and teach yourself."

That was the worst, sitting in the middle of the newsroom, in front of everyone, with a typing book open next to an aging electric typewriter. As soon as Bill's back was turned, I sneaked out. God knows what I did to amuse myself. I was not a self-starter, so I doubt I was tracking down leads or thinking up stories. I actually had no idea how to go about being a journalist. The assistant city editor, Susan Kille, found me at a computer, aimlessly sifting through Associated Press wire news on celebrities.

"I've got a job for you if you're up to it," she said. "It's not much. Just a brief."

She handed me a press release on the recently discovered fact that North Carolina road bridges were in a sad state of repair. In other states, similar bridges of like age had crumbled right out from under cars. Susan wanted just a few paragraphs for the next day's paper. For a seasoned reporter—one who could type—it would have been ten minutes work. It took me about an hour and a half. When it ran the next day, it didn't even have my byline. Still, I found that I enjoyed doing it, and despite the fact I couldn't type, it seemed that writing came naturally. It must have been all those years of having the managing editor of *The New York Times* correct my school papers.

Despite that little glimmer, I did not fit in well at the paper. But that had nothing to do with my writing ability or the fact I couldn't type. I had brought every one of my lousy habits with me from New York. I thought I could outrun them, but I was sadly mistaken. I still had not admitted to myself that the drinking and the drugs were themselves the problem. I had been fooling myself that they were just the effects of something else. What, I didn't know. I told myself it was my grandfather's fame, my upbringing—anything but admit I might have something to do with it myself.

In moving from New York to Wilmington, I did not even break stride. When my new colleagues had a few beers, I had bunches. Within weeks I had made connections and started buying cocaine again. Once more, I was out all night, every other night. I made no distinction between weekends and weekdays. I started calling in sick like clockwork. I don't remember what I wrote—or whether I wrote much of anything at all.

Later, I found out from Bill Coughlin that I had gotten my name on a police watch list of suspected drug pushers and users. Wilmington is not New York. In a small town, it's harder to hide your dirty habits.

At the newspaper, the editors had pretty much gotten disgusted and started shunting me from one department to the other.

Because I was a legacy, I think they were hoping they could just ride out my yearlong internship without my doing too much damage to the paper. Rumor had it that one of the editors finally said, "Let him rot in sports."

There was an area I knew next to nothing about. Tucked away in the back of the newsroom, I sat in the sports department for days on end, reading novels because there was nothing for me to do. I got paid for sitting on my backside. At one point, Jerry Hooks, the sports editor, took pity on me and let me go to a movie in the middle of the day. The one time he sent me to cover a high-school basketball game, he had to explain the game to me first.

Before that could happen, however, in early January 1984, I got called into the office of the publisher, Jim Weeks. Bill Coughlin and Charles Anderson, the executive editor, were there. I had been at the *Star-News* less than six months, but it's not that I didn't know this was coming. Seeing them, I immediately felt sick to my stomach, overwhelmed by guilt and fear and anger. I had thought that I could coast, that things would work themselves out. But here I was, having again to deal with all my shortcomings. And I just knew, could feel it in the pit of my stomach, that this time it was going to be worse than having my best friend mad at me or having a pusher calling the house. I was going to get fired. And then I would be lost. What was I going to do? Go back to New York and start all over again?

"You have a problem," Mr. Weeks began directly. "You have a problem with alcohol, and I think you also have a problem with drugs."

Even as the words came out of his mouth, I was inwardly shaking my head. I didn't believe what he was saying. Drugs and drink were not my problems. They were a symptom of something else, something that I couldn't put my finger on, but something that would work itself out in time. All I needed was time, time and another chance. I always needed more chances. What I didn't realize until later was that Mr. Weeks was about to hand me the biggest chance of my life.

"You have a choice," he said simply. "You can lose your job at this newspaper, or you can get help."

12

The Treatment Center

After that early January meeting in the publisher's office, the *Star-News* packed me off to New York. I was to see *The New York Times* substance abuse counselor to be evaluated and to determine what kind of treatment I needed, where I should go, and how long I should stay. Bill Coughlin, my editor, went with me. Well, he didn't exactly go *with* me, since he wasn't afraid to fly. He went on a plane, and I took an Amtrak train out of Fayetteville.

The New York Times substance abuse counselor was actually called something like the "employee assistance counselor." He was a nice man whom I remember nothing else about. When Bill and I went to the *Times* offices, I must have protested that I didn't have an alcohol problem, because the first thing the employee assistance counselor did was sit me down in front of his desk and hand me a list of the symptoms of alcoholism.

"Do any of those seem like you?" he asked.

I scanned the list. There were eleven or twelve symptoms, most of which I can't recall, but four that stuck out were: Do you think about drinking when you're not drinking? Do you plan your activities around drinking? Do you always drink to excess? Do you have "blackouts" when you're drinking?

The first two were right on target. I argued with myself over the third, because I had been known to stop at one or two drinks—like when I was hungover or had the flu. As to the fourth, well, I never blacked out because the cocaine kept me awake.

Altogether, I found—by my reckoning—that I had about four

of the symptoms listed. This gave me great hope that all the people who thought I had a drinking problem—Mom, Dad, Bill, and my editors and colleagues at the *Star-News*—were nuts and there was some other explanation for my behavior. I wanted very badly to be able to pin it on something or someone other than myself.

The employee assistance counselor apparently anticipated that need. When I handed him back the list and said, smugly, that I only had four of eleven symptoms, he simply smiled. "Well, if you have any two of those symptoms, you meet the definition of an alcoholic," he said.

I thought that was a dirty trick. I wanted him to give me the test again. Instead, he gave me a choice. I could either spend a month at a treatment center in Palm Springs, or I could go to one in some backwater called Kissimmee.

"Palm Springs," I said immediately and with great feeling.

"Well, now wait a minute," he said. "The one in Palm Springs is about three thousand dollars more per month than the one in Kissimmee, and since *The New York Times* is paying for this . . ."

"But I'm paying half," I said.

"Right, but our half will be bigger if you go to Palm Springs."

There was no point in arguing, because I could see his mind was made up. Kissimmee it was. To be fair, money was only part of the reason he was reluctant to send me to Palm Springs. I don't think he liked the way my face lit up when he mentioned the locale. I had only been slightly taken aback when I found out I had twice the number of symptoms required to be defined as an alcoholic. It was obvious to him that I still didn't think I had a problem.

He was right, of course. A man who knew he had a drinking problem would not have gone out that night, gotten drunk, snorted the last of his cocaine, and dragged himself back to his parents' apartment well after midnight.

Back in Wilmington, I called Michael Kendrick. Michael was sort of my man Friday when it came to travel. Since I was afraid to fly, I always took the train, which left from Fayetteville, an hour and forty minutes from Wilmington. Michael's job was to drive with me to Fayetteville and bring my car back. The Fayetteville Amtrak station, nestled like an oasis in a wasteland of topless bars, wasn't the kind of place you wanted to leave your car.

Michael had driven with me to Fayetteville twice before: the first time to get me home to New York for Thanksgiving in 1983; the second, to get me back to New York the following January for the evaluation by *The New York Times* employee assistance counselor.

Michael was nineteen, square-jawed, and perfectly groomed, a youth-group leader. He and I were so outwardly different that I would have thought we would have nothing to say to each other on any of those trips. Yet we got along very well and managed to fill the time between Wilmington and Fayetteville talking about movies, telling lewd jokes, and gossiping about people we knew.

The night in early January 1984 that he drove me to Fayetteville for my trip to the treatment center in Kissimmee was business as usual. I tried to remember that trip as a quiet drive, with me soberly reflecting on what lay ahead of me. Michael, on the other hand, remembers laughing, telling lewd jokes, and eating a box of Godiva chocolates I had picked up before we left. Like everyone else around me, he could see that I had not come to terms with my predicament. He remembers that I seemed unrepentant, even angry, during the drive. Though I explained to him where I was going in Kissimmee and why, I also made it clear that I thought I should not have had to go.

The train left at midnight. Michael and I arrived about twenty minutes early and had to wait, which is not much fun in Fayetteville because of the neighborhood around the station. The city is home to Fort Bragg, one of the largest military bases in the country. On any given night, it seems half the soldiers from the base—plus assorted hangers-on—are crammed into the topless bars or strung out along Hay Street beside the station. Michael and I were lucky that night. The train was on time, and Michael packed me onto the sleeper car and drove off into the night.

I woke up the next morning somewhere in Florida and had an hour or so to kill before arriving in Orlando, the station stop for people going to Kissimmee.

Sleeping and waking up on a train can be a tricky business.

When I was in college, I had no trouble sleeping on trains. Of course, most of the time I got on dead drunk, so it wasn't so much a matter of sleeping as passing out. And passing out on a train can be dangerous, especially if you pass out naked.

Almost every time I've taken the train alone—from college to the present day—I've slept in what's called a roomette. This is not the kind of accommodation my grandfather was used to in the Ferdinand Magellan, the armor-plated private car he used during his 1948 whistle-stop campaign. Nonetheless, it's comfortable for one. The compartment is like a bedroom closet, if your closet comes equipped with a seat, a toilet in one corner, and a wall that folds down into a bed. At night it's nice to stretch out on the bed and look out the window at the lights and towns flicking by in the dark. But you've got to remember to pull the shade before you go to sleep.

I didn't one hot summer night after I'd thrown off all my clothes. I woke up in the station in Wilmington, Delaware, to the sight of four or five elderly ladies staring in at me, their lower jaws swinging in the breeze and their eyebrows stuck in the "up" position.

There was no such committee meeting me in Kissimmee, just a young man named Jim, who would become my rehab counselor for the next four weeks and who turned me over to the detoxification center at Brookwood Lodge.

I looked at my bill from Brookwood not long ago. Though the bulk of the $6,700-and-some-odd dollars went for room and board, several hundred dollars went for detoxification. As I remember it, the money was apparently spent for a medical exam, several showings of *An Officer and a Gentleman* on the waiting-room television, and having a nurse go through my luggage.

"What are you looking for?" I asked as she rummaged among my underwear.

"Anything that might . . . whoops, here we go! Can't have this," she said, holding up my small bottle of Polo cologne.

"Why not?" I asked.

"You might try to drink it."

That was an astounding piece of news. Never in my life, no

matter how badly I wanted a drink, would it have occurred to me to drink my cologne. I took her statement as yet more proof that I couldn't possibly be an alcoholic. Drinking cologne was not one of my symptoms.

"I can tell you right now that I would never drink my Polo," I told the nurse.

She just smiled and kept it, anyway. I got it back upon checking out a month later. I still have it, in fact.

That night I looked out onto the rest of Brookwood Lodge. What I saw were three cottagelike dormitories connected to the main building by a series of covered walks. The offices and the detox center, the medical clinic and the cafeteria, were all in the main building, which was about twice the size of the dorms. The whole complex sat on a two-acre stretch of lawn bordered on one side by the road and on the other three sides by swamp.

Will, who would see Brookwood two weeks later, remembers it as a somewhat run-down, depressing place. The swamp was the source of all wildlife not confined to Brookwood itself. In fact, the first night I was there, I saw something waddling across the grass outside my window. It looked like a bowling ball on legs and turned out to be one of the armadillos that used Brookwood as a throughway to get from the swamp to the road.

I found out later that the swamp was also home to alligators, which I had thought, in my city-boy ignorance, were extinct outside zoos. I have since discovered there are plenty of wild alligators near where I live right now and that they sometimes eat errant house pets. But at the time I was in detox in Kissimmee, the reality of wild alligators was a surprise. The nurse told me the first night that they sometimes came in from the swamp to wander around the Brookwood grounds. Where was that Secret Service agent with the shotgun when I needed him?

When they let me out of detox the next day, the first thing they did was introduce me to the treatment center's health regimen. This included a B_{12} shot, because drinking tends to use up that vitamin, and a daily multivitamin. This was actually appealing to me. Despite my drinking, I'd always been a closet health nut. In between binges, I often huffed and gagged around the jogging track in Central Park. Occasionally I even picked up a pair of dumbbells. It turned out I had a latent instinct for self-preservation.

At Brookwood, I started running again, having laid off for almost a year. Every other afternoon I loped around the perimeter of the complex. It was always at a sprightly jog because I was never sure when one of the alligators was going to make a lunge for me.

Running and some push-ups and sit-ups were about the only exercise options open to me at Brookwood. They were equipped to handle mental, not physical, rehabilitation. In fact, they seemed a little stuck up about the fact I wanted to exercise and insinuated that I should be concentrating solely on my mental recovery. I had to point out that, for me at least, mental and physical well-being went hand in hand. Not that this caused them any great worry. As far as I could tell, I was the only patient who wanted to try to get back in shape.

Still, no amount of jogging would keep me as healthy as a little football-shaped pill called Antabuse. Antabuse was prescribed for almost every Brookwood inmate. The drug blocks the liver's ability to metabolize the toxins in alcohol. As a result, the poisonous byproducts build up in your bloodstream. One taste of a wine-based salad dressing and you were nauseous; knock back a shot of bourbon and you would be violently ill. When I checked out, they gave me a thirty days' supply, plus a prescription for more. For months after I left, I grilled restaurant waiters about the content of salad dressings.

Once I had been medicated, I went over to my dorm, a dingy yellow stucco building with a triangular roof. Just inside the door were a common room with a television, a small kitchen, and a therapy room. Off the common room were two corridors of bedrooms, each with two beds. Each pair of rooms shared a bathroom equipped with a shower.

Throughout the dorm, the floors were gray linoleum. The bedspreads and curtains seemed to be made of the same thin blue material. The place smelled of disinfectant and stale cigarette smoke. Overall, it was like a cheap but not too ratty motel.

My fellow guests were as mixed a group as you could hope to find. They ranged in age from teenagers to men in their seventies. Among them were farmers, students, blue-collar workers, and at least one private detective and one millionaire businessman. Not surprisingly, there were also quite a few who worked at Disneyworld in nearby Orlando. Among these were no mice or pirates; most were maintenance workers and mechanics who cleaned up and serviced the rides. I thought their being at Brookwood was an apt analogy for the stress involved with keeping up a happy face.

I had a room to myself for the first two weeks. After that, I was paired with a young man in his early twenties who was trying to overcome an addiction to marijuana. He didn't look like the sort of person I would have expected to have a problem with pot. He was always freshly shaved and wore his blond hair short and neat. His wardrobe ran to slacks, button-down-collar shirts, and cardigans. He was deeply religious. At home, he had been either a church youth group leader or a fund-raiser for some sort of religious order. I can't remember which.

The second day he was there, he sat down to talk to me in the common room. I noticed that he was having a hard time keeping both his feet and his eyes still.

"I don't know what it is," he said. "I just feel so jittery, you know? Like I'm on edge all the time. I feel like I want to explode."

"When was the last time you smoked any pot?" I asked.

It turned out that before coming to Brookwood he had spent most of the previous seven years stoned. His routine had been to smoke a joint in the morning after breakfast, another one around lunch, and another one or two after dinner. He told me he did this day in and day out without exception. It had gotten to the point that he didn't know what the world looked like outside his haze.

Hearing stories like his was common during our daily therapy sessions. They were so similar, to mine and to each other, that all ran together in my head, and I can't recall more than one or two that stand out.

There was the sixty-year-old Florida farmer who came to therapy every day in his plaid wool shirt and blue overalls. When I first saw him, I expected his story to be about belting back beer and whiskey before climbing up on a John Deere tractor. It turned out he had been impaired while operating his tractor, but not by booze. He was addicted to Valium.

The biggest standout among my peers at Brookwood was Dick, the private detective. Dick was in his mid-thirties, tall and lean, his hawk nose jutting out over a neatly trimmed black beard. His black hair was longish and frizzy, and he had sun freckles on every visible inch of skin, the legacy of years of sunbathing.

Dick seemed supremely self-confident, not only in himself, but in the fact that his being at Brookwood was a big mistake. In therapy sessions, Dick defended his drinking with zeal and conviction. "I handled it," he would say. "I never made a mistake on the job. It never affected my performance. It wasn't causing me the same kind of trouble it's caused the rest of you guys."

Dick's liver was nearly shot, largely because his recent life had been one long drunk. He once told us of meeting a client for breakfast in a diner. The client ordered bacon and eggs; Dick drank two beers. For the rest of the day, he sipped on beer or mixed drinks. He was rarely smashed, but never completely sober. By the time he got to that point, he said, he didn't drink to get drunk, only to feel normal. Without a slight buzz all day long, he couldn't function.

Dick was not at Brookwood because his life had come unraveled by alcohol. Rather, it was because his life would be coming to an end if he didn't stop drinking. He had been told by his doctor—and by the clinic doctor—that if he continued his old habits, cirrhosis would kill him. He had only the smallest part of a functioning liver left. Dick not only took this news in stride; he often bragged about the condition of his liver, as if the disease were a mark of honor.

Will remembers the relationships between the Brookwood patients as being somewhat like the grim camaraderie among prisoners. We were all there for similar reasons and had similar stories to tell. A lot of us, like Dick, wore our pasts—our crimes, if you will—as badges of a sort. We laughed heartily at each other's stories of falling off balconies or waking up behind the wheel of a car going ninety miles per hour.

We were indeed prisoners, of a sort, except that the penalty for breaking the rules was being kicked out, not having time added to your sentence. Brookwood was strict about its boundaries. Patients were not allowed off the little slice of land at the edge of the swamp. The idea was to keep us from going into town for a beer. Do that and you were expelled. The rules also extended to visitors. When Will arrived and asked where he might go for a run, he was told he couldn't leave the grounds. But the rules didn't seem to bother Dick.

If we had been in a prison movie instead of a treatment center, Dick would have been our hardened, street-savvy leader. He did not get along well with authority figures, specifically the treatment-center counselors. The second week I was there, he organized a breakout.

From the first day I was at Brookwood, I had heard stories of the treasures to be found down the road from the treatment center. These were mouthwatering delights, concoctions to make your head spin. Surprisingly, the stories were not about bars, but about food. True, a few patients had been known to walk into town and fall off the wagon, but the majority of us pined not for booze but for pizza.

Will remembered, but did not have to remind me, that the food at Brookwood was terrible. At each meal, we lined up, cafeteria style, to have our trays filled with glops of boiled vegetables and boiled meat. This may have been because the Brookwood chefs had been charged with making our food as nutritious as possible and, therefore, bland. Whatever the reason, we only looked forward to meals as a break from therapy.

To make matters worse, we were not allowed a break in the monotony—no outside food of any kind, especially no fatty pizzas or sugar-loaded candy bars. Brookwood had no such thing as a concession stand. The reasoning was that we were supposed to build up our bodies, not trade our addiction to alcohol for an addiction to junk foods.

The counselors were adamant about this edict. Dick had tried several times to get Brookwood to serve pizza at least one night a week—or at least to let him order one to be delivered—but he was denied. The counselors took his request as just one more sign that Dick was trying to flout the rules. So, one night during the second week I was there, Dick and a couple of others sauntered down the treatment center's gravel driveway and hitched a ride to the nearest pizza parlor. On the way back, they stopped at a convenience store and bought nearly every candy bar in the place.

Brookwood frowned mightily upon this action, but since Dick and the others had not gotten drunk, merely sated themselves on pizza, they were all given a reprieve. When I found Dick later that night, he was standing in the dorm kitchen, reeking of pepperoni and oregano and smiling from ear to ear.

"Hey, Clifton. Check it out," he said, and opened one of the cabinets to reveal boxes and boxes of jumbo-size Snickers and Three Musketeers bars. He gave me one, free of charge. After all, Dick had not escaped to open a black-market candy business, but to strike a blow for freedom—and his taste buds.

While I was not an outward rebel like Dick, I shared his disdain for Brookwood. Despite the fact that my housemates had told me so many stories similar to my own, I still didn't completely identify with them. I recognized enough of myself in them that I now had to admit that drinking was indeed a problem for me, but I still wasn't convinced I couldn't conquer this whole thing on my own. After only a few days at Brookwood, my focus shifted from denying my drinking problem to minimizing it. I told myself that, compared to my Brookwood peers, my drinking was less acute. After all, I only drank in fits and starts, not chronically, like Dick, and my health was still good.

Part of the reason for my continuing denial was that I felt somehow weak for having been sent to Brookwood in the first place. My grandfather Truman would never have considered seeing a therapist for any reason. In his view, you took care of yourself. You knew what was right and you did it. My grandmother Truman was the same way, maybe even more so. When her father, David Willock Wallace, committed suicide in 1904, the family gave no thought to going public with its pain. To the contrary, the shame of suicide was so great in those days that the tragedy was hardly mentioned. They bore their pain in silence. It must have been hardest on my grandmother, because she and her father had been very close.

I have since developed an affinity for my great-grandfather Wallace, especially after I read my mother's 1986 book on my grandmother, *Bess.* That book was the first place I had seen anything in depth written about David Willock Wallace. I was surprised, and somewhat spooked, to find that I bear a strong resemblance to my great-grandfather, both physically and in character. He was an outgoing man, always ready to buy someone a drink and strike up a conversation. He was good with a joke. People liked him. But he was dogged throughout his life by failure. The political career he wanted so badly never panned out. Like me, he was plagued by drink, which ultimately led to his suicide.

I am fascinated by my great-grandfather. Whenever I am in Independence, at the Truman Library or my grandparents' home on North Delaware Street, I ask questions about him. At the library, I discovered what an intellectual, poetic man he had been and what a sometimes bleak outlook he had on life. The library has several of his favorite books, including a leather-bound, handwritten copy of Dante's *Inferno.*

From my family, I derived a dual image of therapy. I prided myself on being open-minded enough to recognize its virtues, but like my grandparents, I didn't think any of those virtues needed to be applied to me. This is contradictory, I know, but while I am grateful to the Brookwood staff for helping me, I didn't like the way they sometimes went about it. The attitude toward the patients was one of benign condescension. It was as if they were saying: "You've screwed up. Only we know how to set you straight. You're incapable of doing it yourself, so you're going to have to do what we say. If you don't, we'll just kick you out and then you've screwed up again."

That attitude rankled me, especially since it was so very like the one at home. My parents had always taken the lead roles in the family. They knew best. It seemed they thought my brothers and I were incapable of managing anything on our own. At Brookwood, the longer I stayed sober, the angrier I got and the more I thought Mom and Dad should shoulder at least part of the blame for helping me turn out the way I had.

But what Brookwood had in mind was asking me to apologize to my parents. The second week there, everyone in our therapy group was asked to write home to family members and significant others and solicit an essay. The topic of the essay was to be: "How Your Drinking Affected Me." The idea was to show us just how much pain our behavior caused the people we loved.

I had no idea what my parents would write. I don't remember that I felt any great dread about seeing their version of my foibles. In fact, I think I was mildly curious. I had lived such a solitary existence under their roof that I truly had no idea how much they knew of my life. I may have thought I had them fooled all along.

My father's letter was much as I expected. He wrote several pages outlining not so much how he had felt about my drinking or how it had affected him but about how much damage he thought I was doing to myself. My father is not one to pour himself out on paper; he guards his emotions. His letter was not accusatory or overly explicit. It was, in all, an objective summation of my behavior—a well-written newspaper article.

I was somewhat relieved to learn from the tone of the letter that he didn't seem to have been yanking out his hair or losing sleep over me. And it didn't strike me as cold that he didn't seem to have suffered. I wouldn't have expected him to. Still, I had hoped for at least some small statement of coresponsibility for my problems, which was nowhere in sight. All in all, the letter left me neither hot nor cold.

Mom's letter made me much more angry. I had seen the pain and worry in her face when she found me bleary-eyed in the library at six in the morning, smoking and babbling with one or two strangers. I thought she might voice some sort of regret for helping lead

Outside the Oval Office when Marti Cariory and I met President Gerald Ford at Thanksgiving in 1975. Marti looks like a deer caught in a truck's headlights. Notice that I am not tickling the president's hand with the secret Deke handshake.

Polly gives Mom a big kiss on arriving on Fire Island in August of 1985. They look very chummy, seeing as how this was the first time they'd met.

A family portrait in Independence in 1971, during the Christmas visit. Grandpa didn't immediately recognize me and Will, ages twelve and fourteen, because we'd grown our hair long.

On a visit to Washington in 1973, Dad took Will and me, ages fourteen and sixteen, to hear a little bit of the Senate Watergate hearings. Earlier that day, Dad had startled two Soviet security men at Blair House by saying "good morning" to them in perfect Russian.

Polly and her bridesmaids on June 28, 1986, while Paul Lowerre, my best man, and I were running around looking for my lost marriage license. Note that Polly isn't the least bit ruffled. *From left:* Polly's sisters Lisa Enright and Phoebe Bryzgalski, Polly, her sister Aimee Parker, and their cousin Linda Aquino.

I found the license.

Paula Grubbs, my mother-in-law, and E. Clifton Daniel Jr., my father. Both were born September 19—about seventeen years apart.

The New York crew at my wedding. *From left:* best man Paul Lowerre; his sister-in-law, Dede Fratt; Clifford Hart's nose and eyes; Ursula Lowerre; Dad; Katie Green; and me. One of the girls has obviously just pinched Dad.

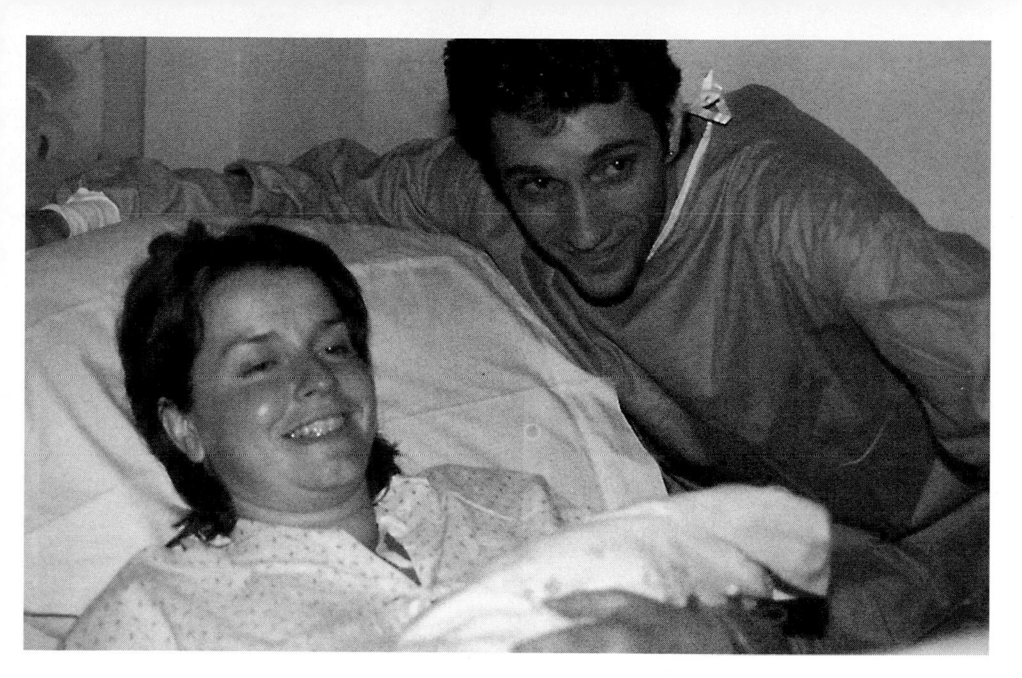

Polly and me just minutes after Aimee Elizabeth Daniel was born, on August 22, 1987. I don't know what we're looking at, unless it's the end of the movie I was watching during Polly's labor.

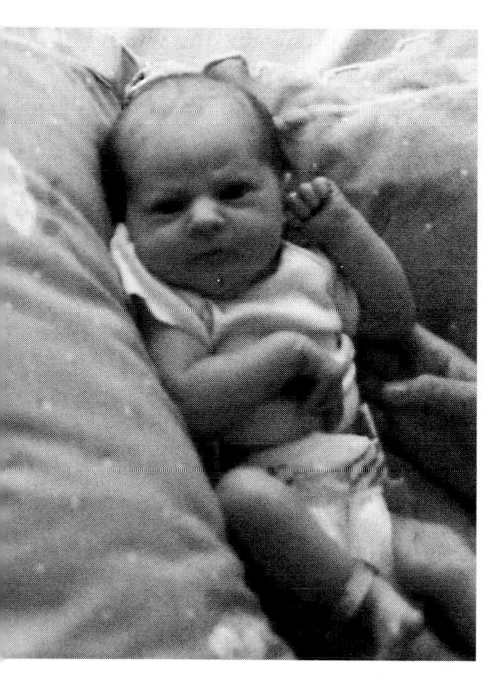

Aimee Elizabeth Daniel on August 23, 1987. This is the same face she makes now when you remind her she hasn't done her homework.

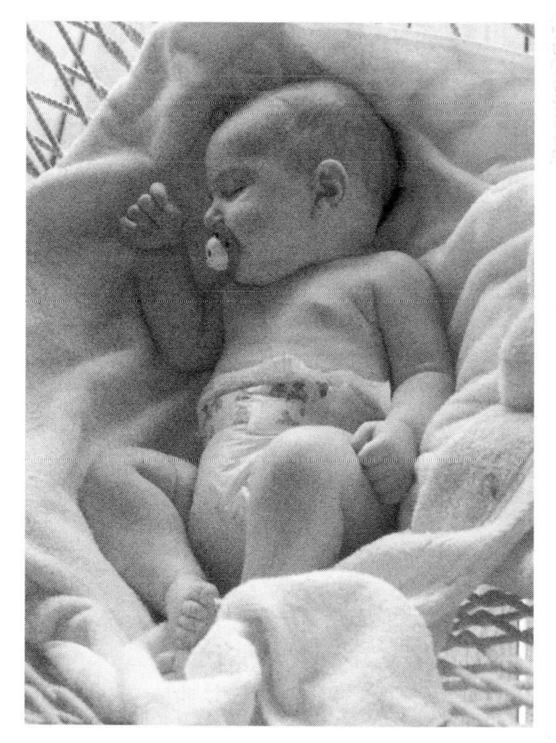

Wesley Truman Daniel in a rare moment of repose.

Above, left: Aimee, age two or three, hungrily gobbling up a handful of chocolate from her grandmother, a known chocoholic. *Above, right:* This is me waving to the crowd during the Fourth of July parade at the Truman Library in 1994. It was ninety-five degrees that day and almost everyone along the parade route was wearing shorts and a tank top. Half were sitting in lawn chairs next to coolers of beer or soft drinks. I badly wanted to join them.

Thomas and Olivia Daniel at home in Vermont in 1993.

Harrison Gates Daniel, circa 1987.

This family portrait was taken in 1970 in New York. *From left:* are Harrison, seven; Thomas, five; mom; Will, eleven; me, thirteen; and Dad.

The Daniel Family South at Thanksgiving in 1993: Aimee, me, Wesley, and Polly.

This is our last walk with Grandpa in Key West in 1968. Thomas, not quite two, is setting a blistering pace. Will is eight, Harrison is four, and I'm ten. (*Courtesy Dr. Voss*)

me there. What I did not expect was the one-sentence note, written in script on "Margaret Truman" personal stationery:

"I thought he'd go out and get hit by a car or something."

My first reaction was incredulity. We were opening and reading the essays out loud in therapy, and I kept turning Mom's note over and over in my hands, looking for a postscript. I searched the envelope in vain for a second page.

"How do you feel about that?" asked Jim, the counselor.

I have no idea what I said. I don't remember if I ranted and raved or just sat there, shaking my head. I remember feeling a lot of things, though—anger mostly. I couldn't believe she didn't care enough to say something more. She was a writer, after all.

In the years since, I think I've come to understand why my mother wrote that one-line note. I think she just didn't want to believe I had a drinking and drug problem. Maybe that wasn't acceptable to her, given her background. So she ignored the drink and the drugs and focused on the possibility of my getting hurt. The fact that I might stumble across the street drunk one night and get hit by a car summed up all her fears.

I think that by the time my mother's letter arrived, I already knew she wasn't coming for Family Week. That's what they called the third week at Brookwood, when family members were invited down to spend five days living at the treatment center, learning about alcoholism and taking group therapy with patients.

At first it looked like no one in my family would show. Jim called me into his office one day to rave about how stubborn Dad was being. No matter what Jim said, Dad wouldn't back off the assertion that Mom was tied up with a book tour. Jim tried saying everything to get at least one of them to visit, including, "He's your son, your flesh and blood. Don't you care?" To that, Dad had replied something like: "Of course I do, but we have commitments. You can't just expect people to drop everything they're doing and go running to Florida when you want them to."

In Dad's defense, Jim probably did not ask very nicely. He was good at his job, and I found I liked and trusted him to look out for my best interests, but tact was not his strong suit. Again, it was part of Brookwood's overall outlook. They knew what was best for everybody. They were the experts.

It made me mad that Mom wouldn't come. Her refusal, coupled with her letter, made me think she was ducking the whole issue of my alcoholism. More than that, it appeared to me that she cared more about her book sales than about me. Not long ago, she told me that she didn't come because she was afraid that having my well-known mother there would somehow throw a wrench into my treatment.

In the end, despite his protests, Dad came down. A few days before he arrived, I was surprised to learn that Will was coming with him. My brother and I had not had much to say to each other for more than a year. But my surprise was also due to the fact that Will was willing to spend a week in the same room with Dad. If my relationship with Dad was strained, theirs was reaching the breaking point.

For the first two days, Will and Dad went through a shortened version of our own indoctrination. From morning until night each day, they watched movies and heard lectures on alcoholism. Will bristled at the confinement and gagged at the food. Dad took in the lectures, the food, and the people like a plucky tourist booked by accident on a Third World vacation. In the end, he later said, he did not find the experience unpleasant.

About the only time his stay did come near unpleasantness was in group therapy. I was very unsure of myself in that area. I was torn between the dread of airing the dirty family laundry and the wish to hurl accusations and, by doing so, forge some kind of new understanding with my father. In the end, I did neither.

In family therapy, we used what they called "the empty chair." This was literally an empty chair that sat in the middle of the room. Patients and their family members took turns talking to the empty chair as if there were someone in it, even if that someone was really somewhere else in the room. The idea was that talking to the chair was easier than confronting someone directly.

The chair was also used to enable patients to talk to people who were not in the room. One of my housemates used the empty chair to apologize to his sixteen-year-old son. The boy had been killed in a car wreck while his father, who was supposed to be caring for him, was on a three-day drunk.

In therapy, I used the empty chair to confront Dad about his emotional distance. It is a complicated issue, and I wasn't then sure of how to proceed, since I had never tried to put it into words before. This was the first time in my life I had ever confronted my father on anything of any emotional depth. He had always been so unapproachable. Afraid of stepping on toes, I proceeded gingerly. I concentrated on physical symptoms of emotional distance.

"You and Mom weren't around a lot when we were growing up," I told the chair while Dad watched from across the room. "You didn't play with us much."

When it was Dad's turn to answer, he did something I hadn't expected him to do: He defended himself. "We had jobs. We had a family to raise. We had to make money to support all of you," he said. "It would have been nice if we could have spent the whole day playing with you kids, but it just wasn't possible."

At that moment, I began to understand my father's point of view. I didn't necessarily agree with it or even like it, but I began to see it. And it was at that moment that I decided I had been wrong for wanting an apology from my parents. They had not set out to mess me up. They were simply who they were. They did things as they saw fit.

Will and I fared better with the empty chair. For years we had harbored a lot of resentment toward each other. There was no question that I had been a bully to him when we were kids. But what had not come out was the emotional bullying Will employed to pay me back.

It's funny how you fixate on one thing, one habit or personality trait, when trying to sum up a person's actions. For me, Will's attitude toward me was summed up in the way he rolled his eyes at me whenever I said something he didn't agree with. For years, that eye rolling had made me feel like a fool. I told that to the chair.

Then Will, like Dad, did something I didn't expect him to do: He apologized.

"I didn't realize that I might have been contributing to your problem," he said. "It just never occurred to me that I was having an effect on you."

At the end of the therapy sessions, Will and I, who had not really spoken to each other for a year, resolved to keep in touch and forge a better relationship. Dad and I didn't make any similar promises, but we had taken a first step toward more normal relations. I had begun to learn to put blame behind me, and I think he realized that he might have done things a little differently.

We ended up, like everyone else in family therapy, being required to give each other a big hug. It was the fastest three-way hug you have ever seen in your life.

I left Brookwood about a week after my brother and father. I had been there a month. When I flew out of Orlando that day, I took with me the phone numbers of a couple of my housemates, as a fail-safe, and a month's supply of Antabuse. I left behind the swamp, the alligators and armadillos, and about five pounds I had sweated off jogging around their territory.

I had felt safe at Brookwood but had not liked being there. I had trusted the staff, but had not liked their attitude. I had disdain for the training films and the group therapy. The food had been awful. I had been convinced that I had a drinking problem, but they couldn't convince me it was permanent. In the back of my mind, I knew I would drink again someday.

But at the same time, I knew for certain that alcohol and drugs were never going to run my life again. I had been sober for a month, long enough to get a good look at what was possible, what kind of human being I might be. And for the first time in a long time, I liked what I had seen.

13

Wedding Bells

I came out of Brookwood Lodge like a blank slate. I had not matured emotionally since I started drinking heavily, which was during my freshman year in college. Here I was at age twenty-six, looking at the world through the eyes of an eighteen-year-old. When I came out, I set about trying to remake myself.

I had very little idea of how to go about it. I had no idea who or what I was trying to become; I just knew that I wanted to be a different person. I remember the first year and a half after leaving Brookwood as very confusing. To create some kind of order, I concentrated first on little things. Since I had previously spent so much of my sober time avoiding people, I now made it a point to look them in the eye and say hello when I passed. Since I had not given a damn about the places I had worked or the communities in which I had lived, I now felt compelled to pick up trash around the newspaper office and report broken vending machines or clogged toilets.

Physically I became a zealot. The thought of the years of abuse I had heaped on my body terrified the health nut within me. I kept up the running I had started on the edge of the Kissimmee swamp and added weightlifting. At meals I ate lots of vegetables, avoided butter, and poured only low-calorie dressing on my frequent salads. Gradually I began to wean myself from cigarettes.

At times I carried my new health kick too far. I became paranoid about toxins in the environment. I moped over newspaper articles about drinking water contaminated by pesticide runoff from farms. I despaired at the malodorous emissions from the paper mill across the river. While running one evening, I got caught for a split second in a cloud of pesticide from a mosquito-spraying truck and was apoplectic for a week.

I was often afraid of getting sick. Celia Riverbank, one of my colleagues at the *Star-News,* rolled her eyes every time I did a medical story and started imagining I had the symptoms of whatever disease I was writing about. The only thing that concerned me more than my health was my relationship with the opposite sex.

Coming out of Brookwood, the first person I chose to have a relationship with had been another alcoholic, although I did not know it. Despite my physical sobriety, I still thought like an alcoholic, so she seemed perfectly normal. And, of course, she didn't know she was an alcoholic. I didn't even figure it out until she broke up with me, which she did in a very novel way—by pretending to me that she had a venereal disease.

We didn't last more than a couple of months. Either I made her think too much about the possibility of her own problem with alcohol, or she just wasn't having fun with a guy who drank ginger ale every night and wanted to go home early. There may have been a host of other reasons, including the fact that I was unsure of myself and therefore somewhat clingy. But whatever her reasons, she couldn't make herself just come out and tell me it was over. She stopped taking my calls when she was at work and didn't bother returning them later.

Finally, when I called her at home one day, she dropped the bomb. She told me that she had herpes and that I might have been infected. She said she had contracted the disease from her ex-husband, who had been a CIA agent. He had apparently picked it up from a prostitute while spying in some exotic locale.

"But I don't think you could have caught it," she told me that day. "It's not always infectious."

"What do you mean it's not always infectious?"

"Well, I mean, sometimes I can pass on the virus, and sometimes I can't."

"Great. Were you . . . was it infectious on the nights we, uh . . ."

"No."

"Are you sure?"

"Oh, yeah. No problem."

Well, I wasn't so sure. She insisted that she couldn't have passed on the disease unless she was having a periodic outbreak. But I didn't know a thing about herpes, and I was concerned for my health. I hoped someday to get married and have children, and it seemed that having incurable herpes might conceivably interfere with that plan. So I asked to speak to her doctor. I wanted some reassurance.

The next day I got a call from someone who said he was her doctor, but he didn't sound much like a doctor to me. To begin with, he seemed extraordinarily uncomfortable talking to me. At first, I thought he was reluctant to discuss a patient, even though he supposedly had her permission. But after I hung up, it occurred to me he hadn't seemed so much reluctant as uninformed. His answers had been very general, and he had not used a speck of medical terminology.

Some weeks later, when I heard that my ex-girlfriend had a new boyfriend and that they liked to spend nights closing down bars together, it hit me that her "doctor" was probably not her doctor but a friend—maybe even the new boyfriend—posing as her doctor to get her off the hook. I thought I recognized the trick for what it was because a few months earlier, if I had been in her shoes, I would have done the same sort of thing.

Although my thinking was changing during my first year out of the treatment center, my own love affair with drinking and drugs was not over.

For the first six months I was back in Wilmington, I stayed completely sober. I took Antabuse daily and attended several Alcoholics Anonymous meetings each week. The latter was a stipulation for continued employment with the *Star-News,* as were regular one-on-one meetings with a substance abuse counselor in town.

After only a few months, I began to hate going to the AA meetings. At Brookwood, they had invited local AA members to conduct meetings in the treatment center so we would all become accustomed to the program. It was assumed we would continue with it after our release. But I had never liked AA. I didn't agree with the program's emphasis on "surrendering to a higher power," as they put it. It may be arrogant of me, but I had always seen the relationship with God as more like a partnership or that of a parent to a child, not a lord to a servant. And I didn't like the idea of letting someone or some "higher power" resolve my problems. I wanted to do that for myself.

In Wilmington, the people in AA began to wear on me. There was an awful lot of whining during meetings. "I didn't have a drink again today, but I wanted to drink real bad, because my day was so awful and my life is so awful and my parents are so awful . . . blah, blah, blah." I had reached a point where staying sober was not the number-one priority for me anymore. Rightly or wrongly, I wasn't worried about drinking or not drinking. I wanted to get on with my life, to talk about the future, to hear something positive, to know that there were great horizons to reach. But these people seemed to be stuck in place.

On top of it all, I let one of my fellow AA members borrow about two hundred dollars from me, and he never paid me back. He even quit coming to that particular group so he wouldn't have to face me. That left me with yet more bad feeling toward my fellow alcoholics.

It wasn't until years later that I found out that there were other AA groups more progressive than the one I was in. That particular group had been largely for newcomers, which was why everyone seemed to be wallowing in self-pity. Still, I don't know that I would have tried a more progressive AA group even if I had known about one. By the time I left my group, I had made up my mind that I wanted to finish up my rehabilitation on my own.

The first time I had a drink after leaving Brookwood was in New York in July 1984, on the outdoor patio of the Lion's Rock restaurant on East 77th Street. It was a glass of Pouilly-Fuissé. I had stopped taking the Antabuse about a month before, knowing that it took at least two weeks to clear out of the bloodstream. Nevertheless I sipped the wine slowly, waiting for it to make me sick.

Earlier that day, I had left Fire Island, where my parents had thrown a party for me to celebrate my sobriety. Their intentions had been good, but I had a hard time enjoying myself. Everybody at the party was drinking except me. It was tough walking around and making small talk amid the jingle of ice cubes and the popping of pull tabs. All I wanted to do was get into New York and fall off the wagon where none of them could see me.

I had looked forward to this for weeks, so I landed with a resounding thud. The whole mechanism for my misguided behavior was still in place, even after six months sober. Still, drinking turned out to be much less fun that I thought it would be. After six months being sober, I found I did not have the capacity I used to. More than that, though, the feeling of being drunk again was unsatisfying. I woke up the next morning feeling not only sick but stupid for blowing six months of sobriety.

But that bad experience didn't keep me from falling off the wagon again. In fact, I have never quit drinking entirely. In those early days, I would go on a toot, then stay stone-cold sober for months. Even after I met and married my wife, I was prone to lapses. It has taken years of learning self-control on my part—and some nagging on hers—to whittle my drinking down to normal dimensions.

I met Polly in the spring of 1985, a year and a half after I left the treatment center. I first saw her at the Pilot House restaurant on Wilmington's waterfront. She was carrying plates of food all up her arm. She was not my waitress, but I kept wishing she was. I had a date that evening, but my eyes kept wandering to Polly.

I can't say that it was any one feature or collection of features that drew my attention, though Polly's features are arranged very nicely. Looking at her, I felt as if I had always been carrying around a mental picture of the woman I was going to marry and here she was, walking around in a black uniform with fetching puffy sleeves and a white apron.

Polly had noticed me as well, a year and half earlier. Before I had been packed off to Brookwood, she had seen me sitting with a large group at the restaurant. It must have been a newspaper party of some kind, but my heart was apparently not in it. I had my chair pushed back from the table and was ignoring the others, looking morose. I looked so sorry, in fact, that Polly wanted to come over and ask me what was wrong.

Even after I "discovered" Polly, it took me months more to ask her out. I was not only shy, but in the middle of a breakup with the woman I had been ignoring at the Pilot House in order to look at Polly. In the meantime, I stalked Polly, often eating lunch or dinner at the Pilot House. I didn't go so far as to figure out her schedule, but a few times I got lucky and drew her as my waitress. The place is expensive, so I ate a lot of salads. Finally, after lunch one day in the spring of 1985, I approached Polly at the restaurant's bar.

"Would you like to go out sometime?"

"Sure," she said with a big smile. "Want to go running this weekend?"

That wasn't at all what I had in mind. I was thinking more of dinner and a movie. And I had no idea that Polly was a runner. As it turned out, she wasn't. In fact, she had never run for exercise in her life; she couldn't even make a mile. She told me later that she had been so nervous when I asked her out that she blurted out the first idea that came to her. That night, she went to her roommate, Becky Brelsford, a competitive runner, and pleaded with her to help get her in shape for her date.

For three days they went running together, Polly lurching along in the lead and Becky jogging behind her. "No, no. You're wasting energy," Becky would shout. "Stop swinging your arms so much. Take a smoother stride."

Polly chugged along, but just as she had feared, she pooped out before she even ran a mile. Finally she gave up altogether. "It's no use," she said to Becky. "When he comes, I'll just tell him you're going running with him."

That would not have been what I had in mind at all. I like Becky, but it wasn't Becky I had a crush on. Plus, she is a heck of a lot faster that I am and would have run me into the ground. As it turned out, she didn't have to. A weekend assignment came up and I had to cancel the date.

I didn't get a chance to ask Polly out again for three weeks. This time, it wasn't running she suggested, but an outdoor jazz concert. Next to the running, this was the last thing I wanted to do on a date. I know nothing about jazz. Will is the jazz expert in the family. I gathered Polly was also a jazz fan, and I just knew I was going to spend our entire first date being dense about jazz.

It turned out that Polly knew no more about jazz than I did. The concert was rained out, and we, and about two dozen others, ducked into a utility shed near the amphitheater where the concert had started. Members of the band ducked in with us and started an impromptu jam session. Near the end of a song, one of the saxophone players began grinding out notes, making the horn squeak and grunt. It sounded terrible to me, but Polly seemed fascinated. So I thought this must be very avant garde and that I was simply clueless. Just then, Polly turned to me.

"I don't know about you," she said, "but I think that sounds kind of like a moose caught on a barbed-wire fence."

Our next date was much better. We just went to dinner, then back to Polly's little rented house, where we sat on the couch and talked until four o'clock in the morning. I was a zombie at work the next day, but it was worth it. I learned the entire Polly Bennett saga.

Aside from being a waitress, she was a jewelry designer who created necklaces and earrings from handmade porcelain. Later on, she and I would spend many weekends at craft shows, sitting at her display table, talking, getting to know each other.

Polly was born and raised in Harvey, Illinois. Her father, Sam Uhl Bennett, was a native Missourian—and Truman fan—who had been a mechanic and garage owner. He died of lung cancer when Polly was seventeen.

Polly was born dyslexic. But though she had been in and out of reading clinics all her life, her dyslexia wasn't diagnosed until she was a senior in high school. She is naturally shy, and her shyness is compounded by the dyslexia. Where I am talkative and outgoing and comfortable in front of large groups of people, Polly gets the willies if confronted with more than a handful.

Polly's mother, Paula, is the oldest of three daughters and a son born to Paul and Bernice Soenksen of Harvey. Mr. Soenksen owned the Big Eagle Department Store in town. The family also had a house on Bass Lake, Indiana, where Paula and her sisters and brother, and later their families, spent summers.

Polly's family could not be more unlike my own small brood. She grew up in a big, rowdy bunch of three older sisters and six cousins—not to mention an army of second cousins and aunts and uncles by marriage. Paula's sister Dannie and her husband, Art Webber, have two girls, Becky and Jody. The other four cousins, three sons and a daughter belonging to Paula's youngest sister Carol and her husband, Jack Pembroke, moved to Australia when Polly was in grade school. Two of the four, Linda and John, came back to the United States, but the other two—and their parents—still live part of the year in Australia. When you meet Paul or Wesley Pembroke, you're less likely to hear "hello" than "G'day, mate."

Two other cousins, Alyssa and Anne Bennett, daughters of Sam Bennett's brother Bill and his wife, Madge, live in La Grange, Illinois, near Harvey. Two more cousins, sons of Polly's uncle, Bill Soensken, live in Hawaii. My mother-in-law and one sister-in-law, Aimee Parker, live in Wilmington. Paula is now married to K. K. Grubbs, so his three kids, Gary, Steve, and Sandy, who all live in North Carolina (Steve lives in Wilmington), are now part of the family equation.

Big as it is, Polly's family is close. Paula sends out annual family newsletters to keep the far-flung elements informed of one another's doings. To keep in touch with those who live closer, she uses the phone. Every week she calls her two oldest daughters, Lisa and Phoebe, who also live in La Grange. She calls Polly and Aimee far more often. Paula lives in Wilmington and sometimes works with Polly all day at their baby shop, yet she calls at least once a day. When the phone rings, I can say, "Give my best to your mother," and I'll be right on target ninety percent of the time. The other ten percent of the time, it's Aimee who is calling.

Paula's involvement spills over onto me as well. Early in my marriage, I came downstairs late one Sunday morning and fell over a chair that hadn't been there the night before. Paula and Polly had kindly rearranged the furniture on the first floor.

It was because Paula is so close to her daughters that Polly insisted I call to ask her permission to marry her in August 1985.

Earlier that summer, I had taken Polly to New York to meet Mom and Dad. After a night in the city, we went out to Fire Island. My mother, who had for years turned a blind eye whenever I sneaked a girl into my room, made Polly and me sleep in separate bedrooms. Since this was a serious romance, she decided to be old-fashioned about it.

When Polly was out on the beach one day, my mother gave me my grandmother Truman's diamond engagement ring, the one Grandpa had bought in New York on the way back from his tour in France at the end of World War I. It would turn out that the ring fit Polly's finger perfectly.

Polly and I had talked often about marriage, so my proposal in August wasn't a surprise. We were soul mates, if not perfectly matched. Polly said that what she liked about me was that I was gentle and caring, but not perfect, which she also liked. She figured she wasn't perfect, either, so there was room in the relationship for both of us to grow. What she didn't like about me was the partying.

In September, we moved in together, planning to get married June 28, 1986, on what would have been my grandparents' seventy-seventh wedding anniversary.

Polly got more than she bargained for that first year, as I continued to indulge in late nights. After an engagement party at Paul and Ursula's New York apartment just before Christmas, I kept Polly out all night. I was so hungover the next day, my father had to take her shopping, something I had promised to do. Needless to say, my parents were horrified. They thought I had returned to the kind of behavior that got me sent down to Florida. To this day, my mother nags me to come home early whenever I visit them in New York.

Personally and professionally, I was still adrift. Since returning from the treatment center, I had been writing features for the *Star-News* Lifestyle Department. The more relaxed format and relaxed deadlines appealed to me, and I had begun to enjoy my work, but I still saw acting as my way to fame and fortune.

In 1984, before I met Polly, I starred in two shows in a small dinner theater in the Historic District, then played in a British comedy at the University of North Carolina at Wilmington. Not long after that, I met a New York actor named Lou Criscuolo, who had come to Wilmington for stage and movie work and stayed to found a professional theater troupe, the Opera House Theatre Company. For his first show, he lured Joe Namath to town to star in *Cactus Flower.* Mr. Namath's new wife, Deborah Mays, was to star opposite him. Lou cast me in the fourth lead, as Igor Sullivan, the neighbor who falls in love with Deborah.

Mr. Namath could not have been nicer or easier to work with. Our director, Lee Yopp, was a former football coach who ran rehearsals like a scrimmage. He even went so far as to count the number of laughs he thought we should be able to squeeze out of each scene, as if they were a series of completed passes.

"There were thirty-one laughs in that last scene," he would snap after a run-through. "You only got eighteen. Let's try it again."

Mr. Namath was in good shape despite his knees, which he guarded like a pair of Ming vases. They slowed him down on the theater stairs, but he had no trouble churning out laps in a local health-club pool every day. He was acutely aware of his famous injuries. When asked during an interview what advice he would give to young people, he said: "Take care of your health. It's the most precious thing you've got."

Deborah Mays Namath worked as hard as her husband, maybe harder. She'd been a television actress when they'd met, and this was her first time onstage. Her nervousness about being a novice wasn't helped when Lou packed her entire family into one of the theater boxes on opening night.

The box hangs practically over the stage, and Deborah started each show on her back on a bed, her head hanging over the end. "Oh, my God," she said coming offstage after the first scene. "I opened my eyes, and there was my whole family staring at me upside down."

I have a signed poster from the Namaths on which he wrote: "Mr. America [which is what he called me in a line from the show], Nice going. However, if I *ever* catch you kissing my wife again, I'll . . ."

After *Cactus Flower,* I did *A Funny Thing Happened on the Way to the Forum* for Lou. At about the same time Polly agreed to marry me, I started rehearsals for the Opera House production of *Arsenic and Old Lace,* directed by movie producer Frank Capra Jr., whose father had directed the 1941 film version starring Cary Grant. It was Mr. Grant's role, Mortimer Brewster, that I was playing.

At the same time I was doing all these plays, I made a foray into a different sort of performing—as Harry Truman's grandson.

Wilmington is a small town with a sizable retirement community. With so many people of my parents' generation around to recognize the name Clifton Daniel, my link to my grandfather has never been much of a secret in Wilmington. Nor has it been a big deal.

From time to time, community groups asked me to speak to their members about my family, but I usually turned them down. I think the most honest reason is that I really didn't think I had much to say. But I told them—and myself—that it was because I wanted to be my own man. Every one of them seemed to understand.

But in the winter of 1984–85, a history professor at the University of North Carolina at Wilmington, Bob Toplin, asked me to speak to his class. He asked me not to talk about my family but to tell his students how growing up in a president's family had affected me personally. For me, this was a chance to try to talk out loud about what I had been through and maybe whine a bit. So I jumped at the chance. I told them all the details, from playing in Harry Truman's backyard to looking out at the swamp in Kissimmee.

A few weeks later, the whole thing backfired. I was doing a play at the university at the same time. When the editor of the university newspaper came to interview me for an article about the play, he asked me only three questions. I was curious about that, and my pride was hurt, but I forgot about the interview until I saw the article, about a quarter of which was about me and my history in New York. Reading it, I realized the editor had been in the history class I had spoken to and had taken most of his story from there, including some of the more lurid details. That put me off speaking about my family—or even telling anyone I was Harry Truman's grandson—for several years.

Polly and I were married in Wilmington on June 28, 1986, one of the hottest days of that year.

Polly wanted the ceremony performed by Thomas Brady, minister of her hometown church. The problem was, we weren't getting married in Harvey. So we approached a Wilmington church where we knew the minister and several members of the congregation and asked if having a guest preacher was possible. Polly and I weren't even sure it would be polite to ask such a thing, but the minister happily said it was, adding that he would be delighted to assist. He proceed to exchange cordial letters with Father Brady, discussing the details.

For reasons we will never know, as the wedding day approached, the tone of the letters changed. They went from "Dear Tom—Looking forward to having you . . ." to "Dear Father Brady—I'm afraid some changes will have to be made . . ." Finally, the night of the rehearsal, the Wilmington minister deposed Father Brady and announced he would be performing the ceremony. My soon-to-be mother-in-law, a longtime parishioner and friend of Father Brady, had to be restrained by the good father himself from throttling the other minister.

I was almost as much of a hazard to my own wedding as that other minister. The day of the ceremony, my brothers and I changed into our strollers in their room at the Hilton. Then I scooped up an armload of official wedding papers, including the marriage license. Minutes later, the four of us arrived at the church to find Paul, my best man, waiting for us. He, Ursula, Dede, Jason, and several other close friends from New York had flown in the night before.

Also waiting for us at the church was the usurping minister. "If you've got the license, we'll just go ahead and sign it now—get that out of the way," he said.

"Sure," I said. We were still on speaking terms, since I couldn't get married without him. "I've got it right here."

But I didn't. The license was nowhere in the pile.

"I can't perform the ceremony without that license," the minister said.

Thomas and Will and I bolted for the Hilton and turned their room upside down. No license. I went back to the church, which was now filling with guests, to plead with the minister.

"I'm sorry, but I can't marry you unless I have that license signed," he said.

It was my mother-in-law's opinion that this was horse hockey. "You're already married as far as the state's concerned," she said. "This is just a formality. He could perform the ceremony and have you sign that license when you find the darn thing."

Father Brady said happily that we could forgo the church wedding and he would marry us at the historic peanut plantation where we were having the reception. By now we had a church full of sweaty guests who wanted to see a wedding. The string quartet we had hired had begun to play its repertoire.

The other minister wouldn't budge on the license requirement, so I went back to the hotel room a second time and tore up my parents' room, though I wasn't sure I had even been in there. Still no license. Again I went back to the church to plead again with the rector, but he was still the Rock of Gibraltar.

The third time I went back to the hotel, Paul went with me. It was four o'clock, time for the wedding. The string quartet had started to play their program through for the second time. It was ninety-five degrees outside, and Paul and I were beginning to broil in our gray wool jackets.

In the car on the way to the Hilton he said, "If we don't find the license this time, we better just keep on going to the airport and hop a plane to South America."

It did seem hopeless. I couldn't for the life of me figure out where the damn thing had gone. In the elevator on the way up to my parents' room, I hung my head, staring at the floor, wondering what I was going to tell Polly. As the elevator doors opened on the fourth floor, I caught sight of what looked like the corner of a piece of paper peeking out from under the bench in the hall. It turned out to be the missing license, which had slipped from that bundle of papers I was carrying and wafted under the bench.

Back at the church, there was a fight brewing. As Paul and I sprinted from the car, Dad had the priest backed up against the wall outside the sanctuary and was jabbing a finger at his chest. He was redder around the collar than the southern heat dictated. Waving the license before him was the only thing that cooled him off.

After all that the ceremony went smoothly. At first I was completely unflappable, having achieved a runner's high sprinting back and forth to the Hilton. My composure didn't even crack when I saw my mother-in-law crying. I didn't flinch when I looked across the aisle and saw tears in my own mother's eyes. But when I glanced at Dad and saw that he looked like he was crying, too, I almost lost it.

At the reception at Poplar Grove Plantation, we stood in a receiving line in the plantation house for an hour in the heat. No one had thought to turn on the air conditioning until the very start of the reception. Despite the temperature, Mom managed to produce a substantial chill when she saw the ceremony-stealing minister coming through the line. "What are you doing here, you son of a bitch?" she said, refusing to shake his hand. "Why don't you leave?"

He did—about ten minutes later. The only reason any of us could think of for his taking over the ceremony was to get his name in the paper. If that was the reason, he was foiled. The paper had already been printed—with Father Brady listed as the officiating clergyman.

After blistering the minister, Mom was cooled down by Michael Kendrick, who, since driving me to the treatment center, had become a New Hanover County sheriff's deputy. He was apparently schooled in dealing with crises. After the receiving line broke up, he handed my mother a glass of white wine and led her into the living room. "Come over here. I think I've found something you'll like," he said.

"I'd like to get out of this heat," she said, looking as though she might melt.

"Stand right here," Michael said.

He stood her over one of the air vents, which was furiously trying to overcome the heat by churning out an arctic blast. In seconds, Mom's violet taffeta dress filled like a balloon with cool air. The smile on her face was beatific. "Oh, thank you!" she said.

14

Settling Down

Polly and I honeymooned in Maine. We had considered about a half dozen other places, including France, Italy, and Ireland—but they were way too expensive. Besides, every time we mentioned a place to my parents, Dad sent an envelope full of brochures, travel books, and hotel pamphlets. So we either had to pick a place fast or open a travel library.

Maine turned out to be a smart choice, not only because it's a beautiful state, but because Mainers mark their roads so well. You could find your way around that state in a blizzard, which, I suppose, given the climate, is the point. Polly and I had also rented a big luxury-model car with a digital speedometer and power steering, which beat hell out of my little no-power-steering Nissan. You could pull a shoulder muscle trying to make a turn in that thing.

The only mistake I made on that honeymoon was taking only a week off for the trip. I used up the other week before the wedding in case Polly needed my help with preparations. She did not. There is apparently nothing more useless than a prospective groom.

The day after we flew back from Maine, I was back at my desk at the *Star-News,* which was about the last place I wanted to be. Despite the fact that I liked my colleagues and thought I owed the newspaper a huge debt of gratitude, my heart wasn't in my work.

I still wanted to be an actor, so as far as I was concerned, newspaper work was just a way to pay the bills. Writing was also hard for me, especially since it was both my parent's profession and both had been successful at it. I felt—and still feel sometimes—that I didn't measure up. As a result, I often put off starting stories while I fretted over where to find sources. I always worried that I wasn't going to be able to cover every angle, think of every point of view. By the time I got around to starting, I had little time left to finish, so the work was often sloppy.

Acting was the only thing that was uniquely my own. My mother had done some acting, but if she'll forgive me for saying so, she did not make the whopping career out of it that she has with murder mysteries. She was good at it. I remember seeing her in a play in a dinner theater in New Jersey when I was eight or nine years old and being very proud of her.

I had some justification for thinking that I might still make it as an actor. To begin with, since I wasn't plastered all the time, I had actually learned to act. I won't be vain or crazy enough to say I turned into a great actor, but I can say that I have been known to get through a play without making the audience want to get up and leave the theater. And I assumed that since I could act, I would, of course, be discovered.

In 1983, the year I moved to Wilmington, Dino DeLaurentiis had opened a movie studio on the outskirts of town, DeLaurentiis Entertainment Group (DEG) Studios. When the studio came to town, so did scads of producers, directors, and casting agents. I didn't think it was farfetched that one of them might spot me and haul me off to Hollywood.

In the year before Polly and I were married, and for about a year after, my entire social life was the theater. I went from one production to another, playing a lead in one, a spear carrier in the next, then a lead again.

Just before the wedding, Lou Criscuolo, founder of the Opera House Theatre Company, gave me the part of Brick in *Cat on a Hot Tin Roof*. I wanted the role so badly that I actually considered postponing my honeymoon to rehearse. But ultimately I gave up the role to Brian Kerwin, who was in town filming the sequel to *King Kong*, *King Kong Lives*, for DeLaurentiis. Kerwin, who became famous playing Sally Fields's wayward ex-husband in *Murphy's Romance*, had met Lou and expressed interest in playing Brick. And he was surely a bigger box-office draw than I was.

In return for giving up Brick—and avoiding being throttled by my bride for trying to give up my honeymoon—Lou promised me the lead in any show I wanted. I chose Randall P. McMurphy in *One Flew Over the Cuckoo's Nest.* I did the role in the spring of 1987, right after playing Salieri in the Opera House Theatre Company production of *Amadeus.* That role was grueling because old Salieri never leaves the stage during the entire two-and-a-half-hour performance.

Both plays were successes in Wilmington, and I thought that since I was on such a hot streak, I should try a musical, so I agreed to play Bobby in the musical *Company. Big* mistake. This was the lead role, so naturally it called for a lot of singing, something I don't do.

Two comments I heard afterward illustrate just how well I did. The first came from Michael Titterton, the manager of Wilmington's public radio station and sometime actor. After he saw the show, he arrived backstage and patted me on the shoulder. "You're very brave, Clifton," was all he said.

A few days later, I was in a field picking blueberries with Polly and a couple of friends when I bumped into Charlotte Parker, a member of an old Wilmington family and an ardent theatergoer. When she saw me, she peeked out from under her wide-brimmed straw sun hat and said, "Saw *Company,* Clifton. Not your best work."

I was lucky that neither Paul Hume nor any of his heirs saw the show. Hume was the music critic for the *Washington Post* who wrote a scathing review of one of my mother's concerts while my grandfather was still in office. Grandpa dashed off a hot-tempered note to Hume and managed to sneak it by his press officers. The note was plastered all over the papers the next day. Grandpa's act drew criticism from the media and government officials, but he got tons of letters of support from other parents like himself.

New York Times photographer George Tames told me years later that after Grandpa managed to squeak that letter by his staff, they bought him a special brass mailbox, should he want to mail any more letters like it. At the bottom, below the slot, there was stamped the word INCINERATOR.

I have actually received only two bad reviews in my short stage career. Neither of them was for *Company,* mostly because the critic at the *Star-News* is far too nice to be a critic. Even the worst of his reviews of local theater have always been mostly constructive.

Not so the review of *Guys and Dolls* written by a theater professor at the University of North Carolina at Wilmington, who implied that I was stiff onstage. He said I acted the part of Nathan Detroit as if I still had the hanger in my coat.

The worst review was written by a woman working for a local weekly, *Encore.* I played Zack, the choreographer, in *A Chorus Line.* The reviewer slathered praise on every member of the cast until she got to me. "Clifton Daniel has one speed: Dull," she wrote. She went on to say that I had dragged the entire show down, which I found hard to believe, since Zack doesn't do anything but ask questions over a microphone. You don't even see him for most of the show.

I found out later that the reviewer was the wife of yet another university professor I had left out of a story on a new art-film series in town. I left him out not to be mean but because everyone connected with the series told me that he hadn't done anything.

Critics notwithstanding, by 1987 I thought I had come to a point where I needed to fish or cut bait as an actor. So I went to New York to meet with an agent for the William Morris Agency. He told me that he would be happy to represent me, but that I would have to move to Los Angeles or New York to be close to the movie and television business.

That left me with a dilemma. Polly's life and mine were in Wilmington. All our friends and part of her family were here. We liked the pace in Wilmington. I couldn't just uproot the both of us and move to a huge city. Los Angeles was out of the question; we didn't know a soul there. And what were we going to do if I went back to New York, move in with my parents? My mother didn't even want me back in New York, for fear that my being in the city would somehow trigger the drinking and drug taking again.

My decision was complicated by the fact that I had not just Polly and myself to consider. We had found out in the fall of 1986 that Polly was pregnant.

I had never really seriously considered having children. I liked kids—other people's kids. Of course, when friends saw that, they said, "Oh, you'd make such a good father!" They probably also said it because they knew I was basically just a big kid myself.

Gammy and Grandpa Truman had wanted more than just the one child they got, but two babies died during childbirth before Mom was born. My grandparents had married late, in an age when people married early. He was thirty-five, she was thirty-four. When Mom was born in 1924, Gammy was thirty-eight, old for a first-time mother even by today's standards.

Mom and Dad also waited to get married and have children. When I was born, Dad was forty-four and Mom was thirty-three. When my youngest brother, Thomas, came along, Mom was forty-two; Dad, fifty-three.

Once married, Polly and I sailed her birth-control pills into the wastebasket. It wasn't only because we were dying to become parents, though we were. Polly also has endometriosis, a condition in which cells of the lining of the uterus grow uncontrolled throughout the abdominal cavity. Because of the disease, Polly wasn't even sure she could have children. If she could, her doctor told her, she had to do it quickly, before the condition worsened.

Aimee Elizabeth Daniel was born about 7 P.M. on August 22. She was named Aimee for Polly's older sister, Aimee Bennett Parker, and Elizabeth for her great-grandmother, Elizabeth Virginia Wallace Truman.

Like me, Aimee was a difficult child from the start. Polly began having labor pains late on Thursday, August 20. That night and all the next day, she paced the floor, having contractions every ten minutes, unable to eat or rest, grousing at those of us who could.

Polly was admitted to the hospital at seven on Saturday morning and went into serious labor about ten. Her sister, Aimee, and I were at the hospital with her.

The hospital had "birthing rooms" with adjustable beds for the mother-to-be and a television set at the foot of the bed so the rest of us could watch movies while she writhed in agony. Aimee and I spent the better part of Polly's labor watching Saturday afternoon movies, including James Cagney in *White Heat.* I kept thinking how dramatic it would be if Aimee had been born at the end of the movie, while Cagney was standing on top of the exploding gas tank yelling, "Top of the world, Ma!"

During each of Polly's contractions, it was Aimee's job to dab her sister's forehead with a damp washcloth. My job was to vigorously massage her lower back, where her labor pains were worst, due to the endometriosis. Watching TV too intently during contractions could become hazardous, as I found out when I chose to change channels in the middle of one.

"Clifton, I'm having another one," Polly called.

"Just a second, honey," I said. "I want to see what Jerry Lewis does here."

Up to that time, I hadn't known my wife could curse like that.

When the time came to push, Polly pushed for two solid hours. The pushing seemed so unproductive, in fact, that the doctor, Donald Pole, didn't think Aimee was going to get born without help, so he marched off to find a suction cup. Polly had heard about these suction-cup-assisted births. A friend had told her they were very painful for the mother. So the second she saw Dr. Pole leave the room, she started pushing even harder. Suddenly, to everyone's great surprise, Aimee's head crowned, and the nurse had to say, "Whoa, whoa, whoa! Don't push anymore. We have to wait for the doctor."

But it was like trying to hold back the tide.

It had been agreed beforehand that I would help with the birth. So, with the help of another nurse, I was putting on a gown and gloves when I heard the first nurse yell, "No, no, no! Don't push! Don't push!"

Dr. Pole had just walked back into the room, holding his suction cup, when Polly couldn't resist any longer and nearly fired Aimee through the television set.

"Whoa!" was all he could say as Aimee came flying into the world.

The nurse had just snapped my rubber gloves in place when he turned to me.

"Here, hold her," he said.

"Oh, my God," I said.

I took my very blue, very slippery child by the heels and shoulders and concentrated very hard on not dropping her. It was like holding a bar of soap. I held her upside down while the doctor cleared her nose and throat so she could breathe. While I wasn't concentrating on not dropping her, I had time to notice two things—that she was a girl and that she had her mother's dimple.

With or without a chin dimple, a girl was big news to the Daniel family, which had produced four boys while trying to deliver a girl. In the weeks before Aimee's birth, Dad wrote a piece for *The New York Times*'s Maturity News Service on his hopes of being blessed with a granddaughter.

"Because we've never had a girl in our family, I want the first grandchild to be a girl," he wrote. "So, for now at least, I live in a fantasy world. As I roam the streets of New York, I stop in front of boutiques that sell children's clothes to admire the teeny, tiny dresses, bonnets, and white slippers.

"I never buy anything. My wife says it is bad luck before the baby is born. Besides, she likes boys, and she wants nothing to do with hair ribbons, curlers, and frocks that must be pressed all the time. But I am counting on the accepted wisdom that girls are more affectionate than boys and are more attached to their fathers and grandfathers."

I, too, was counting on having an affectionate little girl, but both Dad and I were foiled by Aimee. It's not that she's not affectionate, just more like a boy than a girl. If you buy her a toy, it better have teeth or a gun attached. And if you try to get her into a teeny, tiny dress or bonnet, she will gladly try to shoot or bite you.

Aimee did not cry the day she was born until the nurse at the hospital carried her into the nursery for weight, measurements, footprints, and a blood sample. As I followed her into the nursery, I didn't know I was going to have to comfort my daughter so soon after her birth, but Polly had prepared me for the job. A month before Aimee was born, she had me talking to our daughter through her belly at night.

"That way, she'll get to know your voice," she said. "When you talk to her, she'll know who her daddy is."

So I would lie down next to Polly, feeling very self-conscious, and put my face near her belly and say, "Hi, baby. How are you? Are you a boy or a girl? Democrat or Republican?" When we asked if Aimee was a girl, Aimee kicked once. There was no response to the question of political affiliation.

All this seemed to have an effect. When the nurse poked Aimee on the heel for the blood test, causing our baby to let out a howl, I stroked her head and tried some soothing words of comfort. At the sound of my voice, Aimee stopped screaming and turned toward me.

The nurse turned from the counter where she was working and said, "Oh, she knows her daddy."

I left Polly on the verge of sleep at the hospital that night and went to a friend's party, determined to celebrate my fatherhood. But I was so pooped I did what Polly was always trying to get me to do at parties: I had two beers and called it a night.

Having a child forced me to grow up. My work ethic and my ideas on career changed. If I was going to have a wife and small child depending on me, I couldn't wait for some producer to discover me, and I couldn't uproot my family and haul them off to some big, dangerous city where they didn't know anybody. And if I was going to stay in Wilmington, I also couldn't keep doing a half-assed job for the people who were paying me a salary.

None of this happened overnight, but I began to learn, for the first time, that there was pride in doing something well, even—and maybe especially—if it wasn't the thing you wanted most to be doing.

But for all the self-awareness fatherhood brought me, I didn't take to it well. The first nine months left me a nervous wreck. Early on, Aimee had colic. When I was alone with her while Polly worked, she would sometimes cry for hours on end, and I would have no idea of how to soothe her. At night I slept fitfully, springing awake every time I heard the tiniest noise.

What worried me most were the fits of sudden rage that came over me whenever I couldn't make Aimee stop crying. It even got to the point that I yelled at her. It was more than just frustration. It was also selfishness. I had not received the attention I thought I needed as a child, so I resented my daughter for wanting some attention herself. Every time I got mad at her, I was instantly ashamed of myself.

Such ugly feelings left me thinking that maybe I wasn't cut out for fatherhood, and I worked up my courage to tell Polly I thought we ought to stop at one. I didn't think I could handle even one more. Polly had always said she wanted four to six kids—something I couldn't even imagine.

The night I decided to tell her, we sat down in the bedroom. She seemed to be in a very good mood, so I thought this would be the perfect time to talk about curbing expansion in the Daniel family. But I hadn't counted on nature.

"Before you say anything, there's something I have to tell you . . ." she began, taking my hand.

My mind went blank after that.

Wesley Truman Daniel was born on Groundhog Day, February 2, 1989, about seventeen months after his sister. He was named Wesley for Polly's favorite cousin, Wesley Pembroke, and Truman after some obscure branch of my family.

Wesley and his sister had opposite sensibilities. He turned out sweet and cuddly, and she was all elbows and knees, wriggling to get down, poking me in the ribs. Maybe it's payback for all the times I got mad at her for crying.

Wesley is my pal. Whenever we go out as a family, he and I pair off. We get along; we understand each other. He learned to say "Daddy" before he learned to say "Mommy" and liked it so much, he called Polly "Daddy" for a few months, which she found slightly annoying.

I'm not worried about Wesley. Aimee is the one who needs my time and attention. And it isn't easy, because she and I like to butt heads. We are very much alike—stubborn, willful, in need of attention. In fact, it was seeing so much of myself in Aimee that made me realize nature had played a big part in my own development. My parents may not have done everything right, but I may not have been the easiest and most charming baby in the world.

Aimee also made me see that some of my parenting techniques were very much like my parents'. I also realize that Aimee's personality is probably due in part to the way I treated her as a baby.

The trick for me now is to try to figure out how to undo what I've done and avoid some of the mistakes I think my parents made with me. I try to spend a lot of time with the children, Aimee especially, and take an interest in what they do. But like my parents, I have a full-time job. I also work on freelance projects at night. Again, like my parents, I think one of my first priorities is making a comfortable life for my family, but I realize that I'm risking my kids' happiness to do it. Someday soon I hope to strike a balance between the two.

My own parents, meanwhile, have been loving, if distant, grandparents. I don't mean emotionally distant, but physically distant, just the way my grandparents Truman were for me. Like Gammy and Grandpa Truman, Gammy and Grandpa Daniel have their own lives. It would never occur to them to pull up stakes and move to North Carolina just because they had a couple of grandchildren there.

Like my own grandparents, Mom and Dad see their grandchildren about once or twice a year. My parents often come down to see me in plays and squeeze in a weekend visit with Aimee and Wesley. Polly and I don't have a guest room for them, so they stay in a hotel. This means we don't have the weeklong visits I used to have with Gammy and Grandpa Truman.

The ritual visit usually starts in the late afternoon. Polly or I pick up Mom and Dad from their hotel, drive them over to the house, and give them a glass of wine. Then my parents sit patiently for an hour or so while Aimee and Wesley trot out their latest toys or show Gammy and Grandpa how they can turn somersaults. Then we all sit down to dinner together.

On one of their earlier visits, Grandpa Daniel got a taste of just what it meant to have a girl in the family. Aimee was about three and in the middle of potty training. As such, she thought she knew all about bathrooms and bathroom etiquette.

During dinner, Dad pushed himself back from the table and announced that he had to use the bathroom, the "little boys' room," as he put it. Aimee immediately climbed down from her chair.

"I'll show you where it is, Grandpa," she said, and led him out of the room.

But Aimee didn't stop at showing her grandfather the location of the bathroom. She thought he might need to know how to use it as well. So, as my father watched in shock, she hiked up her skirt, dropped her training pants, and hopped up on the seat.

Dad came back to the dining room red-faced and laughing. "I think someone needs to have her bottom wiped," he said.

Polly jumped up from the table to retrieve Aimee as Mom and I burst out laughing. A minute later, she came back with Aimee, apologized to my father, and sat our little potty guide back in her seat.

"Well, fine," Dad said. "Now I shall make another attempt to go to the little boys' room."

Off he went, and Mom and Polly and I fell into a deep conversation. Wesley, who was about one year old, was in his high chair, smearing strained peas all over his face in repeated attempts to get the spoon into his mouth. We adults were paying so much attention to him and to our conversation that none of us noticed that Aimee had slipped off her chair and gone after Dad again.

The secret to potty training is that you have to be positive. Whenever Aimee did what she was supposed to do in the place she was supposed to do it, Polly and I clapped and cheered and made a big fuss. "Good girl, Aimee!" We would shout. "Good girl!"

This had a very positive effect on Aimee's potty training, but it also led her to conclude that clapping and cheering was in order whenever anyone, child or adult, went to the bathroom.

Grandpa Daniel was in the bathroom, attending to his business, assuming he had privacy, when the door swung open. There stood Aimee. When she saw what he was doing, a big, proud smile appeared on her face.

"Good boy, Grandpa!" she shouted, clapping her hands together vigorously. "Good boy!"

15

Stories

We love stories in our family. Aimee loves to hear that last one about how she helped potty train Grandpa. She and Wesley also love to hear any other stories I tell them about themselves, especially the one in which Wesley rolled down the stairs and the one in which Aimee fell on the sidewalk while Polly was in the hospital after Wesley's birth.

They also like to hear stories about me when I was a kid, especially the one in which I fell off the couch and split my head open when I was five and the one in which Will and I rode our bicycles down a hill in Central Park and smashed into a tree.

It seems my children like a lot of violence.

They also like the story about when Morgan, our late Lhasa apso–poodle combo, started hacking up popcorn one night and I got so annoyed by the noise that I chased him around the house stark naked, wielding a pillow.

I like to hear stories about my family, too. The trouble is, I've heard all the good ones already, including the one about Grandpa losing his glasses in an artillery attack during World War I. The concussion from an exploding shell blew his glasses right off his face. It was dark, and bombs were blowing up all over the place, so he didn't think it would be a good idea to get off his horse and search for his glasses. Instead, he reached in his pocket and took out his spare pair and galloped off. The next morning, a glance to his rear revealed his first pair of glasses. They were sitting behind him on the rump of his horse.

One of my favorite short stories about my grandfather was told to me by my Aunt Shawsie, Mary Shaw Branton. Aunt Shawsie is one of my mother's oldest friends, having grown up in Independence. Aunt Shawsie and Mom were premier members of a girls' club, the Henhouse Hicks, which used the old henhouse in my grandparents' backyard as home base. As a grown woman, Aunt Shawsie went to see my grandfather one day late in his life, when he was very frail. They had a short visit, and as she stood up to leave, he grabbed his cane and struggled to his feet as well.

"Mr. Truman, you don't have to stand on my account," Aunt Shawsie said.

My grandfather just smiled and said, "I have never not stood for a lady."

That story was actually one of the newest stories about my grandfather I have heard, and I was beginning to think there were no more out there. But the neat thing about being Harry Truman's grandson is that he liked people and he liked to spend time with them, a lot of them. One result is that there seem to be tons of people who have a good story about him.

Hugh Hill of WLS-TV in Chicago remembers watching Grandpa walk out of the Blackstone Hotel in Chicago on his way to an interview with a CBS reporter and camera crew. This was after he was president. On his way through the lobby, he stopped at the bar, ordered a tumblerful of bourbon, and knocked it quickly back. He didn't have another drink the rest of the day.

That's not something I think I should try.

In July of 1994, Mr. Hill was on a panel of dustinguished journalists gathered for a symposium in Chicago. The event commemorated the fiftieth anniversary of my grandfather's nomination as vice president at the 1944 Democratic national convention, also held in Chicago. I was way out of my league, but I took part in the symposium, as did Gen. Donald Dawson, a former Truman aide and now president of the Truman Library, and Prof. Robert H. Ferrell, who has written ten books on my grandfather and knows possibly more about him than Gammy did.

At that symposium, I heard some fresh stories about Grandpa, including *Chicago Sun Times* columnist Irv Kupcinet's tale of overhearing Grandpa persuade Adlai Stevenson to accept the Democratic nomination for president in 1952. That little pep talk took place in the cloakroom of the Blackstone Hotel, after Grandpa had lunch with Mr. Stevenson. Apparently Grandpa conducted a lot of business at the Blackstone.

Mr. Kupcinet not only covered my grandfather's administration but became a family friend as well. So it fell to him to entertain my mother whenever she was in Chicago. The trip he remembers most fondly took place when my mother stopped in Chicago on her way to Los Angeles to be a guest on Jimmy Durante's television show. "Kup" and Russ Stewart, general manager of the *Sun Times,* picked Mom up at the airport and took her to lunch at the Tap Room restaurant. They invariably took Mom to the Tap Room, where the maître d' always gave them the second-best table in the house.

A few days later, when Mom stopped in Chicago on her way back from Los Angeles, Kup and Mr. Stewart again took her to the Tap Room. This time, however, the maître d' seated them at the best table in the house. After the meal, Kup went back to talk to him.

"I don't get it," he said. "Every time we come to this restaurant with Miss Truman, you give us the second-best table in the house. Now, all of a sudden, you give us the best table. What gives?"

"Well, before, she was only the president's daughter," the maître d' said. "Now she's a TV star."

Kup got a look at a congratulatory telegram Grandpa got from another, slightly better known TV star after he won the 1948 election. The telegram was from Bob Hope. All it had on it was one word: "Unpack."

Kup's connections to my family were impressive to at least one of his well-known colleagues, broadcaster Jack Brickhouse, "the voice of the Chicago Cubs." The first time the pair worked together was during a Rams-Bears football game in Los Angeles in the early 1960s. Mr. Brickhouse, by then a veteran announcer, was calling the game. Kup, a relative newcomer to broadcasting, was responsible for halftime interviews.

To be friendly, Mr. Brickhouse told Kup that if he needed any help lining up halftime interviews, give a holler. But Kup said he thought he had things well in hand, thank you.

At halftime, Mr. Brickhouse watched in awe as the first of Kup's interviews came into the booth: champion boxer Carmen Basilio, fresh from his win over Sugar Ray Robinson. Then Bob Hope strolled in and sat down. "And when Harry Truman stepped in and said, "Where's Kup?" I figured this guy didn't need much help from me," Mr. Brickhouse said.

The Secret Service tried to get a little help from the Chicago press corps during one of my grandfather's visits to the city as president. In those days, when the Secret Service was a little less nervous about rooftop snipers and suicide bombers, the press was allowed to follow at the end of the presidential motorcade in their own cars.

That day, the line of limousines and press cars was gliding slowly enough that you could walk beside the cars without breaking a sweat. Despite the absence of suicide bombers, the Secret Service was a little jumpy as the cars crept along one of Chicago's tougher streets. One or two of them then approached the press cars to ask if the reporters would like to walk alongside the presidential limousine and ask my grandfather some questions. Edwin Darby of the *Chicago Sun Times* was among those asked.

"It did not take us too long to figure out that the Secret Service thought it was a fine idea that one of us get shot instead of the president," he said.

Despite the Secret Service's outlook, Grandpa, as always, had a soft spot for reporters. He even sometimes invited members of the Chicago press corps to play poker and watched over them like a mother hen. Mr. Darby was at one game during which a colleague started losing pretty badly. So Grandpa figured he would run up the pot a little, then lose to the man so he could at least win back his stake. The strategy backfired, however, when Grandpa kept drawing to flushes and inside straights—and making them. Mr. Darby said Grandpa finally had to order the reporter out of the game for his own good.

Bill Hannegan also learned about Grandpa's soft side. He was just a boy in 1944 when his father, Bob, served as chairman of the Democratic National Committee. Mr. Hannegan remembered then—and on every subsequent visit to the Hannegan home—that my grandfather took time to talk to him and his siblings. He seemed genuinely interested in them and always asked how they were doing in school. If they said they didn't really like a certain subject, he would try to talk them into liking it better.

Mr. Hannegan also remembered Grandpa's kindness to a Hannegan family friend, Ruth Harper, during the last year of World War II. Mrs. Harper's husband, Roy, whom Grandpa would later make a federal judge, was a U.S. soldier stationed in Australia in 1944. Because the war delayed the mail, Mrs. Harper, who had only been married to Mr. Harper for three or four months when he went overseas, often had to go months without knowing how or where he was.

As vice president and, later, as president, Grandpa kept tabs on Mr. Harper and sent Mrs. Harper weekly letters on his whereabouts and condition.

Such kindness left a lasting impression on the Hannegan family. In the early 1960s, Bill Hannegan's brother was flying to Washington with his wife and five daughters when he noticed my grandparents were on the same plane. So he sent all five girls over to Gammy and Grandpa to say hello.

"You are going to meet the greatest president who ever lived," he told them. The youngest, who was just starting to learn American history in school, looked at her father with wide eyes. But by the time she and her sisters had walked over to my grandparents and introduced themselves, she was wearing an expression of doubt.

The girls chatted with my grandparents for a moment or two before the oldest Hannegan daughter said, "My father says you are the greatest president who ever lived."

Grandpa had worked hard and tried to do the right thing for the country at every turn, so hearing this comment proved very gratifying. Gammy rolled her eyes, but she needn't have worried about Grandpa's ego getting out of control. The second after her sister made the statement, the youngest Hannegan daughter, still wearing that expression of doubt, looked Grandpa dead in the eye and said, "Are you really Abraham Lincoln?"

"Mrs. Truman let out a howl you could hear all over the plane," Mr. Hannegan said.

Bob Wiedrich, a former *Chicago Tribune* reporter, made sure a big chunk of Chicago had a laugh at my grandfather's expense during a visit in 1949. At that time, as Ed Darby pointed out earlier, reporters could join the presidential motorcade with whatever car they happened to be driving. That day in 1949, Mr. Wiedrich pulled in at the end of Grandpa's motorcade in his beat-up, disreputable-looking 1939 Mercury. The driver's-side door on the ten-year-old car was rusted out, and the car itself passed more oil through it than a drilling rig.

"It burned oil so badly that I had to buy oil by the case at Sears, and about every fifty miles I had to put another can of oil in the thing," Mr. Wiedrich said.

So here came a line of gleaming Cadillacs, wending through the city from the airport to the Blackstone Hotel. "At the end of the parade," Mr. Wiedrich said, "is this god-awful-looking, stinking, smoking 1939 Mercury." The car attracted so much attention that as the motorcade neared the Blackstone, he added, "the crowds began applauding us."

That night, Mr. Wiedrich drew what they called the "death watch" at the Blackstone, meaning it was his job to sit in the lobby all night in case anything momentous happened, say, my grandfather having a heart attack or the hotel burning down. Neither of those things occurred, of course, so Mr. Wiedrich spent the night in a chair in the lobby.

Early the next morning, he woke up in time to see the elevator doors slide open. Out stepped my grandfather with two Secret Service agents. On his way across the lobby, Grandpa spotted Mr. Wiedrich and pointed an accusing finger at him.

"You're the young man who ruined my parade," my grandfather said.

"To make me do penance," Mr. Wiedrich went on, "he said

'Come on, kid. We're going to take a walk.' And off we went into Grant Park, and he ran the pants off me."

One of my favorite stories about my grandfather is one I heard long before that Chicago symposium from *New York Times* photographer George Tames, who had covered my grandfather's administration. It's not a joke I'm always comfortable telling in polite company.

In researching the proposal for this book, I had asked Mr. Tames if he recalled anything that would illustrate Grandpa's sense of humor. Grandpa had a great sense of humor, but he wasn't a joke teller. General Dawson cracked that Grandpa's old friend and military aide, Gen. Harry Vaughn, was in charge of telling jokes at the White House. But Mr. Tames recalled that if Grandpa couldn't tell a joke, he sure knew how to get the most out of one.

During Grandpa's presidency, the chief of the Washington bureau of *The New York Times* was a man named Arthur Krock. Mr. Krock, a courtly gentleman from Kentucky, was not above telling an occasional off-color joke to his friends. In Washington, those friends included generals, senators, congressmen, and cabinet members. Sometimes these friends carried Mr. Krock's off-color jokes back to the White House.

One such joke, borrowed by Mr. Krock from Mr. Tames, concerned a man who went to see his doctor with a voice so hoarse it was barely more than a whisper.

"Doc, you've got to do something," he said. "I thought it was just a cold, but it's been getting worse and worse."

The doctor looked down his throat, in his ears and up his nose, but saw nothing suspicious.

"I'll bring my colleagues in here, and we'll give you a thorough going over," the doctor said. "Strip down. I'll be right back."

The man did as he was told, and minutes later, a phalanx of doctors tumbled into the room. Every one of them stopped short when they saw the size of a particular part of the man's anatomy.

"Well, there's your problem," the first doctor stammered. "Look at the size of that thing. You're having to tighten your stomach muscles and chest muscles and neck muscles to hold it up. No wonder you're hoarse."

"Well, what can you do?" the patient asked.

"Well, there's only one solution," the doctor said. "That thing has to go. Now I've got a refrigerator full of smaller ones in the back and we'll just . . ." The rest of the sentence fell on an empty room. The patient had grabbed his clothes and bolted.

But a week later he was back, more hoarse than ever.

"Doc, it's no use," he said resignedly in a barely audible whisper. "I can't talk to my family and I can't do my job. Go ahead with the operation."

So they did, and a few weeks later, the patient went back to see the doctor with a smile on his face and a song in his heart.

"Doc, you're a miracle worker," he said in a booming baritone. "Just listen to me. I've never sounded so good. And, confidentially, everything else works just fine. So, what do I owe you?"

The doctor gave him a great big smile and said in a hoarse whisper, "Oh, not a thing."

Two days after Mr. Krock told that joke to a group of friends, Mr. Tames got called into his boss's office and found his chief face-down on his desk, his shoulders shaking. When Mr. Krock looked up, there were tears running over his cheeks. He was laughing so hard he couldn't breathe.

About five minutes earlier, he'd gotten a phone call.

"Mr. Krock? This is the White House calling, said a secretary. "Will you please hold for the president?"

"Of course," Mr. Krock said, and braced himself for a bawling out over a column or some piece of momentous news. He received neither. An instant later, my grandfather came on the line and in a hoarse voice said, "Hello, Arthur, is that you?"

16

My Brothers and Me

My brothers and I have each dealt differently with being Harry Truman's grandson.

Thomas, the youngest, lives in Vermont. As of February 1995, he was twenty-eight years old. His birthday is May 28, making him a Gemini like me. Like me, he was not thrilled with formal education. He went to prep school in upstate New York, then to the University of Vermont, which he left after only one year. In the interim, he became an occasional follower of the rock group the Grateful Dead. Once he drove from Vermont to Florida and followed the band all the way back up the coast, taking in twelve or fifteen concerts along the way.

Thomas snapped out of his dissatisfaction with school faster than I did. Not long ago, he earned a two-year business degree from Champlain College in Burlington. Today he is circulation manager for a Vermont magazine. He lives on a mountainside with his wife, Nina, their daughter, Olivia, and their son, Truman. Their house, complete with a Gothic turret, overlooks ten acres of pasture and woodland. There is a pond at the base of a hill on their property where, on our last visit, my kids loved catching tadpoles.

Thomas and Nina also raise chickens and keep a pack of three Siberian husky mixes named Otto, Ivan, and Sasha. Polly and I received a Christmas card from Thomas and Nina in 1994 that shows the whole family sitting on a dog sled tethered behind the huskies.

Thomas, who was six when Grandpa died, worries not so much about living up to our grandfather's legacy as being able to give his children the same financial advantages our parents gave us. In that regard, he is like me. We both feel that we are somehow not going to measure up; that we aren't going to be good enough or smart enough or be able to make enough to support our families.

Both of us have had to deal with the sudden bursts of anger. As Thomas describes it, these spells come out of nowhere, without provocation. Olivia will cry or spill something and Thomas will fly into a sudden rage, wanting to take it out on the baby, like I did with Aimee. The instant he feels it coming on, he tries to direct the anger at himself and becomes his own bouncer, as he puts it.

Like me, Thomas never had this problem until he had children. Having to care for children seems to bring up the selfishness we have each harbored for years. Thomas doesn't necessarily share my view. He has not yet decided why these fits of anger plague him, but he works every day to free himself from them. His consolation, like mine, is that he knows the rage will fade someday. He knows this not because I have told him so, though I have, but just because he feels it in his heart.

As for being Harry Truman's grandson, Thomas doesn't hide the fact that he is but won't go out of his way to let it be known, either. He would rather people get to know him for himself first, then find out about his lineage. It works the opposite way for me. Because of my job and my work for the Truman Library, I meet many people who already know about my family. So I figure I have to work a little harder to live up to the reputation.

Because he is the youngest and didn't know Grandpa as well as his older brothers, Thomas considers himself less Harry Truman's grandson and more the son of Margaret Truman and Clifton Daniel. Yet he admits to feelings of guilt over being Harry Truman's grandson, something I have never felt. I figure it was just luck of the draw. But he sometimes feels guilty that he had the luck to grow up on Park Avenue, in the shadow of a famous president.

Conversely, he also finds that being Harry Truman's grandson doesn't carry the same weight with our generation that it did with our parents' generation. "Being a grandson of Harry Truman just isn't that impressive anymore," he said.

Only twice has he been asked to do things purely because of

the connection to our grandfather. Once, the president of Champlain College wanted him to talk Mom into giving the commencement address. She was backup for their first choice and politely declined. The second time involved a Vermont preservation society that asked him to help raise funds to restore the childhood home of a former first lady. Thomas can't remember which first lady it was and didn't have time to take on the job.

Will, on the other hand, has run into many people who have tried to trade on his name or buddy up to him simply because of his lineage, and he resents the intrusion.

Of all of us, Will has asked the most questions, dug the deepest into his own psyche. Thomas and I have often preferred to let sleeping dogs lie. We don't delve into our pasts unless we have to, unless stress or fear gets to be too much or some ugly emotion surfaces. But Will has always searched for answers.

As of February 1995, he was studying for a doctorate in psychology. It would be simplistic to say that his own inner search led him to psychology, but there seems to be some precedent for it. At least he has always been good at psychoanalyzing me.

Of all of us, Will has the most anger and the most compassion. He has worked on several campaigns for idealistic New York politicians and in the late 1980s started a campaign to register New York's homeless to vote so they would have a say in policies that affected them.

Will's idealism has sometimes brought him afoul of Mom and Dad. In the spring of 1986, my mother was asked to rededicate the USS *Missouri,* which had recently been modified to run on nuclear power and carry nuclear weapons. In 1944, as the vice president's daughter, she had christened the battleship when it first rolled into the water.

Harrison, Polly, and I and Will and one of his closest friends, Miriam Cytryn, went along for the ride to San Francisco. The Navy flew us to California on a private jet.

Will came along for the ride in person, if not in spirit. The day we flew out of New York, he was wearing a black "No Nukes" button on his jacket lapel.

Will wasn't opposed to the *Missouri* specifically, but to the general remilitarization that was then going on under President Ronald Reagan. He objected not only to the buildup but more emphatically to the fact that the escalation was driving the country further into debt and diverting money from social programs.

When we arrived at our hotel, a small group of like-minded protesters had gathered behind police barricades out front. Will said later that if the rededication of the *Missouri* had taken place in New York, he might have been behind the barricades with them.

There was a banquet that night in honor of Mom and the *Missouri.* Several of the speakers, including, I think, a U.S. senator and a Navy chaplain, referred to the protesters as misguided and said they were trying to hamstring the very forces responsible for maintaining their freedom.

"God forgive them" was the phrase used. "They know not what they do."

That was too much for Will. That night, he and Miriam paid their bills and moved out of the hotel where we were staying. The next day they flew back to New York on a commercial airline.

Will came to the hotel the evening of the banquet to tell Mom he wouldn't be at the ceremony and why. He was careful of everybody's feelings and made it a point to meet me and Polly in the hotel bar so he could explain himself to us, too.

Will has often found himself at cross-purposes with our parents. He doesn't speak to them if he can help it. The split began the day Will and I faced Dad during group therapy at Brookwood Lodge in Kissimmee in 1984. Will remembers that session as the first time he saw Dad as being less than unimpeachable. His word had always been law, and Will and I had based much of our self-images on his opinion of us. Suddenly he seemed like a man who didn't have all the answers. At worst, Will found his performance in therapy self-serving.

That's when the split started, but it didn't open wide until Will began to weigh in against Mom and Dad over our younger brother, Harrison.

Harrison has, in many ways, had the worst time of all of us. He has the same fears, the same fits of rage, but he feels them much more strongly. Where my fears are purely mental, Harrison's are physical as well. He is careful about walking so he doesn't fall. Yet his anger is so great that it often overrides his fear of being hurt. Once he passed a gang of young men on the streets of New York and spit out: "What're you lookin' at? Wanna fight?" Thank God he didn't say it loud enough for them to hear clearly. I was with him.

At the group home where he lives in New York—and in all the schools and facilities he has lived in over the years—he has routinely had to be disciplined for outbursts of anger. He has hit people with his shoe and put his fist through panes of glass. He has been doing this for years, seemingly in an attempt to be sent home. But it never gets him where he wants to go. A couple of years ago, all it got him was a daily dose of antidepressants. Mom and Dad can't care for him at home. He needs a structured environment and more attention than they can give.

Will saw Harrison more than anyone else in the family. He routinely took the train from New York to the facility in Pennsylvania where Harrison lived. I have been there once. On these trips, Will and Harrison went out to dinner, took in a movie, or went shopping. Will just wanted to spend time with Harrison; he thought he deserved that. At the same time, he was getting an eyeful of the conditions in which our younger brother lived.

The more he saw, the more he thought Harrison should be moved. The place where he lived was supposed to be one of the best institutions of its kind in the country, but whenever Will went out there, he found it more and more run-down and understaffed. There was talk that the owners were downsizing, getting ready to sell the property.

Will wanted Harrison moved to New York, but his wish had less to do with the condition of the facility in Pennsylvania and more with the level of care Harrison could get in New York, which was very high. He argued to my parents that not only was the care better but that New York was where Harrison wanted to be, closer to them.

Mom and Dad did not react well to Will's suggestion that Harrison be moved. They have never solicited the advice of their sons when it came to family matters. Sometimes we don't know what's going on in their lives—or ours—unless we read about it in the newspaper. When Dad was made Washington bureau chief for the *Times,* I had to hear it on the news that we were moving out of New York. And then there's that incident when we all went to Greece and forgot to tell Will.

Mom and Dad have said that they keep us in the dark sometimes because they don't want to worry us. But neither of them is used to soliciting or taking advice. And Will probably did not offer his advice on Harrison politely. When you take that sort of tack with my parents, the their backs go up. Mom, especially, did not want Harrison in New York, where she felt he would be easy prey for muggers. Will took her reluctance as a sign of fear that she would have to care for Harrison at home again.

The strain of the fight took its toll. During it, the main issue of Harrison's welfare drew out of Will a lot of his own anger and unresolved problems with our parents. It became not so much a fight over a decent living place for Harrison but a fight over how we all had been raised. Will jumped in with both feet, and Mom and Dad defended themselves. Nothing much was resolved. Maybe Will didn't have the right words to make clear what he felt. Maybe he was too angry. Whatever it was, Will barely speaks to them, and they say they can't understand why he hates them so.

I, on the other hand, get along better than ever with Mom and Dad. They seem to have mellowed a lot in the last few years. We don't see each other that much, which apparently suits all of us just fine. We tend to get on one another's nerves when we're under each other's feet for too long.

Dad still sends clippings of articles he thinks we or the kids would enjoy, and both Mom and Dad have been generous with money. In fact, I think I'm going to have to name at least part of my year-old, used Mitubishi after Mom.

Thomas has also forged a relationship with Mom and Dad. His might even be better than mine. After all, he has gotten them to go up to Vermont several times, and I can't imagine my mother dragging herself to a mountainside for a week and liking it.

Harrison may never be completely at peace with Mom and Dad. He sees them more often than the rest of us, coming into New York regularly for holidays and weekends. Mom and Dad take him out to dinner or to a movie. The rest of the time, he sits by himself in the basement and watches television.

Of all Harry Truman's grandsons, I'm the only one visibly connected to Grandpa and the Truman Library. In 1994, I gave the main speech at the Truman Library's July Fourth celebration. Two weeks later I represented the family at the Truman symposium in Chicago. In January 1995, I flew to Los Angeles for a week of fund-raising for the Truman Library.

In April, I will speak to an audience at the Smithsonian about my grandfather. In September, I go back to Chicago to give a speech on Gen. George Marshall and the Marshall Plan. I'm scheduled to share the stage with Britain's Lord Carrington and Winston Churchill's grandson. Not long ago, I handed out the Harry S. Truman 33rd Degree Mason Award at the Scottish Rite Temple in Wilmington.

I am glad to do all these things, proud to do them, in fact, but I am also amazed that people let me. I've been a second banana to my mother for so long that it never occurred to me anyone would want me to represent the family by myself. But Mom has done this for so many years now that she seems happy to have someone else weigh in. And I have to admit I like it. It's undoubtedly somewhat selfish on my part; I'm still a publicity hound. But I also think that working for the Truman Library is worthwhile. My grandfather's legacy ought to be preserved.

For me, that legacy is not only a legacy of decisions that shaped the world for the better, but of a man who helped shape my life. Whenever I think of my grandfather, I tend to think of him not as a president but as a man. The presidency has little meaning for me on a daily basis, and the fame of the office helped push me down the wrong road. So I look to the man, not the office, for lessons on life. It was that man who made a great president.

Not that I want to make a career out of being a president's

grandson. In the end, I think that would be a hollow life. When this book is done, I am not going to write any more about him.

I am no longer tied to Grandpa. Will has said that he was often made to feel that being Harry Truman's grandson was the best part of him. But that's not true. It's only one part of him, one part of me. I have seen what I can do on my own. I have been accepted as a writer and an actor. I'm not knocking 'em dead on Broadway, but I'm not schlepping, either. And someday I might do something spectacular. There's always that hope. And even if I don't, I'll know I tried. Through it all, I try every day to work on my problems, be honest, do my job, try to see the other guy's point of view, be considerate, be straightforward—as my grandfather would have done.

And I have a good life in Wilmington, a loving wife and two wonderful children, if I don't mess them up too badly. I have made a lot of progress as a human being. I'm not as needy of attention as I used to be, thanks to Polly and the children. I have learned that it is important to focus more on them than myself. I don't drink like a fish anymore. These days, when I drink too much, it's five beers, not a whole weekend of drinking, drugs, and debauchery. I may be deluding myself. They say you are never cured of alcoholism, so I may be playing with a loaded gun by not quitting completely. But I don't think so. I have figured out what's important—family, friends, and work, not drinking.

On top of it all, I get that little bit of fame I always wanted, even though it's not really mine. But that's fine. I have learned to enjoy it for what it is, a chance to honor my grandfather. And if that little bit of fame swells my head too much, Polly will always gladly jerk me back down to earth.

During the July Fourth celebration, they set up television and radio interviews, gave me dinners, let me throw out the first ball at a Kansas City Royals game, and rode me through Independence at the head of a parade. After my speech, about a hundred people came up to me for autographs. It was a scene I had been dreaming about all my life. I was still flying when I called Polly from inside the library about an hour later.

"Well, the speech is over with," I said.

"How'd it go?"

"Good. They gave me a standing ovation, and about a hundred of them asked for my autograph afterward."

"Oh, I'll bet your head's really swelled now."

"No."

"Well, you enjoy yourself, because when you get home, I'm going to hand you the brush."

"What brush?"

"The brush to clean out the toilets."